Still Here!
The Apocalypse is Now

by

Braxton DeGarmo, MD

Christen Haus Publishing

COPYRIGHT

Still Here! The Apocalypse is Now – Copyright © 2021, 2023 by Braxton DeGarmo. All rights reserved under International and Pan-American Copyright Conventions. By payment of the required fees, you have been granted the non-exclusive, non-transferable right to access and read the text of this e-book on-screen. No part of this text may be reproduced, transmitted, down-loaded, decompiled, reverse engineered, or stored in or introduced into any information and retrieval system, in any form or by any means, whether electronic or mechanical, now known or hereinafter invented, without the express written permission of Braxton DeGarmo.

Paperback and eBook Edition Publication Date: November 2021
Paperback ISBN: 978-1-943509-43-0
eBook (Mobi): 978-1-943509-44-7
eBook (epub): 978-1-943509-45-4

Unless otherwise noted, Scripture quotations are from the ESV® Bible (The Holy Bible, English Standard Version®), copyright © 2001 by Crossway, a publishing ministry of Good News Publishers. Used by permission. All rights reserved.

Scriptures marked KJV are taken from the KING JAMES VERSION (KJV): KING JAMES VERSION, public domain.

For more information, go to:
www.braxtondegarmo.com

Introduction

[Note: It's now July 2023 and I'm reviewing and updating my original text. Additions or significant changes will be highlighted by brackets, such as with this note.]

In my earlier book, *Still Here! Surviving the End Times*, I presented an overview of eschatology as I had come to understand it three years ago. I gave the background of each of the four major viewpoints—idealism, preterism, historicism, and futurism—and then discussed Daniel's 70 Weeks prophecy, the Olivet Discourse, and the major scriptures used by some futurist believers in teaching about a rapture. Hopefully, I showed how those scriptures are used errantly to support that false teaching, with my goal being to prepare people for what's to come instead of their hope lying in being whisked away. I then offered a line-by-line exegesis of Psalm 91 in support of understanding the Lord's name, Jehovah Machaçeh, and why we need to take refuge in Him.

So, now, three-plus years and much additional study later, have I learned anything that would make me change what I said in that book? My perspective on some things has changed—broadened, in a good way—as I've read more on certain areas, such as Idealism, and learned more about the Preterist view of the Olivet Discourse.

I mentioned Idealism a moment ago. While strict Idealism seems to be followed by few in eschatological circles, a viewpoint of *modified* Idealism is claimed by many prominent theological scholars. I mention this because they offer valid points of study, IMO, particularly when it comes to the Book of Revelation. In truth, even supporters of the other views hold various idealist perspectives about Revelation because much, if not most, of the book is indeed symbolic.

And yet, Revelation is not symbolic in the sense that John envisioned things that require deciphering. It's not a code book with secret meanings that require lemon juice or holding up to a light to reveal. Those symbols are portrayed in the Old Testament (OT) and knowledge of the OT is critical to understanding Revelation.

In my previous book, I also mentioned a dream I had in December of 2017 in which the Lord warned me of upcoming economic upheaval, famine, and pestilence. In my logical mind, I saw economic upheaval leading to famine, leading to pestilence. Instead, all three seemed to arrive at once as COVID-19 shut down the world and its economies, and locust plagues hit eastern Africa, the Middle East, and China. And, while the experts' predictions that the locusts would spread to other areas of the world in the summer of 2021 didn't pan out, we're seeing extreme drought, wildfires, and flooding drastically affecting world food supplies. The next time the Lord sends me a warning, I won't try to apply my own logic to it <forehead slap>.

One other area where my understanding deepened is about Daniel's 70 Weeks Prophecy. Although many believe that specific prophecy points to Jesus's first advent, it more clearly pointed to the reign of Antiochus IV Epiphanes. Indeed, it seems to be broadly accepted that the prophecies of Daniel 7-12 were fulfilled during that tyrant's reign. Key to that timing is the Zadokite calendar, which we'll have more on when we get to Revelation 12.

While that period could also be seen as a foreshadowing of the destruction of Jerusalem in 70 A.D., there is little doubt in my mind that it foreshadows the persecution of God's people in the End Times. As we'll see, much of Daniel, as well as Isaiah, is prophetic of the End Times, confirmed by the repetitive "allusions" to Daniel, especially chapters 7 and 12, in the Apocalypse.

So, what I didn't do in the other book was delve into the Book of Revelation, the Apocalypse. That is my goal for this book. However, it is not my intent to do a line-by-line or even a chapter-by-chapter study of this important book. There are dozens of books out there, by more knowledgeable scholars than me, which can offer you varying forms of exegetical study on the book in whichever eschatological perspective you wish to explore. I would suggest Steve Gregg's *Revelation: Four Views, Revised and Updated*. While his introduction also looks at the four major views of eschatology, he then presents Revelation using a parallel commentary format so that you can learn each of the traditional four ways in which the book is interpreted. At over 500 pages, however, it's not light bedtime reading.

Other books used in my research included Dr. Gregory Beale's *The New International Greek Testament Commentary, the Book of Revelation*, which is considered by many as the "gold standard" for commentaries on Revelation. Sir William Ramsay's *The Letters to the Seven Churches in Asia* provided a depth of insight into those assemblies that I'd never read before. Dr. Michael Heiser's books, *The Unseen Realm* and *Reversing Hermon*, also offered great insights into the background of the Apocalypse. He also recently posted a lengthy series of podcasts on Revelation that suggested excellent secondary materials for review. For that, go to NakedBiblePodcast.com. Dr. Voddie Baucham, formerly a pastor at Grace Family Baptist Church in Texas and now serving as the Dean of Theology at African Christian University in Zambia, participated in a series of teachings on Revelation while at Grace Family Baptist. His videos are quite good but only covered parts of the book. Other sources will be footnoted as needed, although my reading took me to many places I haven't directly referenced.

I hope that I can make the Book of Revelation more understandable. Until a few years ago, I, like so many, saw Revelation as this daunting book of mystery. That was in large part due to my becoming born again in a Dispensational church and accepting that view of eschatology for years. Who is The Antichrist and when is he coming? Who are the 144,000? Who are the two witnesses? Was John seeing helicopters when he spoke of locusts with fire in their tails but faces and hair like humans? To the Dispensational mind, all of Revelation is literal and the book is one huge codebook that must be decrypted. No wonder Revelation is so confusing to so many in today's church.

And thanks to books like Hal Lindsey's *Late, Great Planet Earth* (1970) and the popular *Left Behind* series (1995-2007), much of that Dispensational thinking seeped into popular culture to the point where many accept the idea of a seven-year tribulation period, a global tyrant—The Antichrist, and a rapture of the church, even if they don't identify as Christians.

While all I can offer is a personal take on Revelation, and it no doubt will have its share of shortcomings, I hope you find it helpful. Let's see if we can clear up some of that confusion.

Note: As with my previous book, in any quoted scripture with bold emphasis, the emphasis is mine, not part of the ESV from which the quote comes. Scripture quoted from other translations will be so noted.

Before Delving In . . .

Eschatology Revisited

While I presented the four main viewpoints on eschatology and their widely accepted origins in my earlier book, *Still Here! Surviving the End Times*, that book was focused on debunking the concept of a rapture and presenting what believers may be called upon to do to survive the End Times since we're all *still here* during that time of tribulation. In looking at the Book of Revelation, I think it's important to take another look at those four views because each one alters how you look at Revelation, as well as scripture in general.

A Quick Rehash . . . and Discussion

Over the course of history, four major viewpoints on eschatology developed: historicism, preterism, futurism, and idealism. Most students of the End Times find their place in one of these four boxes, and sadly, many won't look outside their box. Let's take a quick look at the four views. For more details on each, please see my other book.

Historicists see many prophecies of Revelation as having been fulfilled already during the church age, throughout history. Thus, the name. Yet, they are also futurists to a degree in that they acknowledge that some aspects of Revelation will be fulfilled in the future, leading to Christ's return and a 1,000-year reign. To them, the church will go through the tribulation foretold by Jesus. The historicist sees prophecy in a very literal sense, and over history they've tried to accredit this or that event—such as Muslim invasions or the rise of Hitler—with one prophecy or another from Revelation. Different individuals throughout history were heralded as the Antichrist. They also equate a day with a year, so the 1,260 days mentioned later in Revelation 12 became a 1,260-year span with a beginning date that keeps changing. At first, it was to be the 1,260 years following the reign of Emperor Domitian. When Christ didn't return in the 14th century, they adjusted the starting point. That is the biggest problem with this viewpoint; the goalposts keep moving.

The **futurist** sees all of Revelation as occurring at some future time. Today, most futurists are dispensationalists, too. By that, they believe there have been seven ages, or dispensations, throughout the church age. The ideas of dispensationalism arose in the 1830s and were popularized by John Nelson Darby, who brought his teachings to America where they quickly became standard theology in the major Bible schools. Dispensationalism is the most common eschatological viewpoint in the U.S. but not elsewhere.

Dispensationalists promote a rapture, a great apostasy, the rise of a global leader—The Antichrist, seven years of worsening tribulation for the Jews (because Christians will have been taken to heaven), Christ's return after the seven years, and a final battle—Armageddon, which takes place after a literal 1,000-year reign of Christ and His church. Indeed, they promote a strictly literal interpretation of all of Revelation, except where it's clearly symbolic. Curiously, dispensationalists place great importance on Revelation's prophecies, giving them a sequential timeline that's critical to their viewpoint, and yet, if they're correct, they won't even be here for that time in history.

Besides having no real scriptural support for their beliefs, they always point to some future time because they see a tribulation so severe, they have trouble accepting that maybe they're already in the time of tribulation. We'll see that John has something to say about that when we move into chapter one.

Both of these viewpoints—historicism and futurism—are also **premillennial** views. By that, both see the 1,000-year reign of Christ mentioned in Revelation 20 as being a literal 1,000 years that precedes the battle of Armageddon and the final judgment by God. So, they see most of the prophecies of Revelation as occurring *before* that millennium. We'll get into the concept of the millennium later.

The **preterist** viewpoint believes that all of Revelation and the prophecies of the Olivet Discourse and major prophets were fulfilled with the fall of Jerusalem and the destruction of the temple in 70 C.E. (or A.D., if you're 'old school' like me). To them, we are in the 1,000-year reign of Christ now—what we call the church age, and the 'return of Christ' is symbolic of a final judgment on Israel, not a physical return of the Lord. This is what's considered the *full* preterist view.

Today, most are *partial* preterists in that they've modified their beliefs to acknowledge that parts of Revelation have yet to be fulfilled. However, partial preterism is split further, as they can't agree on the definition of what "partial part" they believe. Some accept that all prophecy has been fulfilled except for the physical return of Christ, and some say that the antichrist, great tribulation, and Day of the Lord, with Christ's return, have yet to happen. Classically, no matter which view is taken, the preterist camp has been heavily dependent upon the date of the writing of the Book of Revelation. More on this shortly.

Most preterists are also what's called **postmillennial**. By that, it means that they don't accept a literal 1,000-year reign of Christ but see it as symbolic. Since we are currently in that period of reigning with Christ, they believe that the church will grow and grow, becoming a bright beacon to the world and entering a Golden Age of the church that will usher the Lord back to earth as His unstained bride.

The **idealist** sees all of Revelation as metaphor or allegory. Likewise with the major prophets. All of prophecy is a metaphor for the battle of good versus evil. In its fullest sense, idealism sees no final victory of God over evil, but most today accept God's final triumph. Today, again, most idealists are *modified* idealists. They still see Revelation as metaphor, taking few prophecies literally, but accept that there will be a final judgment and the return of Christ. Most modified idealists are also **amillennialists**. Like the postmillennialists, they see the 1,000 years as symbolic of the church age. Unlike the postmillennialists, however, they see the tribulation worsening and the church diminishing before the return of the Lord.

Today, most within these two groups expect Christ to return at the end of the age, at which time the final battle of Armageddon and judgment will occur. Then the new heaven and earth will arrive with no additional 1,000-year period of reigning on the old earth.

Please realize that these are "nutshell" descriptions of the four major views. There are nuances to each that would take up too much space here to present. However, when it comes to the study of Revelation, a person's perspective of eschatology will affect their study. Is it symbolic? Is it literal? Is there a literal 1,000-year reign, or not? This last question has particular relevance.

Why? The Book of Revelation is the only place in the Bible where "the millennium," a 1,000-year reign of Christ, is mentioned (Revelation 20:4). We'll get into that later, but it is a major point of division within the study of eschatology and the study of Revelation itself. Some theologians believe this to be the most problematic verse in the entire Bible. To them, how you interpret this verse affects how you interpret not only the rest of the Book of Revelation but also much of Biblical prophecy.

The Timing of Revelation

As stated above, the timing of John's writing of the book comes into play when looking at the major views of eschatology. Of the four traditional perspectives, preterism is heavily dependent upon this timing.

Since the preterist camp believes that the prophecies of the Olivet Discourse and most of Revelation were fulfilled with the destruction of Jerusalem and the temple in 70 A.D., they maintain that John wrote Revelation during the reign of Nero in the mid-60s A.D., prior to Paul's death in 67 A.D. Without such dating, John's visions would not be prophetic but simply a rehashing of history regarding the destruction of Jerusalem. For the other viewpoints, this is not a problem since they see the fulfillment of the prophecies as occurring after 70 A.D., at some point during or at the end of the church age.

Christians certainly faced great tribulation under Nero. Yet, there are equally strong arguments for the writing of Revelation to have occurred in ~96 A.D. during the time of Domitian, whose reign of terror against Christians was much worse. Among those arguments, history reports that it was Domitian who exiled John to Patmos in ~95 A.D. and that upon Domitian's death, John was allowed to return to Ephesus where he died in 100 A.D. Irenaeus—the early Christian historian who was trained by Polycarp, a disciple of John—supports this date. If the book was written in 95-96 A.D., then its prophecies could only apply to some undefined time in the future and thereby would debunk much of the preterist viewpoint.

Some see another potential issue. All of the various preterist views hold that all of Jesus' prophecies in the Olivet Discourse from Matthew 24:5-34 were fulfilled with the fall of Jerusalem in 70 A.D. So, in Matthew 24:34, in the lesson of the fig tree, He states, "*Truly, I say to you, this generation will not pass away until all these things take place*"—"these things" being the destruction of the temple. The term "this generation," in Greek, points to the presently living generation. Thus, the preterist argument holds that Jesus' reference to the generation living with him not passing away until the destruction occurs is proof of its fulfillment in 70 A.D.

As we'll see later, there is strong evidence that Jesus was born in 3 B.C. The discrepancy—ie., not the year 0 A.D.—is due to glitches in both the Jewish calendar and in changing over to the Gregorian calendar which we use today. Since we believe that He "died" at age 33, that means He "died" in the spring of 30 A.D. The final siege of Jerusalem started just before Passover in 70 A.D., but the city didn't fall until August, five months later. The temple was burned and destroyed on Tisha B'Av, the same day as the destruction of Solomon's temple. So, with the Biblical generation being generally accepted as 40 years, can we say that the destruction of Jerusalem and the temple in 70 A.D. happened within that generation of Jesus' time? Or was it several months outside that time window?

I know. It's nit-picking. Now, I did say this was a *potential* issue, and it's one that mainly the strict literalist will hold to. To me, the term "this generation" of Matthew 24:34 doesn't require a rigid time frame. Many who were alive with Jesus lived to see the destruction.

Amillennial or Postmillennial . . .

Now, getting back to my rehash of eschatology, amillennialism has been the primary perspective of the church through most of history and still is outside of the U.S., as well as in the orthodox (Catholic and Eastern Orthodox) and reform (Presbyterian and Lutheran) groups within the U.S. Dispensationalism dominates in the U.S. due to the great number of Southern Baptists and evangelical churches in this country.

As I stated, modified idealists tend to fill the amillennial tent. As such, they see the Book of Revelation as metaphorical, with, as an example, the seven seal, trumpet, and bowl judgments depicting the same thing just from different perspectives—much like witnesses of an accident whose statements differ because they saw the event from a different angle. As we'll see, most of the Apocalypse has been foreshadowed in the OT but now has universal application to the church. Yet, to me, there is an intensification between these sets of seven judgments that doesn't seem consistent with the idea of different perspectives and needs consideration. We'll get to that.

Although postmillennialists and amillennialists agree on most aspects of eschatology, amillennialists view the world as getting worse and worse with tribulation occurring for all mankind prior to the Lord's return at the end of the age. They look at such scriptures as Matthew 24:10, 21-22; 2 Timothy 3:1-5; Daniel 12:1, Jeremiah 30:7, Isaiah 24-27 (his mini apocalypse), and the judgments of Revelation as pointing to such deterioration. They look at history and current events as a form of confirmation, with the great apostasy foretold by Christ as occurring during this time, not necessarily a great falling away within a brief time.

[The 2023 American Worldview Inventory done by the Cultural Research Center at Arizona Christian University reveals that only 4% of

American adults hold to a biblical worldview.[1] At least within the U.S., this would seem to point to a great falling away. Most hold a syncretic worldview, which means believing in a little bit of this and a little bit of that, with Christianity being part of the mix. This isn't new. Reading through the books of Kings and Chronicles show that the people of ancient Judah were much the same—believing in Yahweh while also worshiping other gods, sacrificing at their Asherah poles, and burning incense on altars in the high places. We see how that worked out for them.]

Postmillennialists see this as pessimistic, and yet some will hedge by saying that just because the church is growing doesn't mean believers won't be persecuted or put to death. And some amillennialists will hedge by admitting that the world's getting darker will make the church shine brighter and persecution always results in church growth. We see this already happening in countries of the Middle East, SE Asia, and China where tribulation and persecution against the church have been great, and yet, the church is increasing by leaps and bounds. Could such persecution lead to a third great awakening? Sure, it's possible. Time will give us all 20-20 hindsight.

As I see it, each of the four main viewpoints requires compromise at some level. Or if you think compromise is too strong a word, inconsistency might be better. Idealists appear to ignore anything that could have a literal meaning and much that is actually literal. Thus, they become "modified" idealists to give them more flexibility. Dispensational futurists have to manipulate God's Word in many ways to make scripture fit their concepts of a seven-year tribulation, a rapture, and more.

Partial-preterist postmillennialists (few, if any, are full preterists these days) do some of the same in making scripture fit their ideas. How? Let's look at the following three verses:

---

[1] https://www.arizonachristian.edu/wp-content/uploads/2023/02/CRC_AWVI2023_Release1.pdf

> And this gospel of the kingdom will be proclaimed throughout the whole world as a testimony to all nations, and then the end will come. (Matt 24:14)
>
> Now there were dwelling in Jerusalem Jews, devout men from every nation under heaven. (Act 2:5)
>
> Go therefore and make disciples of all nations, baptizing them in the name of the Father and of the Son and of the Holy Spirit, (Matt 28:19)

Some define the "whole world" as the Roman Empire (although in Thayer's Greek lexicon, this phrase in this verse is defined as the whole inhabited earth), while others claim it to mean the known world. The same word, *ethnos*, ἔθνος, with similar phrasing, is used in all three verses for every or all nations. In the first two verses, most preterists teach that the phrases "all nations" and "every nation" refers to all people groups within the Roman Empire. Thus, they claim that the proclamation of the testimony to all nations was fulfilled on that day of Pentecost because all nations were represented. The "end" they refer to in Matthew 24:14 above is the end of the temple.

Honestly, I see an inconsistency here. If "every nation" in Acts 2:5 means those peoples of the Roman Empire, then, to continue being consistent, "all nations" in the Great Commission of Matthew 28:19 should also mean the peoples of the Roman Empire. Instead, they teach that "all nations" in this verse means the entire world. Some will say that they mean the "known" world. Yet, all nations of the "known" world are not listed in Acts 2:9-11, nor were Jews known to be among the Scythian peoples or many known African nations, Jews who might have been in Jerusalem on Pentecost in order to fulfill Matthew 24:14.

Of course, they respond by saying that the Great Commission is universalized to include us. The command is one for every generation to reach the known world of their time. That understanding should also apply to Matthew 24:14 but at that time, the gospel was far from being proclaimed throughout their known world. As for us, today, what "end" to come is implied for us?

I don't mean to seem as if I'm picking on preterist postmillennialists. This was an example of using scripture inconsistently, as I see it, that I recently came across and seemed to be a good one to highlight. Besides, I "picked on" dispensational futurists in my last book, and if I tried to criticize examples from modified idealism, they'd simply claim my comments are a metaphor for something else. Plus, it's our faith in Him that counts, not our view on eschatology, as interesting as this is. As one pastor friend told me, it's best to be panmillennial, it all pans out in the end.

(Note: Today's amillennialist believes we're currently in the Kingdom of God (which we are) but that with Christ's return we will be ushered to some unknown ethereal location (heaven?) to spend eternity. I think the Bible clearly shows that our eternity is to be spent here on earth in God's new Eden/Jerusalem. For my purposes in this book, I will "define" amillennialism as simply a belief that there is no separate 1,000-year period after Christ's physical return, that most of Revelation is metaphorical, and that the church will not enter some glorious Golden Age to usher Christ back.)

My Personal View

Personally, because I see points of compromise, or inconsistency, in all of the viewpoints, I don't claim to sit inside any one of those four boxes. Call me eclectic. I see some of these prophecies having been fulfilled at Christ's first advent and the fall of Jerusalem in 70 A.D., primarily Daniel and parts of the Olivet Discourse (preterist). Some prophecies, such as the "birth pains" of the Olivet Discourse, have been occurring over time both before and after the temple's destruction (historicist+futurist, kinda). To me, several of the prophecies of Revelation, such as the first four seal judgments, have been taking place over time, too (historicist?). And yet, much of Revelation is still on the horizon (futurist). Or are we beginning to see that acceleration now?

The Bible tells us that the latter days are followed by the end of the age, not a 1,000-year reign (post/amillennial). In a similar vein, most of Revelation can be seen as metaphorical (modified idealist), just as much of OT prophecy is. Could a third revival occur before His return? I believe it's already started in parts of the world. And as the world gets darker, I believe we'll see many more people turning to Christ, but such a revival is unlikely to be as publicly evident as prior great awakenings because of the persecution.

Once upon a time, I was taught that much of prophecy held a dual purpose. We see that frequently in OT prophets, who while proclaiming judgment on a nation of their time also made statements pointing to Christ's first advent, or the End Times, or the Second Coming. I've come to realize that much, if not most, of the major events of the OT were foreshadows of what's coming in the End Times. Even the destruction of Jerusalem can be seen as a type of what's to come on unbelievers. The "birth pains" foretold by Jesus could readily apply to both the fall of Jerusalem and the latter days of the church age.

Dr. Michael Heiser, and many others, also use the term "already and not yet" for this idea that some prophecies have already seen fulfillment in the spiritual realm but have not yet seen their earthly consummation. We can only speculate that this duality might be the case because it hasn't, to date, been proven by scripture.

There's a fine nuance of difference between saying that John alluded to, or referred to, say, Daniel or the plagues of Egypt when giving a prophecy and seeing that those OT references were actually foreshadowings. Is John referring to Ezekiel or Isaiah when he describes the throne room of God? I prefer to think he was shown the same thing. After all, he was instructed to write down what *he* saw, not what the OT prophets saw. Differences between them could be simply his visual perspective, or they could be relative to his historical perspective and his knowledge of Christ. An example of this would be the four beasts of Daniel 7. Daniel sees them as four separate beasts rising from the sea because they have yet to arrive in history. John sees them as one beast rising from the sea (Revelation 13) because they are history to him.

When one views the prophecies and events of the OT as a

foreshadowing of the Apocalypse, it becomes more difficult to sit inside any one of those four traditional eschatological boxes. Eclectic? Is perplexic a word? I'm sure some will find my mishmash of understanding perplexing.

The Millennium

Let's dive deeper into the millennium. As stated earlier, the concept of a millennial reign is mentioned only in Revelation 20:4-5,

> *4 Then I saw thrones, and seated on them were those to whom the authority to judge was committed. Also I saw the souls of those who had been beheaded for the testimony of Jesus and for the word of God, and those who had not worshiped the beast or its image and had not received its mark on their foreheads or their hands. They came to life and reigned with Christ for a thousand years. 5 The rest of the dead did not come to life until the thousand years were ended. This is the first resurrection.*

There's also the statement about Satan being bound for a thousand years in Revelation 20:2 and released after 1,000 years in Revelation 20:7. The idea of a 1,000-year reign occurring after Christ's return, as a separate epoch in history, comes from two things, (1) reading the number 'thousand' literally, and (2) seeing a sequential timeline in John's prophecies. Both are accepted by dispensationalists and historical futurists, who also often argue—using the verse about a day being like a thousand years—that man "ruled" the earth for 6,000 years and that adding Christ's 1,000-year reign totals 7,000 years, with seven being the number of perfection. Of course, one could also say that God rested on the seventh day and such a rest can only occur after His final judgment and the establishment of His new Eden. We'll look at all of these—being literal, being sequential, and the meaning of numbers—in a bit.

However, does the Bible say anything about a separate era or

1,000-year epoch? Nothing in the above verses would indicate that this is a distinct period of history, so what do we need to do? That's right. We look at other scripture—scripture supporting scripture.

Here's a sampling of verses that might help.

> *And whoever speaks a word against the Son of Man will be forgiven, but whoever speaks against the Holy Spirit will not be forgiven, either in this age or in the age to come. (Matt 12:32)*

> *And this gospel of the kingdom will be proclaimed throughout the whole world as a testimony to all nations, and then the end will come. (Matt 24:14) —if this verse applies to more than the fall of Jerusalem*

> *29 And he said to them, "Truly, I say to you, there is no one who has left house or wife or brothers or parents or children, for the sake of the kingdom of God, 30 who will not receive many times more in this time, and in the age to come eternal life." (Luk 18:29-30)*

> *... far above all rule and authority and power and dominion, and above every name that is named, not only in this age but also in the one to come. (Eph 1:21)*

This age and one to come, singular, not two to come. Nothing in these verses even suggests a millennial period. Even the disciples' question in Matthew 24 points to a single age to come:

> *As he sat on the Mount of Olives, the disciples came to him privately, saying, "Tell us, when will these things be, and what will be the* **sign** *of your coming and of the end of the age?" (Matt 24:3)*

The sign (again, singular, not plural) of His coming and of **the end of**

the age point to one thing, Christ's return which marks the end of the age and judgment.

Perhaps these verses will also help:

> *23 But each in his own order: Christ the firstfruits, then* **at his coming** *those who belong to Christ. 24* **Then comes the end**, *when he delivers the kingdom to God the Father after destroying every rule and every authority and power. (1Co 15:23-24)*

> *38 The field is the world, and the good seed is the sons of the kingdom. The weeds are the sons of the evil one, 39 and the enemy who sowed them is the devil. The* **harvest is the end of the age**, *and the reapers are angels. 40 Just as the weeds are gathered and burned with fire, so will* **it be at the end of the age.** *(Matt 13:38-40)*

> *Now these things happened to them as an example, but they were written down for our instruction,* **on whom the end of the ages has come.** *(1 Co 10:11)*

In all of these verses, we see no reference to a separate millennial reign on earth. These verses point to the end of the age—that age being the latter days, or church age—occurring with the return of Christ. At this time, the harvest takes place and men are judged, with "the weeds" being burned. To paraphrase, we have the latter days and then comes the end . . . not the latter days, a thousand-year interlude, and then the end.

If you did before, do you still believe in a 1,000-year reign of Christ in the literal sense? Having once accepted that idea myself, I know how these scriptures hit me when they were pointed out. <forehead slap-again>

Is it literal?

In the previous section, I mentioned that we'd look at the idea of literally interpreting Revelation. In *Still Here! Surviving the End Times*, I stated that ". . . one of the basic tenets of sound Bible study is to first look at the most literal, common-sense understanding of any scripture and then dig deeper." I then defined the term 'literal' to say that it doesn't mean a word-for-word account. For historical books, yes, such an interpretation is valid. For poetry, such as the Psalms, the interpretation will be more figurative.

While it starts and ends like an epistle—having a greeting in the beginning and a closing at the end, Revelation sits alone in the Bible as the sole book of apocalyptic literature. Indeed, it's the sole book of prophecy in the New Testament. There are prophetic sections in other books that show an apocalyptic vision, but only Revelation holds to that genre in its entirety. From 200 B.C. to 100 A.D., this was a common and very popular genre of writing among Jews and Christians.[2] The receivers of John's letter would have been quite accustomed to reading and understanding it. As such, its interpretation is unique.

What is apocalyptic literature? There are several well-known pieces of the genre from that Second Temple Period—1 Enoch, 4 Ezra, the Book of Jubilees, and more. Typical of the genre are angels being used as guides or interpreters, as well as its use of numbers, dramatic images, and striking symbols—such as dragons and beasts—in portraying the battle between good and evil. Like other books of the genre, it was written during a period of intense persecution of believers, whether under Nero in 66 A.D. or under Domitian in 96 A.D. Apocalyptic literature also uses numbers to convey bigger concepts, instead of pure statistical data.

Unlike other books of the genre, however, the Book of Revelation claims to be prophecy given *by* God to John through a series of visions. And, where some of the other apocalyptic books are pseudepigrapha—

---

[2] Gregg, Steve. *Revelation: Four Views, Revised and Updated.* (Nashville, TN: Thomas Nelson, 2013), pg. 20.

works attributed by the author to someone in the past, such as Enoch—the true author, John, is attributed by name to the work. The final difference is that the Book of Revelation actually predicts the future, bolstering its claim of being God-inspired prophecy.

As a quick side note, the concept of visions brings to mind dreams or mental images. In John's case, these visions were possibly astrological in nature. John was called a seer, and seers of that day interpreted things they saw in the heavens. This was understood and accepted by earlier historians, such as Sir William M. Ramsey.[3] More recently, *The Social-Science Commentary on the Book of Revelation*,[4] by Bruce J. Malina and John R. Pilch, looks at this extensively. It's a fascinating look at the Book of Revelation, although as you read it, their eschatological viewpoint is evident. We'll look at a few of the astral aspects of Revelation as we move along through the book.

So, as apocalyptic literature, how should we interpret it? The book is highly symbolic, as shown from chapter one on. Images like golden lampstands, stars in Christ's right hand, and a sword coming from His mouth are obvious metaphors. The ideas behind the numbers in the book are important enough that I'm dedicating an entire section to the numerology/gematria of Revelation—how numbers are used and the system of how numbers assigned to names and letters are used. I am *not* talking about fortunetelling or the use of numbers by the mystic sect of the Jewish Kabbalah.

We also need to recognize that the symbols used are those that are believed to have been commonly known to the ancient Eastern world, not our Western one. After all, John was writing to seven assemblies in Asia Minor with a mix of Greek, Semitic, and other mindsets. Many of those receiving his teaching came from a pagan background. As such, even his use of Jewish symbols and idioms needs to be considered with that in mind.

One of the commonly accepted concepts of that time (as well as

---

[3] Ramsay, William M., *The Letters to the Seven Churches of Asia*, (Hodder, 1904)
[4] Malina, Bruce J and Pilch, John R. *The Social-Science Commentary on the Book of Revelation*, (Augsburg Fortress Publishers, July 25, 2000)

ours) is that of two planes of existence. Friezes from a variety of ancient cultures often depicted both the earthly plane and the heavenly one. The bottom half of the sculpture might show a priest or college of priests making a sacrifice to his/their god while the upper half showed that god accepting it. Curiously, when Zeus was the subject of the frieze, he was often shown accompanied by his son Hermes. So, the idea of God as father and son was not foreign to them. We see this idea of two planes of existence in the stars/angels and lampstands/churches. It will also be evident later in the book, where some events are taking place in heaven while others are happening on earth.

Colors also have meaning. While we've been taught certain meanings for some colors, such as white, red, and black, some of those might have provoked different ideas in the ancient Eastern mind. We understand white to represent righteousness and purity. In that day, a person on trial received a verdict by either a white or black stone, with the white one declaring innocence. Also, a white horse was specifically associated with the Parthians. Historically, the Parthians never went to war without being accompanied by sacred white horses. A victorious Parthian general would be shown on a white horse holding his bow, the national weapon for which they were widely known. Romans had no bows in their arsenal and victorious generals were shown wearing the purple and gold robes of Jupiter, riding in their chariots drawn by four horses.[5]

Likewise, beasts rising from the sea or from the earth were common motifs from ancient Mesopotamia to the Greek art of John's day. Even ancient Jewish literature made use of those symbols. The popular apocalyptic literature of his day, such as 1 Enoch, no doubt influenced John. However, that's not to say he simply copied this material for his images. As will be discussed in the following chapter on the use of the OT in the book, John took these images and put them to a new use, one that fit his theology and what he was trying to portray. After all, if the early church had developed its own form of Christian-speak that was foreign to the cultures around them, how successful do

---

[5] Ramsay, William M., *The Letters to the Seven Churches of Asia*, (Hodder,

you think they would have been in spreading the Gospel? Those cultures had to be approached on terms they understood in order for the Gospel to make sense. The same holds true for missionaries today.

In closing out this section, we have to recall that John was instructed to write about what he **saw** in the visions given to him. Those visions consisted of "*those* (things) *that are and those that are to take place after this*" (Revelation 1:19) We can't forget that these are things that he saw and heard, and it's unlikely that God would give him visions of things so far removed from his cultural understanding, and that of the recipients of his letter, that they would make zero sense to them. The whole idea of his seeing helicopters or other weapons of modern warfare is a bit bizarre.

So, as we work through the book, we will be looking at it from its OT (mainly symbolic) perspective and consistent with the post/amillennial viewpoint, with splashes of "eclectic" historicism and literalism, where appropriate, thrown in.

Is it sequential?

One other detail that should be mentioned is that of chronology. Is there a timeline of events provided by the Book of Revelation, or the Olivet Discourse for that matter? Regarding the Olivet Discourse, I take the position that it foretold both the coming destruction of Jerusalem (as a foreshadowing) and the End Times. We'll look at that below.

Regarding Revelation, some see the visions presented by John as sequential. Thus, the first seal (judgment) is broken before the second, which precedes the third, and so on, and the breaking of the seventh seal unleashes the seven trumpet judgments, which also take place in order. Likewise, the seventh trumpet makes way for the seven bowl judgments, which also occur in progression. Some loosen their standard by saying the trumpets and bowls might not occur one after the other within their given array but that the scroll judgments lead into the trumpet judgments, which occur before the bowl judgments.

1904), pg. 50.

The stricter concept of sequential happenings comes from the literal reading of "After this I . . ." saw, looked, or heard something, statements made by John **seven** times throughout the book. The literal understanding of these statements assumes that John saw the visions in chronological order. Yet, to say "After this I saw . . ." simply says that after one vision, he saw another. Nothing in the text explicitly states any prophetic timeline.

The various judgments could occur sporadically over time. I believe that to be true of the first four scroll judgments—the four horsemen of the Apocalypse— which, to me, have been occurring throughout the church age. These four "punishments" are generalized and random. There are dozens of accounts in history, or even in current events, of ethnic groups and nations conquering their neighbors (the white horse). Millions of people have died at the hands of tyrants, in wars, or by family and friends (the red horse). Likewise, history shows famine and inflation in various places at various times (the black horse). And of course, death by sword, famine, and pestilence has followed (the pale horse). As for the trumpet and bowl judgments, there is no indication that any or all are cataclysmic events, even though some sure sound like it. There is much to say about them being metaphorical.

As I pointed out in *Still Here! Surviving the End Times*, these four judgments correlate remarkably well with Jesus' declarations in the Olivet Discourse (again, taking the stand that these statements have a dual meaning or fulfillment).

> *6 And you will hear of wars and rumors of wars. See that you are not alarmed, for this must take place, but the end is not yet. 7 For nation will rise against nation, and kingdom against kingdom, and there will be famines and earthquakes in various places. 8 All these are but the beginning of the birth pains. (Matt 24:6-8)*

The word for 'nation' here is *ethnos*, ἔθνος, again referring to people groups, whether ethnic, tribal, or even family groups. The reference to kingdoms is closer to how we define nations today, such as Germany warring against the rest of Europe in WWII. And, of course, we've seen famines (and pestilence), as well as earthquakes, repeatedly in history. Already and not yet?

Once again notice how Jesus described these events above in Matthew 24:8. These are only the "*beginning of the birth pains.*" The **beginning** implies a timeline. Is the end marked solely by the destruction of the temple, or is that, too, part of the birth pains? His reference to birthing is noteworthy. The labor of childbirth might start with a few Braxton Hicks contractions of false labor, but when it's time, labor pains become increasingly intense.

So, while trying to put the judgments of Revelation into a strict timeline might be futile, the visions of John do indeed show an intensification of trouble. With the scroll judgments, the events described are generalized, occurring in various places and, seemingly, continually at different times throughout history. Then, in the trumpet judgments, a third of the earth is involved, followed by the bowl judgments in which the entire world is affected.

Without reading more into the images described by John, and not assuming a physical third of the earth, this again implies a timeline of intensifying tribulation but gives us nothing specific. Several scholars that I read see the scrolls, trumpets, and bowls as being simply recapitulations of the same events, and therefore, not sequential. (And "events" is the word used by at least two prominent scholars.) To me, that doesn't account for the escalation of judgment.

Showing the same "events," but with increasing intensity, still implies a time sequence. Think of a wildfire. If observer one sees the fire after it's burned 20 acres and observer two sees it after it's burned 1,000 acres, yes, the second description could be said to be a recapitulation of the first. It's the same fire, the same "event." Yet, how did the fire grow from 20 acres to 1,000? It required time for that fire to grow.

To me, there's a nuance in calling these "events." How do we define an event? A wildfire in California is one event, while a fire in Australia is another. Is the fire in one place a recapitulation of the fire in the other place? Not at all, in the sense that they are geographically different events, but they could be part of the same judgment, a judgment that intensifies over time.

Isn't that what we're seeing today? Where once we heard about an occasional fire here or there, this year we saw not only record-breaking fires in California but also in Oregon and Washington. And Greece . . . and Turkey . . . and Australia . . . and Israel, among other places. [As I review this in 2023, Canadian wildfires have burned over 19 million acres in the first six months of the year, and the smoke from these fires has reached Europe.]

Also, as we look about, don't we see society fulfilling the descriptions of 2 Tim 3:1-5?

> *1 But understand this, that in the last days there will come times of difficulty. 2 For people will be lovers of self, lovers of money, proud, arrogant, abusive, disobedient to their parents, ungrateful, unholy, 3 heartless, unappeasable, slanderous, without self-control, brutal, not loving good, 4 treacherous, reckless, swollen with conceit, lovers of pleasure rather than lovers of God, 5 having the appearance of godliness, but denying its power. Avoid such people.*

Sure, there have been people filling those descriptions throughout history, but in my nearly 70 years on this planet, I've never seen it so intense. Maybe it's just more obvious thanks to social media and this era of instant news, but I don't think so. And the great falling away that Jesus foretold? We're seeing not just the occasional prominent pastor and entertainment figure denouncing their faith, but entire denominations leaving Biblical Christianity. Even the stalwart Southern Baptist Convention seems on the verge of splitting.

A recent study (March 2020) by George Barna—for the Center for Biblical Worldview at the Family Research Council—looked at the worldviews of U.S. adults. While 51% claimed to hold a Biblical worldview, upon deeper questioning, 49% of those people accept reincarnation as a possibility and only 33% of that group believe that humans are born with a sinful nature and can only be saved by the grace of Jesus Christ. Indeed, after answering 51 worldview questions, only 6% of American adults hold to a truly Biblical worldview. [Now just 4% in 2023] Even among a group called SAGE Cons—Spiritually Active Governance Engaged Conservative Christians, only 44% actually held a Biblical worldview (88% claimed to hold one).[6]

As a result of our society falling away from a Biblical worldview, we see increasing persecution of the church. Believers are being beheaded in Muslim nations when they were previously tolerated. In Communist China and other totalitarian nations, the church must meet underground, while the government now destroys church buildings they once sanctioned and even built. In the U.K., believers are singled out and charged with hate speech crimes for speaking out on what the Bible teaches. In Canada, pastors are being arrested, churches have been closed under the guise of pandemic restrictions, and some burned down in clear hatred of what they represent. Even here in the U.S., restrictions were placed on churches in some states, while bars and mosques remained open. Such things were unheard of just two decades ago. Yet, they are likely to accelerate as Satan sees his time growing short.

[Indeed, now in 2023, we're seeing an increase in this persecution. Pastors being arrested for hate crimes for stating the biblical teaching that there are but two genders. College professors are being fired for teaching that biological fact. The LGBTQI+ movement has taken hold in crazy ways, leading to every major corporation feeling the need for DEI execs and training. For those who don't know, DEI stands for diversity, equity, and inclusiveness, and the LGBTQI+ activists demand that their rights supersede your rights. If you use the wrong pronoun for some guy dressed in women's clothing, you'll be "retrained" at the minimum or prosecuted at the worst.]

Let's consider natural phenomena, earthquakes in particular. While Seneca wrote of earthquakes occurring often before the fall of Jerusalem, we have no actual records, nor did any type of scale exist regarding magnitude. Looking at today, is God using the planet to tell us

---

[6] https://downloads.frc.org/EF/EF21E41.pdf

something?

Despite a few "slow" years, we've seen a steady progression in the number and intensity of earthquakes since 1900. In fact, up through May 19th of this year (2021), there have already been 66 M6+ earthquakes across the globe,[7] and over 40 active volcanoes (when, historically, only 20 or so are active in any typical week). When averaged, that's almost one major quake every other day so far this year, although they do tend to cluster.

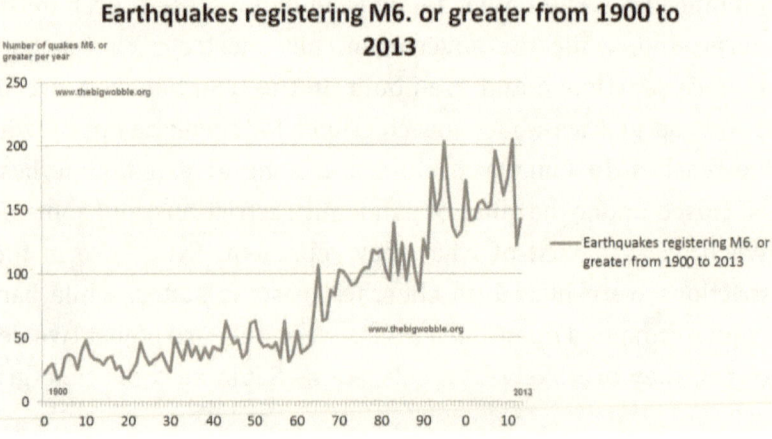

In the Olivet Discourse, if there is any relevance to duality, did Jesus foretell future events, both near future **and** far future (as it ends up)? Either way, He offered no timeline. Indeed, He said of that hour and day we wouldn't know (although I discuss that Jewish idiom in the other book). The discourse is offered in the synoptic gospels—Matthew, Mark, and Luke—but not in John. In essence, the Book of Revelation is John's Olivet Discourse—on steroids. It, too, while offering a prophetic look at the future, provides no "schedule." Yet, although we can't place specific events into a defined timeline, I believe we can see that we're moving into an era of increasing tribulation and persecution of the church, and that, as we'll see, is what the Apocalypse shows us.

Will this lead to a third great awakening with the church moving

---

[7] https://earthquake.usgs.gov/earthquakes/browse/m6-world.php

into a golden age? Or are these just pessimistic amillennial observations? Have we entered the period of tribulation preceding Christ's return and feared by so many? Hang onto your hats and keep your focus on Him.

The Numbers Game

Gematria & The Use of Numbers

What is Gematria?

Gematria is often thought of as a form of fortunetelling with its origins in Jewish mysticism, the Kabbalah. Because of this, some search the Scriptures for secret codes and hidden phrases which will unlock some hidden meaning within the Scripture. One example that comes to mind is that on the day Yitzhak Rabin, Prime Minister of Israel, was assassinated in 1995, the daily scripture reading in Jewish synagogues throughout the world allegedly had the phrase, "Rabin . . . Rabin . . . die . . . die" encoded within.

Hmmm, maybe. While I have no doubt that the Bible is full of hidden stuff we might never know in this lifetime, I tend to doubt such specificity. This is what makes many people look at gematria as a form of fortunetelling.

On a positive side note, the Kabbalah gave us the science of codes, cryptology aka cryptography. Without this, we'd have no secure methods of encryption for banking, email, and the like.

naokewJpwoshlelloewdsttuenouqwaroosgbkoisspazmiwaghj desvowtisnebbsoeqs.

The key is hidden elsewhere in this chapter. haha

Gematria is the method of assigning numbers to a name, word, or phrase based upon the number associated with each letter. In ancient Hebrew, there was no separate numerical system. Each letter had a number assigned to it, and it was interpreted as a number, rather than a letter, based upon its context. As such, names, words, and phrases could be numerically coded and different meanings could be discerned based upon the cipher used.

In fact, gematria has a longer history than the Kabbalah, which is believed to have started in the Middle Ages as a formal method or school of thought. It was used in ancient times and had its basis in astrology and divination. The Babylonians had a system called *aru* in which numerical valuations were assigned to whole words, which made sense because their writing form was logographic. However, these values were assigned arbitrarily, given through tables.[8] The ancient Greeks had a system called *isopsephy*, which was similar to Jewish gematria in that the alphabet was used for numbers. We don't know which came first, Jewish gematria or Greek *isopsephy*, but they led to other systems such as Arabic *abjad* numerals and English gematria. So, gematria is not unique to the Jewish culture.

However, the use of numbers in Revelation—actually, throughout the entire Bible—involves numerology, not gematria. Why, then, do I bring this up? To the multitudes, perhaps the most famous gematria in the modern world is in Revelation. Famous to the point that it holds a firm place in modern culture—Christian and non-Christian alike: 666 . . . Ever hear of it? But what if the 666 has nothing to do with gematria? Again, more on that later.

Recently I learned of two other interesting gematria numbers in the NT. When reading about Simon Peter and the others catching 153 fish (John 21:11), did you ever wonder who took the time to count them? I mean, such precision is unusual for numbers in the Bible. Well, 153 is the gematria for "sons of God." Jesus *did* say they'd become fishers of men. And the net didn't tear. Ponder that for a moment.

A second gematria of interest lies in the accounts of Jesus' baptism by His cousin in all four gospels. The word for 'dove,' *peristera*, περιστερά, has the same gematria as the first and last letters of the

---

[8] Lieberman, Stephen. "A Mesopotamian Background for the So-Called Aggadic 'Measures' of Biblical Hermeneutics?" (Hebrew Union College Annual, 1987), 58: 157–225

Greek alphabet, the alpha and the omega. The writers could have used a generic word for 'bird' or some other description, but instead, they chose this word. Coincidence?

In actuality, gematria is rare in the Bible. Numerology, however, is common. And by saying numerology, I mean it in the broad sense of its definition: the study of numbers. I don't mean using numbers like a horoscope to determine one's future. That is a form of idolatry. Biblical numerology is the study or use of numbers in a symbolic sense, as we'll see.

The Importance of Numbers in the Bible

In the latter half of the last century, popular teachings led to an upsurge in the popularity of kabbalistic mathematical concepts. In the previous section, I mentioned one such issue—the hunt for hidden codes in the Bible's text. Many of these practices led to the increased use of numbers in occult, mystic, or metaphysical teachings. These, in turn, led biblical scholars to become highly skeptical of any use of numbers in the Bible.

As such, we've likely missed out on some very interesting aspects of the Bible. They've been there the whole time, hiding in plain sight, but ignored by theologians and schools of theology because they involved numbers. Sorry, but the whole "I'm not good at math" argument fails to add up.

There are two aspects to the use of numbers that I want to bring up here. First, numbers are integral to the structure of the Old Testament in a purely technical way. I've yet to find similar studies of the New Testament (and I don't know Greek, so I won't attempt such a thing for Revelation). Much like haiku poetry of today that has a specific structure, the Pentateuch, many Psalms, and Daniel have been studied and found to hold to a specialized form of writing utilizing a numeric structure. The number seven and its multiples, in particular, are critical to this structure, and that construction leads to certain words or phrases being emphasized. The work of Claus Schedl, in the 1960s-1970s, and Casper Labuchagne, from 1995-2017, brought this logotechnical (as they coined it) aspect of the Bible back into the light. Their work was met with a hostile reception at first, for reasons mentioned above. However, more recently, scholars are warming to the concepts and beginning to realize they're missing out on something. Further discussion of this is beyond the scope of this book.

Second, some numbers hold special, or symbolic, meaning. For most of us, the meaning of the numbers three and seven have been taught without fail, with three being the number of God, as in the Trinity, and seven being the number of Jesus, completion, and perfection. However, there are more numbers than three and seven that hold special significance, and those two numbers mean much more.

Looking at the number three once again, it held a different symbolism during biblical times. The Holy Spirit, as we know Him today, was not acknowledged as an individual member or person of the Godhead at that time. Yet, *Ruach Elohim*, the Spirit of God, was very much at work in the Old Testament, mentioned roughly 100 times.[9] We see the Spirit of God being active from creation (Genesis 1:2) through Job (Job 33:4), Joseph (Genesis 41:38), the time of Moses (Exodus 31:3-4), the judges, Saul (1 Samuel 16:14) and David (1 Samuel 16:13 and many Psalms), and the prophets to name a handful of instances. Finally, in Acts 1:8 and 2:4, He arrived to permanently indwell believers, something He didn't do in the Old Testament.

While ancient Israelites had no understanding of the Holy Spirit as a member of a triune Godhead, they did hold to the concept of two Yahwehs—the spiritual, unknowable Yahweh, God the Father, and the physical manifestation of Yahweh who walked with Adam and Eve in the garden and met with Abraham under the oak of Mamre. The binitarian concept of "Two Powers in Heaven" was commonly accepted up to the Second Temple Period and was dismissed entirely after Jesus came onto the scene, perhaps in the Jews' desire to deny His being that earthly Yahweh.[10]

---

[9] Charles C. Ryrie, *Basic Theology* (Chicago, IL: Moody Publishers, 1999), 399.
[10] nakedbiblepodcast.com/podcast/naked-bible-355-revelation-17-20/

The use of 'three' in the Bible isn't always obvious. The patriarchs of Israel were Abraham, Isaac, and Jacob. That's pretty recognizable. Yet, before the flood, three men were mentioned as being righteous—Abel, Enoch, and Noah. How many books are in the Old Testament? 39(=3x13) (Note: 13 has its own use in the Bible but for that, I refer you to "The 13th Enumeration" blog[11] by William Struse. More fascinating material.) What about the 27 books of the New Testament? 27=3x3x3. Then there's Jesus' crucifixion. He was placed on the cross at the third hour (9 am) and died at the ninth hour (3 pm), after three hours of darkness. In the Bible, three is also a number symbolizing completeness, although not used to extent that seven is for that.

In ancient times, the Near Eastern world, both Jews and gentiles, viewed the number three as representing the cosmos on a vertical plane—the heavens, the earth, and the netherworld. Just as three stands for the vertical plane of existence, four was symbolic of the horizontal plane—the four corners of the earth, the four winds, the four cardinal points of the compass.

So, yes, four is another important number in the Bible and represents extensiveness, as well as the wholeness and the expanse of creation. On the fourth day of creation, God finished creating the material universe. Like this example, the use of four in scripture is typically more subtle. The river coming from the garden of Eden split into four named rivers. Rainbows are mentioned only four times in the Bible. There are four Gospels, each with its specific emphasis. God bore witness to the message of salvation by (1) signs, (2) wonders, (3) miracles, and (4) the gifts of the Holy Spirit (Heb 2:4). Jesus' garments were divided into four at the foot of the cross for the four soldiers guarding the cross. And from a logotechnical perspective, the fourth item in a list of seven is highlighted by its central location in the structure of those verses.

This brings us back to seven. More than being the number identified with Jesus, the Israelites of the ancient Near East, in the time of the Bible's writing, saw the number seven as symbolically meaning

---

[11] www.the13thenumeration.com/

fullness, totality, completion, abundance, and wholeness. It symbolizes the totality of the cosmos . . . three (vertical plane) plus four (horizontal plane). As Christians, we see the fullness and completion of history in Christ, thus seeing the number seven in Him.

The number seven could be considered a key to the Bible, its most important symbolic number. It and its multiples are used throughout the Bible. We see it in the creation and time cycles set by God—seven days of the week with the Sabbath as the seventh day, the seven-year sabbatical cycle of rest and release—the *shmita*, and the 49-year cycle of the Jubilee. The lunar cycle is, in a practical sense, 28 (4x7) days. We see it mentioned explicitly—seven, multiples of seven (49, 70, 77), seven times, seven-fold, its ordinals (seventh, seventieth), and more. Oh, and please forgive me; I forgot 70 times seven. By the way, the phrase '70 times seven' doesn't mean 490. It's a Jewish idiom meaning to do something completely. Those following Jesus would have known that He meant to forgive someone completely.

Seven is also seen implicitly—the seven intentions of the Lord's Prayer; seven parables in Matt 13; feeding 5,000 men, plus women and children, with five loaves of bread and two fish (5+2=? -- yep, 7); feeding the 4,000 with seven loaves; and more. Those are just some New Testament examples.

In the Old Testament, we see creation in seven days. Noah takes seven pairs of clean animals and seven pairs of birds onto the ark. Jacob labored for Leah and Rachel for seven years each and bows to Esau seven times as he approaches him upon his return to Canaan. Moses went up onto Mt. Sinai with the 70 elders of Israel, and later, the Sanhedrin consisted of 70 men. Joshua had seven priests with seven trumpets march around Jericho seven times. Daniel tells Nebuchadnezzar that he'll be out of favor for "seven times" or years, while at another time, Nebuchadnezzar has the fiery furnace heated seven times its usual. Elijah had his servant look west for rain seven times at the end of the drought. The Shunammite woman's son sneezed seven times as God used Elisha to raise him from the dead. If you take time to count (I didn't), one source says there are over 390 occurrences of seven in the Old Testament-- and 88 in the New Testament, the majority of which are symbolic.[12] Another source states that there are 562 instances of seven and its derivatives in the Bible.[13] Again, I didn't count to see who has bragging rights on being correct.

I didn't even mention Revelation, which has the most references to the number of any book in the New Testament. We'll get to that after seven more paragraphs.

Closely related to seven is 12. Do you see the connection? Three plus four equals seven. Three times four equals 12. There are 12 hours in a day (plus 12 in a night) and 12 months in a year. There are 60 seconds in a minute and 60 minutes in an hour—60=5x12. The number for a dozen wasn't just random happenstance. To the Greeks, even before Pythagoras, the perfect rectangular triangle had sides of 3, 4, and 5, the sum of which is 12. Like seven, 12 represents completeness, totality, and perfection.

Where do we see the number 12 in scripture? Jacob had 12 sons, as did Ishmael and Nahor, Abraham's brother. Jacob's sons, the 12 tribes of Israel, were represented by 12 spies sent to the land and 12 men carrying 12 stones out of the Jordan to build a memorial, as well as the 12 gemstones on the Breastplate of Judgment of the high priest's ephod.

In the New Testament, Jesus stayed behind in the temple when he was 12 years old and, later, had 12 named disciples, called His apostles. One woman healed by Jesus had had a discharge of blood for 12 years. After feeding the 5,000, 12 baskets were filled with broken bread. Jesus states that He could appeal to His Father and 12 legions of angels could be sent to aid Him. The young girl, the synagogue leader's daughter, whom Jesus raised from the dead was 12. Again, I'll leave the Book of Revelation to the next section, but I'm sure your mind is already working toward that.

Upon having the prominence of these four numbers—three, four, seven, and twelve—highlighted to me, I began to notice them in my daily readings. Actually, it was more like they jumped off the page at

---

[12] Labuchagne, Casper. *Numerical Secrets of the Bible* (North Richland Hills, TX: BIBAL Press, 2000), 26.
[13] https://revelationlogic.com/articles/the-number-seven/

me. You might experience the same.

One other number needs to be mentioned—ten. And in case it hasn't already hit you, 10=3+7. In ancient times, again for both Jew and gentile, ten was a mark of authority, law, government, responsibility, and completeness. Ten is considered to be one of the four spiritually perfect numbers (3, 7, 10, & 12).

While creation took but seven days, God spoke— "God said . . ."— ten times to complete His work in Genesis 1. In Exodus, God gave us the Ten Commandments and met with the 70 (7x10) elders who joined Moses and Joshua on the mountain. In scripture, where we see multiples of a number, it is often a multiple of ten. The 70 elders and members of the Sanhedrin. Moses on Mt. Sinai for 40 days. The 40 years of wandering by the Israelites. Jesus in the wilderness for 40 days (Elijah, too). Many of the judges of Israel judged for 40 years, which is the symbolic length of a generation in the Bible. David's chief men, the *Gibborim* (הַגִּבֹּרִים) were called "the Thirty." (Yes, I know 37 names are listed in 2 Samuel 23. Although mentioned in the 37 names, "The Three" was a separate, more renowned trio, and others, such as Uriah the Hittite, had died, so only 30 were probably active at any given time.)

There's a lot more that could be said about these five numbers. As I stated earlier, the number seven is critical in the actual structure of much, if not all, of the Old Testament. For that, I refer you to Casper Labuchagne's *Numerical Secrets of the Bible* and his other logotechnical work. It's fascinating (I know. I find them all fascinating). That work also gets into the gematria of יהוה, YHWH (26), and "the glory of the Lord" (58) as two other important numbers that play a role in scripture. We might touch on those as needed, but now let's look at the symbolic use of numbers in the Apocalypse.

Numbers in Revelation

In the previous section, we looked at five numbers that are used extensively throughout the Bible. These same numbers are used within Revelation, and just as in the rest of the Word, the number seven is preeminent. In fact, of the 88 times that 'seven' or a derivative is referenced in the New Testament, 55 of those are in the Book of Revelation, contained within 31 verses. This time I counted.

The symbolic use of 'seven' starts right in the first chapter. In v4, John offers his epistolic greeting to the *'seven churches that are in Asia . . .*" and mentions the "*seven spirits who are before His* (God, the father) *throne, . . .*" Further on, he tells us of the "seven golden lampstands" (a menorah) and of the "seven stars" held in Christ's right hand, which represent the seven churches and the angels of the churches, respectively.

The use of seven continues throughout the Apocalypse—a scroll with seven seals, the lamb with seven horns and seven eyes, seven trumpets, seven plagues, seven bowls, seven thunderclaps, the beast with seven heads and 10 horns. These are examples of explicit uses of the number. One implicit use is less obvious; there are seven visions shown to John.

Since the use of 'seven' as a symbol goes back to the beginning of time, we need to understand it as the ancients did. 'Seven' in the original Aramaic is *sheba* (שֶׁבַע), and its root word is *saba* (שָׂבַע). This also the root for *shaba* (שָׁבַע) which means 'swearing an oath'—the only difference between it and *sheba* is the accent, or cantillation mark, under the *shin* שׁ. Thus, in addition to the symbolic meanings of fullness, wholeness, abundance, and completeness, as mentioned earlier, it holds the meaning of being sworn to be true.

So, in Revelation, when John lists seven churches, he's referencing the whole church—present and future. And when he relates his vision of, say, the seven trumpets, we also know that what he's relating is true; these things **will** occur. Likewise, the revelation of Christ in seven visions is God's way of saying it's true.

Another aspect of 'seven' is that when we see a list of seven things, the seventh is often special. Example: on the seventh day of creation, God rested. We see this in Revelation where the seventh seal of the scroll is opened to reveal the seven trumpet judgments and likewise with the seventh trumpet introducing the seven bowls. And with the seventh bowl, God pronounces, "*It is done!*" (Revelation 16: 17).

The use of 'three' within Revelation is less obvious, but it's there. It starts right in chapter one as well. Take another look at that chapter. Do you see them? It starts in v2 where John bears witness to three things:

> 2 who bore witness **to the word of God** *and* **to the testimony of Jesus Christ,** *even* **to all that he saw.**

It continues in v3:

> 3 *Blessed is the one* **who reads aloud** *the words of this prophecy, and blessed are those* **who hear,** *and* **who keep what is written in it,** *for the time is near.*

When it comes to lists of three in Revelation 1, the hits keep coming, all the way to Revelation 1:19:

> 19 *Write therefore the things* **that you have seen,** **those that are** *and* **those that are to take place after this.**

As I count them there are 12 instances of such trios. We'll get to the use of 12 momentarily.

Some of you might say there are a couple more, and you're likely to bring v8 to my attention.

> 8 *"I am the Alpha and the Omega," says the Lord God, "who is and who was and who is to come, the Almighty."*

Yes, there are "the Alpha," "the Omega," and "the Almighty" which seem to comprise a trio as they're all preceded by "the." However, I can't think of an instance where He's called just "the Alpha" or only "the Omega." They are always used together. Interestingly, that "title"—the Alpha and the Omega—is unique to the Book of Revelation where you'll find it used ... three times. More curiously, the alternate phrasing, "the first and the last," also occurs only in Revelation ... three times. Leave it to the phrase "the beginning and the end" to ruin the streak. Although it, too, only occurs in Revelation, it's found only twice. To use an American baseball metaphor, John swung for the fences but left a man on third.

And what about "who is and who was and who is to come...?" Yep, there are indeed three components to that as well, and it's another title used only in Revelation. You'll find it used twice, in chapter one, v4 and v8. Even though it's composed of three phrases, I treat it as a singular description, or title, for reasons I'll get to later. So, to me, the three-count in this verse consists of (1) the Alpha and the Omega, (2) who is and who was and who is to come, and (3) the Almighty, as three separate titles.

Three also comes into play through its ordinal, a third. Notice that the trumpet judgments all involve either a third of the earth or a third of mankind. But we'll discuss this a bit more later, as well.

Before moving to the number 12, let me briefly discuss the number ten. I've already mentioned one use of it, the ten horns on the beast. In Revelation 2:10, believers in Smyrna are warned that some will be tested by prison for ten days. There are ten kings—represented by the ten horns—who will receive authority for one hour during which they will also hate "the prostitute" and "make her desolate and naked."

More importantly, however, ten is used more often as a multiplier or ordinal in the Apocalypse. The number of mounted troops unleashed by the sixth trumpet to kill a third of mankind is "ten thousand times ten thousand" (Revelation 9:16). In Revelation 11:13, we read of a great earthquake in Jerusalem that destroys a tenth of the city and kills seven thousand people. Satan is bound and then released after a thousand years, while Christ and His saints rule for a thousand years (Revelation 20). And of course, how can one ignore the 144,000 of Revelation 7?

In all of these references, a thousand is simply symbolic of a large number, just as it does in the remainder of the Bible where you might note that those considered wealthy had large flocks of thousands of sheep, or x-thousand donkeys, or x-thousand camels. Armies were described as x-thousand chariots, horsemen, or soldiers. Even in the New Testament, Jesus fed 5,000 and 4,000 men, not 5,253 men. One thousand was a mark of wealth, which makes sense when a man worked for a single denarius a day (Matthew 20:2). BTW, have you noticed it yet? A thousand is 10 to the third power—10 x 10 x 10. The number 1,000 cannot be taken literally.

The mention of 144,000 is a nice segue back to the number 12. After all, 144 is 12 x 12. We'll look into the 144,000 later, so suffice it to say right now that it represents a large, complete number. Regarding 12, we also see 24 (2 x 12) thrones occupied by 24 elders sitting before the throne of God. There is mention of the 12 tribes of Israel. In Revelation 21, we read of the new Jerusalem descending from heaven with its 12 foundations inscribed with the names of the 12 apostles, the 12 gates made of 12 pearls and named for the 12 tribes of Israel, and the 12 angels guarding those gates. On both sides of the river flowing from the throne room, we read of the tree of life bearing its 12 kinds of fruit, one for each month.

Again, as stated earlier, 12 is a number symbolizing completeness or totality. We certainly can see that in the Book of Revelation. And like the numbers three, seven, and ten, its use in Revelation is symbolic. Don't get caught up in trying to understand these as literal numbers.

The Old in the New

While numerous scholars have written on John's use of the OT in the Apocalypse, the use of the OT in this book is not typically taught to most lay believers today. Unlike the people to whom John wrote directly in the first century, we don't have their almost innate understanding of the OT. For them, the words of Moses and the prophets were taught starting at an early age. By the age of accountability, most Jewish teen males knew the books of the law, Daniel, Ezekiel, and the other prophets. (Oh, and for that next Bible trivia night, the age of accountability is . . . 12.)

Have you ever heard the phrase, "The Old Testament is the New Testament concealed, and the New Testament is the Old Testament revealed?" There's a lot of truth in that statement, but in reality, the exploration of the use of the OT in the New Testament (NT) is relatively recent. Until the mid-20th century, most studies of the OT looked at parallels in the rabbinic literature. The translation and publication of the Dead Sea Scrolls, starting in the 1950s, changed that. The first "landmark" publication regarding the Book of Revelation was *The Use of Daniel in Jewish Apocalyptic Literature and in the Revelation of St. John* by Dr. Greg Beale in 1984. In 1995, Dr. Steve Moyise published *The Old Testament in the Book of Revelation*, and Dr. Beale put out *John's Use of the Old Testament in the Book of Revelation* in 1999. Between them and other scholars, numerous articles and books on the topic have been published.

According to Dr. Moyise and many others, John's allusions to the

OT focused more on the prophetic literature and worship language in the Psalms than he did on the Torah, while other NT writers paid more attention to the Torah (the Pentateuch, or first five books of Moses). As such, John alluded to the Torah 82 times, but he referenced the Psalms 97 times and the count for the prophets is: Isaiah-122, Ezekiel-83, Daniel-74, the minor prophets-73, and Jeremiah-48. It's noteworthy that there is more OT in the Book of Revelation than in the rest of the NT combined.

Why might this be the case? Why would John "allude" to things described by, say, Daniel? Was he just trying to copy him? Of course not. Some scholars infer that John used the OT to present his NT theology. Was he simply mining the OT for scripture he could use to make his point? Nope. Isaiah, Ezekiel, and Daniel (and others) all had visions of God's heavenly court, His throne room. God granted John access to the throne room as well. Unless God redecorated, John saw the same things as the other three had hundreds of years earlier. It makes sense that he would appear to refer to those earlier visions by highly esteemed prophets when, in fact, he was describing what he, too, saw. John's target audience was largely familiar with those prophetic visions already and would understand what he was relating to them. Our basic **un**familiarity with the prophetic writings is one reason we find Revelation confusing.

Yes, John simply described the things he saw—as he was commanded to do—which sound the same as the other prophets because they were the same. There's a fine nuance between "alluding" to OT prophets—as the scholars like to point out—and describing the things he, in reality, saw—which the OT prophets also saw. This gets back to the concept that the OT prophecies were types or foreshadows of events at the end of days.

But, you might say, John's accounts differ from the others. Sure, his perspective and understanding would be different, just as Ezekiel's differed from Isaiah's. If two people describe the same car, one might emphasize the lights while the other offers details on the shape and styling. Differences would be expected.

One way or the other, John also does something unique to these references in the Book of Revelation. Where other NT writers directly quote an OT source word-for-word, John appears to take a source, mash it together with other prophecies, or utilize it differently from the original, to combine them and create a "new" theological statement.

Dr. Beale, in *John's Use of the Old Testament in the Book of Revelation,* lists eight ways in which John uses the OT.

1) Uses segments of the OT as literary prototypes. That is, he models his material after patterns he saw in the OT. Example: Daniel 2 and 7 where he finds the beast with seven heads and ten horns.
2) Makes thematic use of the OT. Examples: the divine warrior theme, frightening celestial events, and other word pictures from OT Day of the Lord passages
3) Uses analogies from the OT using persons, places, and events. Example: the plagues of Exodus
4) Takes OT content and universalizes it. Example: the description of Israel as a kingdom of priests becomes universal to the church, Jews and gentiles alike
5) States that OT prophetic material is directly fulfilled by Christ, but in an informal way without directly quoting the OT prophet. Example: in Revelation 1:7 John states, *"Behold he is coming with the clouds, and every eye will see him, even those who pierced him."* This is an indirect quote from Zechariah 12:10, which says, *". . . when they look on me, on him whom they have pierced . . ."*
6) Shows fulfillment of OT prophecy indirectly. Example: Isaiah 22:22 holds a prophetic statement about *"the one having the key of David, the one who opens and no one will shut, and who shuts and no one opens."* In Revelation 1:18, Jesus is described as holding ". . . *the keys of Death and of Hades . . ."* but in Revelation 3:7, that phrase is replaced by the quote from Isaiah 22.
7) Makes inverted use of the OT. By this, Beale means that on the surface an allusion looks to contradict the OT

contextual meaning. Example, several passages in Isaiah (45:14 and 49:23) contextually show gentiles bowing down to Israel as God's chosen people, but then John directly inverts that in Revelation 3:9 to show those Jews of the synagogue of Satan having to bow before the feet of Christians.

8) Makes stylistic use of OT language. This is a technical area but essentially involves what are called grammatical solecisms, or mistakes. John has been criticized by many for his poor Greek in some areas, and yet those mistakes appear to be on purpose. Though he's writing in Greek, he phrases something the way it would be written grammatically in Hebrew. It looks like lousy Greek, but in fact, is there to call attention to something specific.

John's use of the OT in Revelation is unique and stylistically his own. In so doing, he created, in a sense, NT theology, and yet, that theology is not in contradiction to the theology of the OT. Why not? Because the Holy Spirit inspired and directed him to do so, just as the Spirit directed the other NY writers.

Another aspect of John's use of the OT brings to mind the two disciples on the road to Emmaus after Christ's resurrection. Jesus hid Himself from them as He joined them and began to teach.

> *25 And he said to them, "O foolish ones, and slow of heart to believe all that the prophets have spoken! 26 Was it not necessary that the Christ should suffer these things and enter into his glory?" 27 And* **beginning with Moses and all the Prophets**, *he interpreted to them in all the Scriptures the things concerning himself. (Luk 24:25-27)*

Just as Jesus revealed Himself to Cleopas and Simon (Peter??) through Moses and the prophets, John has done the same for us. We can only hope that our hearts will burn within us as the Scriptures are opened up to us.

Enoch's Here, too

One of the things that modern Christians don't understand is the influence that Second Temple Period writings had on the authors of the NT, including John. We're taught that if it isn't in the canonical books of the Bible, it's not useful. Yet, the NT writers didn't have the canon to go by. Our understanding of scripture can be greatly enhanced by knowing what motivated the NT authors, what their worldview might have been, and what writings affected their thinking.

Books such as Jubilees, 2 Baruch, 4 Ezra, the Book of Wisdom, and a wide selection of rabbinical writings heavily influenced the writers we esteem today. Perhaps the most influential was the book of 1 Enoch. It's referenced in 2 Peter 2:4 and Jude, and early Christian writers, such as Tertullian, Irenaeus, and Origen, firmly believed in the writings of Enoch. Tertullian, in particular, believed the book to have been written by Enoch himself, Noah's great grandfather and a man so highly esteemed by God that he was taken up by God and did not die.

By ignoring the teachings of Enoch, we miss out on a major theme of the Bible—the restoration of mankind and the earth following their corruption by the Watchers, the fallen angels. For today's Christian, evil entered the world through "the fall," Adam's original sin. Yet, to a Second Temple Period Jew, evil entered the world through the fallen angels who introduced mankind to cosmetics and seduction, metallurgy and the art of war, pharmaceuticals, sorcery, and more. These are the same angels mentioned in Genesis 6:1-4:

> *1 When man began to multiply on the face of the land and daughters were born to them, 2 the sons of God saw that the daughters of man were attractive. And they took as their wives any they chose. 3 Then the LORD said, "My Spirit shall not abide in man forever, for he is flesh: his days shall be 120 years." 4 The Nephilim were on the earth in those days, and also afterward, when the sons of God came in to the daughters of man and they bore children to them. These were the mighty men who were of old, the men of renown.*

The Nephilim were the offspring of these illicit unions between angels and the daughters of man, and as such were half mortal and half immortal. When the Nephilim were killed by the great flood, their spirits could not join those of men, nor could they ascend to heaven. Instead, they roamed the earth becoming what we call demons today. Those spirits are still with us, causing havoc.

The Nephilim were also known as giants. We see reference to descendants of them post-flood as the Rephaim, Anakim, Zamzummin, Zuzim, Horites, and Emin in the OT. The first mention of them is in Genesis 14:5 as a confederacy of these giant clans did battle with Chedorlaomer and his allies. The Amorites are also believed to have been giants, being largely Mesopotamian in origin and tying into the *apkallu* of that culture. The latter ties in with Nimrod, founder of Babylon, being described as a giant in some literature. He was, after all, the *"first on earth to be a mighty man."* (Genesis 10:8)

How the giantism of these peoples arose after the flood is a source of great speculation among scholars. Did some of the Nephilim survive the flood? Did other fallen angels try to resume their misdeeds and procreate with human women? Did those genes get passed on through Noah's daughters-in-law? Your guess is as good as any scholar's. Either way, they were living in those days. And God was just as determined to remove them, as these were the clans "devoted to destruction" by God, which Moses and the Israelites seemed to go out of their way to annihilate. For much, much more on all of this, I strongly recommend Dr. Michael Heiser's *Reversing Hermon*.[14]

How does this apply to Revelation? In 1 Enoch, we learn not only how the fallen angels corrupted man, but we also read that they were chained up in the darkness of Tartarus, the deep abyss that is their prison, because of their transgressions (Revelation 9:1). The lake of fire in Revelation 19 and 20 (also Matthew 25:41) has no OT precedent. It's found in 1 Enoch. While the term "antichrist" is of Christian origin, the belief of a demonic army led by a military tyrant figure and joining the

---

[14] Heiser, M. *Reversing Hermon*, Defender Publishing, Crane, MO, May 22,

nations of the earth against the Messiah in the End Times predates Jesus' earthly ministry and has much of its origins in 1 Enoch.

As we'll see, the ideas presented in 1 Enoch permeate the Book of Revelation. The number 666. Gog of Magog. The 144,000. All have connections to Enoch.

* * * *

So, as we now move into the Book of Revelation, I'll point out OT references throughout. However, without making this a major tome, I won't get into every OT allusion. My goal is to make Revelation understandable in a broad sense, not to provide such a detailed analysis that one's eyes glaze over and brain goes numb.

2017.

The Declaration of Christ as God

Revelation, Chapter One

While many see chapter one of the Apocalypse as an epistolary opening, greeting the seven churches to which John is writing, there is much more involved here than a "simple" epistle. As noted previously, some things presented in this chapter are **only** in this chapter of the Bible and others that are presented here and seen only in this book.

After the first three verses, which make it clear where these visions originated and by whose hand the book is written, John wastes no time and comes out swinging in his presentation of Jesus as the Most High (*hypsistos*) incarnate God. He starts in v4:

> *4 John to the seven churches that are in Asia: Grace to you and peace from him* **who is and who was and who is to come**, *and from the seven spirits who are before his throne, 5 and from Jesus Christ the faithful witness, the firstborn of the dead, and the ruler of kings on earth . . . (Rev 1:4-5a)*

Here John describes God as "*who is and who was and who is to come*," which I mentioned earlier. We also find one of those "mistakes," or solecisms, that John made. The Greek he uses for 'who is,' *ho ōn*, **ὁ ὤν**, refers back to the burning bush where God tells Moses 'I am who I am' —*egō eime ho ōn*, **ἐγώ εἰμι ὁ ὤν**. Yet, John presents it not with proper

Greek grammar, which would be in the genitive case, but keeps it in the nominative case as it was written in Exodus 3:14 by the translators of the Septuagint. As with his other "mistakes," he appears to do this to emphasize the words and to make clear the OT reference.

But then he adds "... and who was and who is to come." Why? With an audience in Asia Minor that would more likely come from a gentile background than a Jewish one, John possibly wanted to make clear who God is—the Most High God, the same God Who greeted Moses at the burning bush and led the Israelites out of Egypt.

By the first century, Zeus was considered by the pagan world as the highest god and creator of life. While this was a step up from the earlier days of Homer when he was seen as a lustful tyrant, it nevertheless placed him as a rival to Yahweh.

Sean McDonough, in his book *YHWH at Patmos: Revelation 1:4 in its Hellenistic and Early Jewish Setting*,[15] looked at Greek writers of the Hellenistic period, which corresponds to the Second Temple Period. In various references to Zeus from that time, he found parallels to this phrase used by John. The closest was a reference by Greek writer Pausanius, citing an oracle at Dodona that described Zeus as "Zeus was, Zeus is, Zeus shall be. O mighty Zeus." It would seem that John, by using his phrase to describe God, is delivering a left jab at Zeus and making it clear that the God of Israel is the Most High, not Zeus.

In v4 we know that this title refers to God the Father because the greeting then states in v5 "*and from Jesus Christ the faithful witness, the firstborn of the dead, and the ruler of kings on earth*" differentiating the two. Then we get to v8:

> "I am the Alpha and the Omega," says the Lord God, "who is and who was and who is to come, the Almighty."

where the title is linked to another, the Alpha and the Omega, which is also stated later in Revelation as "the first and the last" (Revelation 1:17, 21:6, and 22:13). At this point, we can't be sure which member of

---

[15] McDonough, Sean. *YHWH at Patmos: Revelation 1:4 in its Hellenistic and*

the Godhead is speaking since the "Lord God" title can apply to both the Father and Jesus. However, by the time we get to Revelation 1:17-18, there's no ambiguity that John is going for the knockout by equating Jesus with God:

> *17 When I saw him, I fell at his feet as though dead. But he laid his right hand on me, saying, "Fear not, I am the first and the last, 18 and the living one. I died, and behold I am alive forevermore, and I have the keys of Death and Hades. (Rev 1:17-18)*

And He holds the keys of Death and Hades, an assurance that He can deliver His people from both.

The *"keys of Death and Hades"* deserve attention. The Greek grammar can be translated two ways. One, as being the keys **to** Death and Hades, as in they are places which have keys to lock and unlock the gates. The second is the keys **belonging to** Death and Hades, personifying the two.

We can readily understand them as places usually associated with the "underworld." After all, the common belief is that everyone who dies goes there and stays there, much like a prison. One problem we have today is that people think of Hades (Hell) as just that, a prison, a place of punishment. The OT shows that both righteous and unrighteous, good and bad, go there after death. The story of Lazarus, the beggar, says a great chasm separates the righteous and unrighteous, but we all end up there. Only one person has ever descended to there and returned, Jesus. While there, He conquered Death and Hades and took their keys.

And He also set His people free. The righteous no longer wear prison orange, but rather robes of white. In Matthew, we read:

> *52 The tombs also were opened. And many bodies of the saints who had fallen asleep were raised, 53 and coming out*

Early Jewish Setting, (Eugene, OR, Wipf and Stock Publishers), 2011.

of the tombs after his resurrection they went into the holy city and appeared to many. (Mat 27:52-53)

Later, in Revelation 20:4, we read of "thrones, and seated on them were those to whom the authority to judge was committed." Note that 'thrones' is plural and not numbered. Plus, as we'll see, **we** are the ones whom Christ has promised to sit on the thrones and to whom He gives authority to judge. For those who have died in Christ, whether 2,000 years ago or today, Hades has no hold on them.

What about Death and Hades being personified? In the pagan writings of the Ugarits, Greeks, and Romans, we see that happening. For the Ugarits, Mot (Death) battled Ba'al and lived in the underworld of decay and decomposition. Hades was the brother of Zeus and the most hated of all of the gods. In the Greco-Roman world, the goddess Hekate held the keys to Hades. So, just as John took down Zeus, declaring that Christ is the one true God, he now brings down Hekate in her role as keeper of the underworld.

But that's the pagan world, you say. Well, we also see them personified in both the OT and NT. Death uses waves of the sea against his victims (2 Samuel 22:5-6), uses cords and snares (in multiple Psalms and Proverbs), terrorizes people (Psalm 55:4), and has many more such personified traits that can be seen in the OT. In Isaiah 28:15,18, we see the people making a covenant with Death and an agreement with Sheol (Hades). Sheol is seen as having an enlarged appetite and in opening its mouth beyond measure in Isaiah 5:4. Paul quotes Hosea 13:14 in saying, *"O death where is your sting? O grave where is your victory?"* (1 Corinthians 15:55). The personification of this pair was not restricted to the pagan world.

Of note regarding Revelation, Death is mentioned four times in the book, each time together with Hades. We've seen them here in Revelation 1:18. In Revelation 6:8, Death is the rider of the pale horse and is followed by Hades. In Revelation 20:13, Death and Hades give up the dead who were in them. Finally, in Revelation 20:14, Death and Hades are thrown into the lake of fire, which is described as the *"second death."* While a place can be burned down or destroyed by fire, for

Death and Hades to meet a second death implies more of a personification than simply fiery destruction. So, again, we see Death and Hades both as a place and as being personified. The great news, however, is that Christ holds the keys, has complete control over this duo, and, as believers, we need not worry about them.

The phrase, "*the first and the last*," also has OT roots. In Isaiah, we read,

> *6 Thus says the LORD, the King of Israel and his Redeemer, the LORD of hosts:* "**I am the first and I am the last; besides me there is no god**. *(Isa 44:6)*

and,

> *10 "You are my witnesses," declares the LORD, "and my servant whom I have chosen, that you may know and believe me and understand that I am he.* **Before me no god was formed, nor shall there be any after me**. *(Isa 43:10)*

You'll find this in Isaiah 41:4 and 48:12, too. Again, John makes the claim that Yahweh, the God of Israel, is the Creator of all things and the Most High God . . . and that Jesus is God.

In fact, to me, the primary purpose of chapter one is to declare to the world that God is the Creator of all things, that He existed from the beginning, and that there is no other God before or after Him . . . and that Jesus is God. This is also John's way of assuring believers that Jesus will deliver them under persecution . . . because Jesus is God. (Three times for emphasis, in case you didn't catch that.)

We see this in other phrases, some that I mentioned in the previous chapter. V6 equates Jesus with God when John tells us that Jesus made us a kingdom of priests, universalizing the allusion to Exodus 19:6 in which Yahweh calls Israel a kingdom of priests. Other descriptions of Jesus likewise are those of deity and kingship or those that equate Him with God:

> *13 and in the midst of the lampstands one like a son of man, clothed with a long robe and with a* **golden sash** *around his chest. 14 The* **hairs of his head were white,** *like white wool, like snow. His* **eyes were like a flame of fire,** *15* **his feet were like burnished bronze,** *refined in a furnace, and* **his voice was like the roar of many waters.** *16 In his right hand he held seven stars, from his mouth came a sharp two-edged sword, and* **his face was like the sun shining in full strength.** *(Rev 1:13-16)*

All of these descriptors have OT precedents, and some had importance in the pagan world as well, referring to deity or royalty. The golden sash is seen in Daniel 10:5. Daniel 10:6 talks of arms and legs like burnished bronze, *"eyes like flaming torches,"* and *"words like the sound of a multitude."* He later explains the seven stars in His right hand, but the remaining description has its references as well. The idea of a two-edged sword from His mouth comes from Isaiah 11:4 and 49:2. There's another place in the NT where we read of Christ's face shining like the sun, and that is the account of the Transfiguration on Mt. Hermon in Matthew 17:2, which would have been well-known by first-century Christians.

We see in the above example how John was not content to simply quote Daniel 10 in his description of Jesus. While Daniel 10 appears to have been a template, a pattern used by John to form his depiction, he went deeper by using Isaiah, Matthew, and, as we'll see below, Zechariah. The following OT references are additional examples of how John takes bits and pieces of OT scripture, twists the threads, and weaves them into NT theology. Look at the following:

> *9 "As I looked, thrones were placed, and the* **Ancient of Days** *took his seat;* **his clothing was white as snow,** *and the* **hair of his head like pure wool;** *his* **throne was fiery flames;** *its wheels were burning fire. (Dan 7:9)*
>
> *4 As I looked, behold, a stormy wind came out of the north,*

> *and* **a great cloud**, *with brightness around it, and* **fire flashing forth** *continually, and in the midst of the fire, as it were gleaming metal. ... 24 And when they went, I heard the sound of their wings like the* **sound of many waters, like the sound of the Almighty**, *a sound of tumult like the sound of an army. When they stood still, they let down their wings. (Eze 1:4, 24)*

> *And behold, the glory of the God of Israel was coming from the east. And* **the sound of his coming was like the sound of many waters**, *and the earth shone with his glory. (Eze 43:2)*

In these passages, we find references to God, the Ancient of Days, and yet, John uses these to point to Jesus and equate Him with the Most High God.

In v7, "coming with the clouds" not only infers His *Shekinah* Glory but also makes a statement of deity. In the Jewish Bible, some variation of "riding the clouds" is seen five times. Of those, four—Deuteronomy 33:26, Psalm 68:32-33, Psalm 104:1-4, and Isaiah 19:1—refer specifically to the God of Israel. The fifth, Daniel 7:13-14, refers to the "Son of Man," pointing to Jesus and His deity.

> *13 "I saw in the night visions, and behold,* **with the clouds of heaven there came one like a son of man**, *and he came to the Ancient of Days and was presented before him. 14 And to him was given dominion and glory and a kingdom, that all peoples, nations, and languages should serve him; his dominion is an everlasting dominion, which shall not pass away, and his kingdom one that shall not be destroyed. (Dan 7:13-14)*

However, that phrase also denoted deity in the pagan world. Phrases such as "coming on the clouds," "riding a chariot in the clouds," or "the cloud rider" were standard descriptions for Ba'al. So, just as John went after Zeus, he went after Ba'al to show that the God of Israel is the true God. And again, he equates Jesus with God.

Having pointed out Daniel 7, the verses above play heavily into the Two Yahwehs theology of the OT that I pointed out earlier. This is perhaps the clearest example of the two being delineated. Yet, Daniel 7 has a greater role. I mentioned Daniel 7:9 above, where the Ancient of Days is depicted as having a robe as white as snow and hair like pure wool, attributes given to Jesus by John. These descriptions in Daniel 7 set a frame of reference to the first-century reader and lead into the next two chapters of Revelation, as will be discussed,

As for the symbolic use of seven in this chapter—seven stars in His right hand, seven angels, seven lampstands, and seven churches, we find these explained as we read from Revelation 1:4 through verses 10, 16, and 20. The seven stars represent the angels of the seven churches, which are likewise symbolized by the seven lampstands, or more appropriately, the seven lamps on the menorah. We'll discuss the seven churches in the next chapter, but the general consensus of scholars is that these churches represent the worldwide church, as seven is the number of completeness.

Certainly, the number seven points to the wholeness of the church, but is that alone enough to universalize these seven churches to the worldwide body? Where do these references come from? For that answer, we turn to several passages from Zechariah.

> *And he said to me, "What do you see?" I said, "I see, and behold, a lampstand all of gold, with a bowl on the top of it, and seven lamps on it, with seven lips on each of the lamps that are on the top of it. (Zec 4:2)*

For whoever has despised the day of small things shall rejoice, and shall see the plumb line in the hand of Zerubbabel. **"These seven are the eyes of the LORD, which range through the whole earth**.*" (Zec 4:10)*

In these verses, we find the lampstand reference made by John. In addition to being described as the seven eyes of the Lord that range through the whole earth, lamps provide light in the dark, thus illuminating the world. So, who is Zechariah talking with? Going back to Zechariah 1:7-10, we read that he was talking with a man on a red horse standing within the myrtle trees. There were additional horses with him that are described as those that patrol the earth. Again, we see the whole earth theme. Then, in v11, the man is identified as the Angel of the Lord. Following the Two Yahweh theology of the OT, the Angel of the Lord is time and time again identified as the second, physical personification of God, that is, Jesus. When we tie together the lampstand here in Zechariah with that of Revelation, it's clear to see how scholars universalize the churches to the worldwide body throughout time.

As a side note, there has been much written on the "eyes of the Lord." In 2 Chronicles 16:9, Hanani the seer tells Asa, king of Judah, *"For the eyes of the LORD run to and fro throughout the whole earth, to give strong support to those whose heart is blameless toward him."* In Zechariah 3:9, we read, *"For behold, on the stone that I have set before Joshua, on a single stone with seven eyes, I will engrave its inscription, declares the LORD of hosts, and I will remove the iniquity of this land in a single day."* In these and other scriptures, the term is a metaphor for God's omniscience and omnipresence.

Before moving on to the seven churches—Revelation 2 & 3—I'd like to mention a couple of points that might seem minor yet are anything but. First, notice in v9 how John describes himself. He is our *"brother and partner in the tribulation."* Clearly, the tribulation is not some far future event—as many believe it to be—if John is our partner in it and he lived 2,000 years ago.

Second, where is the Son of Man in this picture? He's not seated upon a throne but is standing amidst the seven lampstands, in with His churches, with us. He is there as our intercessor, and John goes to some lengths to confirm to us that Jesus is fully capable of delivering us from Death and Hades.

Third, what was John directed to write about? In Revelation 1:19, he is instructed to write about the things he has *"seen, those that are and those that are to take place."* I've mentioned that much of what John saw in his seven visions were images that other prophets had also been shown. He refers back to Daniel, Isaiah, Ezekiel, Zechariah, and others not just because the Jewish believer of the first century could use those prophets' words as familiar reference points, but because he was privileged to see the same things. Does that mean we are to take these images literally? No, images of stars, lampstands, and other things obviously hold symbolic meaning and are to be seen as metaphors. And yet, other images could very well be showing us physical events. As we'll see later, he alludes to the plagues of Egypt. Those were real, physical events. There's a good chance there will be physical events once again.

We all recognize the book as one of prophecy and expect John's words to show us things that have yet to take place. What about the things that are? Just as John was a partner in the tribulation, some of the events/things depicted in this book are *"those that are."* The next two chapters will show us some of those things in the comments about the seven churches. Could there be more to the things that are?

Finally, let's look again at Revelation 1:3:

Blessed is the one who reads aloud the words of this prophecy, and blessed are those who hear, and who keep what is written in it, for the time is near. (Rev 1:3)

Who does John say is blessed by the words of this book? The one who reads aloud doesn't mean you should read it aloud to yourself. Most likely, his reference is to whoever reads the letter to his church, as would have been the custom of the time. And of course, those who hear the words will be blessed as well. But there's a third group mentioned here, and it's a group few ever have in mind when discussing this verse—those *"who keep what is written"* in the book. To keep something is to hold fast to it or attend to it carefully. All of us need to be part of this group. When Christ returns, it will be a glorious event for those of us who believe, trust, and find refuge in Him. For those who don't—even those who claim to be part of the church but don't hold to His teachings—it's going to be an awful time.

The Seven Churches

Just Seven?

As we move into chapters two and three—Christ's messages to the church—have you ever wondered why just seven, or more specifically, why those seven assemblies? I have. One thing I do suspect is that Jesus wasn't concerned that because Paul wrote letters to seven churches, John, His beloved disciple, also needed to. No one was keeping score.

Seriously though, while I understand that seven shows completeness, I've often wondered why those specific seven *ecclesias* were chosen. After all, there were a lot more assemblies in the empire. Colossae was just ten miles east of Laodicea. Philippi was a major Greek city whose Christian body was likely larger than many of the seven selected. Plus, it would have provided easier access to all of the Greek congregations. But then, Paul did already write to them.

All of the groups targeted in Revelation were in Asia Minor, or Turkey, as we know it today. Ephesus was the nearest port to Patmos, the barren island used as the Roman penal colony to which John had been exiled. It was also John's home church at that point, as it's believed that John, Mary (Jesus' mother), Peter, Andrew, and Philip moved to Ephesus to escape Jewish persecution in Jerusalem. The home of Mary and John's tomb can be visited today, and the others are all reportedly buried there as well.

So, certainly a letter to that body—the church in Ephesus—would seem fitting, and the church there would be the first to receive it from Patmos. The other churches sat along a circular trade route, and some speculate that they were selected because they formed a central hub from which the letter could be distributed out to other congregations. One source suggested they followed a mail route on which these seven cities posed as central "post offices" for their region. That seems fitting since the church, like other organizations of the time, relied upon carriers to take their messages from point A to point B, and an efficient route for delivery would be essential. Larger cities within their districts, which might seem more logical as distribution points, were out of the way for such efficacy.

While the efficiency of mail delivery might have played a role, after much reading, thought, and prayer for discernment, I believe they were chosen because they represented problems in or concerns about the *ecclesia* which Christ wanted to stress to present (those that are) and future (those that will be) members of His body. As we'll see, the assemblies chosen were in cities that embodied the problems of that particular church as well. John doesn't separate the church from the city but rather emphasizes the connection between the two. The church in each city is, in a sense, the city itself and Christians are the people of that city. We are to be in this world, but not of it. In most of these churches, the problems arose by its members being **of** the world, not just in it.

Some scholars also see these letters as forensic examinations of the church preceding the meeting of the Divine Council in which the judgment of the world takes place. Divine Council? Huh? For those who are aware of this, it's also called the Deuteronomy 32 worldview, best popularized by Dr. Michael Heiser's book, *The Unseen Realm*.[16]

> *8 When the Most High gave to the nations their inheritance, when he divided mankind, he fixed the borders of the peoples according to the number of the sons of God. 9 But the LORD's portion is his people, Jacob his allotted heritage. (Deu 32:8-9)*

---

[16] Heiser, M. *The Unseen Realm*, Laxman Publishing, Bellingham, WA, 2015.

While the King James and many translations say *"according to the number of the sons of Israel,"* the ESV above and a few other translations say *"according to the number of the sons of God"* or *"according to the number of the heavenly assembly"* (NET). These newer translations are based upon the Septuagint in which the 'sons of God' in the Greek is *angelos Theos*, ἀγγέλων Θεοῦ. According to this worldview, when God dispersed the nations and confused the tongues of man at the Tower of Babel, they were separated into the 70 nations of Genesis 10. Control of each was given to an angelic being from God's Divine Council, while God chose Israel to be His elect, His people.

What council? It's easy to look past, but the Bible clearly speaks of it.

> **God has taken his place in the divine council**; *in the midst of the gods he holds judgment: (Psa 82:1)*

> 9 *"As I looked, thrones were placed, and* **the Ancient of Days took his seat**; *his clothing was white as snow, and the hair of his head like pure wool; his throne was fiery flames; its wheels were burning fire. . . . 26 But* **the court shall sit in judgment**, *and his dominion shall be taken away, to be consumed and destroyed to the end. (Dan 7:9, 26)*

These 'gods' in Psalm 82:1 are those of the 70 nations. The Divine Council in heaven was mirrored on earth as the 70 elders of Israel, which became the 70-member Sanhedrin. Some also believe that these *'ĕlōhîm*, אֱלֹהִים, are the same who laid with human women and led to what we know as the gods of the Greek, Roman, Norse, and other pantheons—not mythical beings, but real beings whose existence became tied up in myth. This idea goes back to the pseudepigrapha *1 Enoch* and is referenced in Jude 1:6, where *"the angels who did not stay within their own position of authority, but left their proper dwelling . . ."* What were their positions of authority? Their positions over the nations.

As we'll explore when we get to chapters four and five, there are several descriptions in the Bible of this Divine Council meeting in heaven. Daniel 7 (above) is a prime example, and that chapter of Daniel holds a prominent position in the Book of Revelation. You could say that Revelation is one large council scene mirroring Daniel 7.

Since judgment begins in the household of God (1 Peter 4:17), it is only proper that the judgments of Revelation start with this examination of the *ecclesia*. Yet, because of God's grace and His forgiveness through our faith in Jesus, the church garners only two chapters in this book, while the judgments on unbelievers consume chapters four through 18. We see this pattern also in the prophets. In Isaiah, for example, the prophet pronounces God's judgments on Israel first and then on Egypt, Babylon, and others who persecuted His people.

There are those who won't keep what is written in this book while claiming to be followers of Christ, and they'll be in for a shock. As we'll see, one of the issues facing the church is those who hold to the idea that grace covers them to the point where they can do whatever they want—once saved, always saved. Nothing could be further from the truth. Let's move on.

A Uniform Pattern

One of the things about the letters to the seven assemblies is that each follows a common structure. This is consistent with the recognition that the Apocalypse is not a letter to a specific body—as were Paul's epistles—but that the seven letters are part of a larger piece aimed at the universal church. Such a pattern would also be in line with the idea of a forensic examination, as mentioned, with a checklist of items that need to be covered. That pattern goes like this:

1. To the angel of the church in a given city, write:
2. Jesus is depicted in terms of His Glory, often using descriptions from chapter one
3. He offers praise or encouragement—I know your . . .
4. But this I have against you . . . offering some reproof or call

for change
5. The one who has an ear, let him hear what the Spirit says
6. An eschatological promise

There are three things to mention about this pattern. First, note that there are only six points to this pattern. Second, the letters are written to the angel of the church. Finally, regarding point #5, there are two things to note.

The number six in the Bible is the number of man and human weakness. Mankind was formed on the sixth day of creation. Man is to work six days and rest on the seventh. It is a number symbolizing incompletion and the manifestation of sin. And as mentioned, three sixes form the most famous gematria of the book, 666. It's appropriate that the examination of the church bears six points. Likewise, the judgments to come upon unbelievers consist of three sets of six afflictions, with the seventh (of the first two sets) leading to six more.

Regarding the recipient of each letter, just who is the angel of the church? Some argue that it's the leader of the congregation. Some think it refers to the congregation itself. However, to this point in the book, John has made no mention of human leadership, only of the supernatural guardians of each body represented by the seven stars in the right hand of Christ. Throughout the Bible, stars are used as symbols of angelic beings. Also, of the 77 times—yes, there's that number seven again—that *angelos*, ἀγγέλων, is used in the book, 69 refer specifically to supernatural angelic beings. The other eight occur in relation to the churches—once in Revelation 1:20, where we're told that the seven stars are the seven angels; and in chapters two and three where the angel of each church is addressed.[17] What are the odds that these eight references also apply to angelic beings and not human leaders? No bookie is gonna take that bet.

So, with it being clear that the angel spoken of is a divine being, what, or who does the angel represent? We know from the book of Daniel that Michael was the "great prince" and protector of Israel—in

---

[17] Aune, David E. *World Biblical Commentary 52A, Revelation 1-5*, Zondervan

essence, its guardian angel. Similarly, the churches had their angels representing the Divine presence and power in the assembly. That being was placed there as the Divine guarantee of the vitality and effectiveness of that church, so will he be judged along with the church? Indeed, the letters address the angel as being as guilty of the church's shortcomings and sin as the offenders within the body. But we have no confirmation that such heavenly beings will be held accountable for earthly transgressions, except perhaps by the scripture that states we will judge angels (1 Corinthians 6:3).

Prior to addressing the two things I wish to mention about the fifth point, I should mention that there are strong OT and NT precedents to the concept of having ears to hear (as well as eyes to see). In Deuteronomy 29, Moses addresses the Israelites and tells them the Lord had not given them hearts to understand, eyes to see, or ears to hear. The wilderness was a test and most of them failed. At several places in Ezekiel (3:10, 12:2, 40:4, and 44:5), we see examples of this. We see this in Matthew, Mark, Luke, and Romans as well. The good news is that He gives His followers eyes that see and ears that hear, while He speaks in parables to everyone else.

So, getting to the fifth point, first, the verse talks about the one who has an ear **hearing** what the Spirit says. The term for hearing in these verses implies listening. I can hear music in the background while I read, but it's just that, background. To listen to that music means comprehending the lyrics or following the notes of the melody. The word used for 'hear,' akouō, ἀκούω, means to attend to, perceive, and consider what is being stated. We are to comprehend what is being said, which is another way of saying we should keep what is written. Also, note that we are to hear what the Spirit says to the **churches**. Not singular. This, to me, clearly means the universal church is to hear what is being relayed about each specific assembly. These messages are for all of us.

The universality of these messages brings up another point. The dispensationalist teaches that there are seven eras or dispensations—

the dispensations of innocence, of conscience, of human government, of promise, of Law, of grace, and of the millennial kingdom of Christ. Those are man-made definitions depicting history since creation, which some believe are represented by the seven churches of Revelation.

However, there is another level of this teaching—that the seven churches stand for the state of the church in different periods since the resurrection. There's the Apostolic Church from 30-100 A.D. represented by Ephesus, the Persecuted Church from 100-312 A.D. represented by Smyrna, and so on until we reach modern day where Laodicea, the lukewarm church, represents today's church.

I, personally, don't hold much to this. After all, these characteristics have existed in various churches throughout the last 1,990 years, just as they all existed in John's time when he wrote the book. And the admonition to hear what the Spirit is saying to the church**es** also speaks to understanding **all** of these warnings no matter what time you live(d) in. Curiously, we'll also see that the very thing which Ephesus, the so-called Apostolic Church, was criticized for was losing their first love, the zeal to evangelize, to share the Gospel. Not very apostolic IMO.

The Cities and Letters

Ephesus

Ephesus—the root of its name being "permitted"—was a large port city on the Icarian Sea that was founded around 700 B.C. by a Greek prince. Its history was tumultuous, but after the Romans defeated Syria (Antiochus the Great) in 189 B.C., it was given to the king of Pergamum. Later, Attalus III, the last of the Pergamum kings, bequeathed it, along with his entire kingdom, to the Roman citizens at his death in 133 B.C. Under Augustus Caesar in the first century B.C., it became the first city of the Roman province of Asia. Its ruins today sit just outside the modern Turkish city of Selc̀uk.

At the time of John, with a population believed to have numbered between 60,000 and 200,000, depending on whose research you like, the city was wealthy and more powerful politically than Pergamum (aka Pergamos), despite the latter continuing to be the provincial Roman capital. When Augustus became emperor in 27 B.C., some believe he moved the proconsular capital from Pergamum to Ephesus, but if so, it appears that the "move" was ceremonial, not official. The city's importance as a port on the main trade roads, as well as being the "entrance" to Asia from the west, made it the province's primary city. In addition, the fame of its Temple of Artemis had spread, to the point where it became part of the imperial religion. As a result, the city prospered. The city was known for that Temple of Artemis (Diana, in the Roman pantheon), which was one of the Seven Wonders of the Ancient World, the Library of Celsus which held over 12,000 scrolls, and its 25,000-seat amphitheater, the largest of the ancient world. The imperial cult, or emperor worship, was also very strong here, to the point that Christians were seen as atheists because they didn't believe in or sacrifice to the Roman gods.

It's believed that Paul founded the church here very early on in his ministry but spent no significant time there until later. Apollos built up the body teaching the repentance of John the Baptist until Priscilla and Aquila *"explained the way of God more accurately."* (Acts 18) By the time Paul returned, it had a flourishing body of believers. The city is mentioned numerous times in the NT, and the riot led by the silversmith Demetrius, depicted in Acts 19, occurred here.

Following the pattern of the seven letters, Jesus commended them as follows:

> *2 "'I know your works, your toil and your patient endurance, and how you cannot bear with those who are evil, but have tested those who call themselves apostles and are not, and found them to be false. 3 I know you are enduring patiently and bearing up for my name's sake, and you have not grown weary. (Rev 2:2-3)*

and criticizes them for:

> *But I have this against you, that you have abandoned the*

> *love you had at first. (Rev 2:4)*

Many pastors teach that abandoning their first love means they no longer loved Jesus. However, v2 and v3 seem to contradict that idea as they patiently endured and bore up for His sake. So, what is meant here? Some point to the Israelis in the wilderness who abandoned God time after time; wanted only an indirect connection to him (Exodus 20:19-21); and preferred being ruled by men (1 Samuel 8:5). God, on the other hand, wants direct communication with each and every one of us.

Dr. Beale, in his lengthy commentary on Revelation,[18] connects this loss of first love to Matthew 24:12-14:

> *12 And because lawlessness will be increased, the love of many will grow cold. 13 But the one who endures to the end will be saved. 14 And this gospel of the kingdom will be proclaimed throughout the whole world as a testimony to all nations, and then the end will come.*

Here we see that the one who endures is linked to the proclamation of the Gospel to the whole world. On the other hand, we can infer that love growing cold is tied to the failure to spread the Gospel. In other words, the ardor of the Ephesian body for sharing the Gospel had cooled down. Under persecution, as we read in Acts 19, they apparently lost their zeal to evangelize. When persecution comes our way, do we strive to bring our enemies to the Lord, or do we simply think, "The Lord's coming back. You're gonna get yours . . .?"

The Ephesians were commended for one other thing . . . hating the works of the Nicolaitans. Also mentioned in the letter to Pergamum, who were these mysterious and nefarious folk whose works Christ also hates? Many scholars believe that the teachings of the Nicolaitans were identical to those of Balaam, who will be mentioned shortly. These also get linked to the mention of the "woman Jezebel" in the letter to the

---

[18] Beale, G.K. *The New International Greek Testament Commentary, the Book of*

church in Thyatira.

The specific practices here were the eating of meat sacrificed to idols (while in the presence of and paying homage to the idol) and sexual immorality. Some contend that the prohibition against eating meat sacrificed to idols extended to the same meat that was later sold in the marketplace—a common practice. Ben Witherington III, in an article titled "Not So Idle Thoughts," showed that all uses of *eidōlothytos,* εἰδωλόθυτος, for 'sacrificed to idols,' refer to meat eaten in the presence of an idol or within its temple precincts. And Paul, in 1 Corinthians 10, appears to agree that by eating such meat in the presence of the idol, one enters into fellowship with demons, but that finding it in the marketplace was not the same thing.

One of the aspects of the culture in that day that we need to recognize was the strength of the trade guilds, as well as the prominence of the imperial cult. The trade guilds each had their patron deity, and of course, the emperor was the deity of the imperial cult. The worship of these deities involved orgies in which meat was sacrificed and eaten in homage to the god, and promiscuous sex played its role as well, both hetero- and homosexual. These were the practices linked to Jezebel of the OT, as well as Balaam, who convinced Balak, king of Moab, to use women to lure Jewish men into sexual liaisons as a way of defeating Israel by leading it into idol worship and sexual immorality.

Because so little is known about the Nicolaitans, many Bible teachers simply lump them together with these other two. Others have labeled them as a sect of Gnostics, and some place them into the realm of antinomianism. That two-dollar theology word means a person who believes that Christians, by virtue of divine grace, are freed from all moral law, as well as biblical law and church-prescribed behavior. Part of that heresy was the idea that since the body was evil, only what they did spiritually counted. So, the body could participate in sexual immorality and eat meat sacrificed to idols as long as one was spiritually "in tune" with God.

An offshoot of that which is common today is the teaching that

---

Revelation, William B. Eerdmans Publishing Co, Grand Rapids, MI, 1999.

since "God is love" everybody goes to heaven. While, yes, God is the epitome of love, He is also holy, and sin has no place with Him. You can't do whatever you want, participate freely in sin, worship other gods, and expect His love to pass you through the "Pearly Gates." How many other forms of spiritual deception follow this pattern? Most, I would gather.

All of this may well be true of the Nicolaitans. However, I came across a citation about these people that expressed a perspective about them I'd never seen before, from Cormenin's *History of the Popes*. Here's what that 19th-century historian had to say:

> "The Nicolaites, the disciples of Carpocratus and his son Epiphanus, taught promiscuous concubinage, and rendered themselves guilty of great crime in so doing in the sight of God."[19]

Is this the same group referred to by Christ? This reference by Cormenin was mentioned concerning the time of the 14th pope, Eleutherus, in 179 A.D. Certainly, the period seems to fit.

Concubinage treated women as halfway between wives and slaves, which brings to mind the relationship between Abram and Hagar. That story is told in Genesis 16 and 21. Paul, equating her with the Old Covenant, says this about Hagar:

> *24 Now this may be interpreted allegorically: these women are two covenants. One is from Mount Sinai, bearing children for slavery; she is Hagar. 25 Now Hagar is Mount Sinai in Arabia; she corresponds to the present Jerusalem, for she is in slavery with her children. (Gal 4:24-25)*

Add in the "promiscuous" aspect of Cormenin's statement and I can see why this group was hated by both the Ephesian believers and our Lord.

---

[19] Cormenin's *History of the Popes*, Vol 1, 1851, pg. 30.

I'm going to summarize all of the eschatological promises in one section, but before I move on to the next letter, there's one other point worthy of mention. In v5b, the Lord says:

> *If not, I will come to you and remove your lampstand from its place, unless you repent.*

Does this mean that Christ would remove the church from existence? Since the Ephesian church continued on, either the believers corrected themselves or this doesn't mean what it seems. Well, with human nature being what it is, I'm prone to go with the latter. We see many examples in the Word where God's judgment on individuals or on His people as a group consisted simply of His removing His presence from them. When the Israelites tried to enter the Promised Land under their own power, God didn't go with them, and they were roundly defeated. When Saul lost favor as king, God's spirit left him. Here we see an example of negative motivation, but as a kingdom of priests, the last thing we want is to lose God's presence, protection, and provision.

By the way, this verse implies a certain intimate understanding of the city that its populace could understand. The city had been built along the harbor at the mouth of the Cayster River. However, by the time of this letter, the river had silted in much of the harbor and created marshlands where mosquitoes caused malaria and death. Lysimachus, one of Alexander the Great's four generals who took control of his empire after his death, commanded that the city be moved roughly two miles away in 290 B.C. So, in a literal sense, the city had been removed from its place.

Smyrna

Smyrna was a harbor city, 40 miles north of Ephesus, which was known for its export trade in myrrh, an oil used primarily for burial and as a beauty treatment (Esther 2:12) in those days. The city's name is from the Greek word for myrrh. It was also the home of respected schools of medicine, science, and philosophy, and is known as one of the residences of the Greek writer, Homer. Smyrna was a prominent city in the Attalid kingdom, which, along with Pergamum and Ephesus, was bequeathed to the Romans in 133 B.C. Although Pergamum was named the capital of the new Roman province, Smyrna thrived as a major seaport. Today, the physical ruins of the city sit within the boundaries of Izmir, Turkey.

The *ecclesia* of Smyrna was founded early in the history of the church. At one time 12 separate congregations existed totaling roughly 500 members. It owed its origin to the apostles and held a succession of bishops who were taught directly by the apostles. The best known of these bishops was Polycarp, who was a disciple of John himself. The Jews of Smyrna aided in the martyrdom of Polycarp at the age of 86 in 153 A.D. Ireneaus, the early Christian writer and bishop who led the expansion of the church into southern France, was also a native of Smyrna.

Of the seven letters, the one to the assembly in Smyrna is the briefest. As with the letter to Ephesus, this letter reveals an understanding of the city that the Smyrnaeans could identify with. The introductory verse says, ". . . *who died and came to life.*" Indeed, the Lydians had destroyed the ancient city, which was dead for four hundred years before Alexander the Great and Lysimachus rebuilt it into a thriving port city. The city was known as one that had died and come back to life.

Smyrna is also one of the two congregations for which Jesus had no criticism.

> "'I know your tribulation and your poverty (but you are rich) and the slander of those who say that they are Jews and are not, but are a synagogue of Satan. (Rev 2:9)

Why tribulation and poverty? In the last section, I mentioned the trade guilds. It is believed that the guilds in Smyrna were particularly prominent. To find customers and work in your trade, you had to take part in your guild, and that meant going to the regular "meetings" that included feasts, which included meat to be sacrificed to their deity's idol, along with orgiastic sex.

Failure to be a member of a guild meant little or no work and a life of struggle. Thus, the tribulation and poverty, while being rich in the Lord. The real message here is that these people put Christ first to the point of losing jobs, work, and a lifestyle like those around them. How many of us today are willing to do the same? As the persecution of the church grows, I believe many of us will have to face that test.

The tribulation they faced was not solely the result of facing poverty. They also encountered slander and persecution by the local Jews, who utilized the Roman authorities to target the assembly. As was the case elsewhere, the true conflict was between the Old and New Covenants. Why would John call them a "synagogue of Satan?" John isn't being anti-Semitic here. He is, after all, a Jew himself. He does appear to be angry, though, with those Jews who fought against them. The Torah says that Jews are to treat each other with justice, and these people weren't following that law. As such, John likely did not see them as true Jews, but as liars. And who is the father of lies? Also, the word used here, and in most of the NT, for 'Satan,' *satanas*, Σατανᾶς, can mean 'adversary' in a generic sense, as well as the "prince of evil spirits." Both definitions could come into play here.

In addition to the Jewish opposition, they were under pressure to join the imperial cult worship. Smyrna's history of Roman cult worship actually preceded that of Rome itself. In 197 B.C., the city ended its relationship with the king of Pergamum and appealed to Rome for help. As an enticement, they created a cult of Rome and the worship of the goddess Roma. Within two years, that cultic worship had spread across the empire. By the time of Augustus in 29/30 B.C., the political balancing act between monarchy and republican values in the eastern empire led to a merging of emperor worship and the cult of Roma into the "imperial cult." Smyrna helped lead the way, and the pressure on its citizens to join was great. The refusal of Christians to do so increased the antagonism already being fueled by the Jews.

Instead of criticizing the church in Smyrna, Jesus gave them a warning about what they would soon face.

> Do not fear what you are about to suffer. Behold, the devil is about to throw some of you into prison, that you may be tested, and for ten days you will have tribulation. Be faithful unto death, and I will give you the crown of life. (Rev 2:10)

Some members of the assembly were about to be tested by imprisonment. To my knowledge, we have no record as to what later happened. However, in that day, imprisonment was but a short-term situation. Fines, exile, and death were the typical sentences at trial. For Christians, death was the usual outcome, so imprisonment was solely an interlude before death for most. Thus, the call to *"be faithful unto death."* As we read in chapter one, Jesus holds the keys to Death and Hades. So, here again, He encourages His followers to hold tight to their faith because even death holds no power over them.

Take note that the word for 'devil' is not *satanas*, **Σατανᾶς**, this time but *diabolos*, **διάβολος**. This word has no direct reference to the "father of lies" or "prince of the evil ones." It refers instead to a man who opposes the cause of God and may act on the part of or to side with Satan. While this person is a false accuser or slanderer, as is Satan, he is a mortal, not a supernatural being.

As for the ten days, many try to pin down a literal meaning for this. Does it mean ten actual days or ten years, or what? If you'll recall, ten is the number of law and government, so this could mean the believers there would face tribulation from the Roman authorities as a result of the Jewish opposition, which ties together the references to the "synagogue of Satan" in v9 and "the devil" in v10. However, the phrase "ten days" also points to such tribulation lasting only for a limited time.

V10 holds two other things that would be special to the Smyrnaean reader, the mentions of faithfulness and of earning *"the crown of life."* Smyrna was known for its faithfulness to the Roman Empire. In his writings, Cicero called it "the most faithful of our allies." Their faithfulness was rewarded by giving them permission over all of the other Asian cities to build and dedicate a temple to Emperor Tiberius and his family. Regarding the second point, the "crown of Smyrna" was a symbol of the city learned by its citizens from childhood, and its patron goddess was depicted wearing a crown. The city itself, as seen from the sea, appeared to be built on a rounded knob of land, Mount Pagos, and to be wearing a crown, as its stately public buildings nestled the top of the hill.

We will see this in subsequent letters also. It seems clear that John "did not discourage such feelings of attachment to one's native city but encouraged local patriotism and used it as a basis on which to build up a strong Christian life. The practical effect of such teaching as this is that a Christian could be a patriot, proud of and interested in the glory and the history of his own city."[20]

Pergamum

Pergamum (aka Pergamon and Pergamos, meaning height or elevation, and known today as Bergama, Turkey) was the recipient of the third letter. The name comes from the word for parchment, *pergamena*, for which they were well-known.

Situated on a high mesa at an altitude of 1,095 feet, north of the Caicus River (the Bakırçay River today), it was the capital city of the Kingdom of Pergamum under the Attalid dynasty. Under the Attalids, the city became a major Greek cultural center known for its 200,000+ scroll library, which was second only to the famed Library of Alexandria, and for its acropolis.

In the Roman wars against Macedonia and the Seleucids, together known as the Macedonian Wars (214-148 B.C.), the Attalid rulers of Pergamum sided with Rome and were rewarded with the territories of the Seleucids, greatly expanding the kingdom. The Attalid brothers Eumenes II and Attalus II (who succeeded his brother as king) greatly expanded the city and undertook a major remodeling of the acropolis and the areas below it in an attempt to become another Athens. As such, great temples were built to Athena, Dionysus, Aesculapius/Asclepios, and other gods, as well as the Great Altar of Zeus Sotēr (Zeus the savior), with its friezes showing the

---

[20] Ramsay, William M., *The Letters to the Seven Churches of Asia*, (Hodder,

Gigantomachy, the war between the Olympian gods and the giants.

When the last of the Attalid rulers, Attalus III, who was childless, bequeathed his kingdom to Rome in 133 B.C., Pergamum also became part of the Roman Empire. Because of the city's early support for Rome, it became the capital of the new province of Asia. That role diminished under Augustus, who preferred Ephesus, as mentioned earlier. So, while Pergamum is believed to have continued as the administrative capital of the province, Ephesus took the lead in many provincial affairs. Also, although Smyrna appears to have originated what led to imperial worship, Pergamum became a leading center for it with multiple temples dedicated to it as well as temples dedicated to worshiping specific emperors, such as Augustus. The first such imperial temple, the Temple of Augustus, was built in Pergamum.

The church in Pergamum was also an early congregation, with its first bishop, Antipas, being ordained by John. The body of believers there was commended for holding fast to the name of Jesus and not denying the faith, even during the events that led to the martyrdom of Antipas.

> "'I know where you dwell, where Satan's throne is. Yet you hold fast my name, and you did not deny my faith even in the days of Antipas my faithful witness, who was killed among you, where Satan dwells. (Rev 2:13)

Before I discuss Antipas, we need to look at the mentions of Satan. Today, we don't know with certainty what John referred to. Candidates for the throne include the temples of Augustus and Asclepios (the city's patron deity), the city itself as a center of persecution and the imperial cult, and the judge's bench or seat of the proconsul—although by John's time the proconsul personally may have moved to Ephesus. However, many scholars believe the scripture talks about the Great Altar of Zeus Sotēr. The friezes of the Gigantomachy were found in the late 19th century and taken to Berlin where a recreation of the altar, along with

---

1904), pg. 208-9.

the restored friezes, now resides in the Pergamon Museum.

© Raimond Spekking / CC BY-SA 4.0

As you can see, it does look something like a throne, and with John's rebuttals against Zeus, this seems to fit well. As for the reference to Satan dwelling there, the word for 'dwell,' *katoikeō*, **κατοικέω**, can mean to inhabit someplace, such as God inhabiting His temple. However, metaphorically, the word can also mean to govern, influence, or pervade, such as a divine power governing one's soul. I think this latter definition satisfies the situation John described more so than to think of Satan physically residing there. Pergamum was, after all, a major cultic center.

On a more symbolic level, idealists connect the throne of Satan to a kingdom. Within the book of Revelation, Satan is represented by the Dragon. When, in Revelation 13:2, the Dragon gives his throne—whether literal or figurative—to the beast from the sea (representing chaos), he's giving it to a power or authority that represents that chaos. In John's day, that power or kingdom was Rome, and this associates the throne with Rome, both the imperial cult and governmental authority.

We see this in the greeting to the church. Just as the previous letters held specific references to their respective cities, the phrase *"him who has the two-edged sword"* would be understood by a first-century audience as pointing to Roman authority, as well as to Christ, who has the ultimate power. Unlike the scimitar of Oriental armies or the cutting sword (one edge) of the Greek armies, the pointed, two-edged sword—a cut-and-thrust sword—was the weapon identified with Roman armies, and the sword was the symbol of the highest order of official authority. In the two-tiered structure of authority in the Roman Empire, where there were higher- and lower-class governors, only the highest class, the Proconsul, had the power of the sword. The "right of the sword," *jus gladii*, was the power over life and death. Historically, Pergamum was the official seat of the provincial Proconsul.

And, as the administrative capital of the province, Pergamum was typically where Christians were tried and executed. By the time of John's letters, Christianity was no longer tolerated. Those who refused to perform the ritual of the state religion—offering sacrifice to the Imperial God, the Divine Emperor—were seen as traitors and enemies of the state. The first temple in the province of that state religion was the Temple of Augustus in Pergamum, and that was where Christians were given a final opportunity to "redeem" themselves. Failure to comply meant condemnation to death. Pergamum is where both Antipas and, later, Polycarp, along with many unnamed martyrs, were tried and executed.

As such, I suspect that John's reference to the "throne of Satan" was not an either-or statement. Nor are we given a multiple-choice question, unless "All of the Above" is the final answer. Taken together—with the Temple of Augustus representing the state religion, the seat of Rome's power as the historical city of the proconsul, and the various temples to cultic deities—and all being in Pergamum, Satan's throne consumed the entire city.

Regarding Antipas, I'm sure his death grieved John. We know little about Antipas except that he was martyred by being placed inside a brass bull used for burning incense and/or human sacrifices to one of the gods. It's reported that after being tied up, his head was placed into the head of the bull so that as the fire under the bull blazed to heat up the bull, the man's moans and cries would echo through pipes in the head and bring "life" to the bull. Antipas, however, prayed and praised God, and those prayers echoed from the bull until he succumbed to the heat. Some reports place the bull at the top of the Altar of Zeus. Others place it in front of the temple of Serapis, also known as the Egyptian god, Isis. The bull represented the bull god Apis. Yet, another account places the bull at the temple of Artemis.

Just as the date of John's writing Revelation is debated, the date of Antipas' martyrdom is disputed. Some sources say it occurred during the reign of Nero at a point shortly before Nero's suicide in 68 A.D. Others place in in 92 A.D. at the request of Domitian. Of the dozen or so resources I looked at, the later date seemed to be favored. The date plays a significant role in understanding the timing of John's writing the book. After all, if Antipas died in 92 A.D., John could not have written about it in the mid-60s A.D. That would place the date of Revelation in 96 A.D. as some argue.

Yes, I realize I just took you down a rabbit trail of little real importance to us today. Does the year of Antipas' death affect us? Well, not really, at least for me. I did so to show you an example of how the timing of the writing of Revelation comes into dispute. With the Preterist viewpoint relying so heavily on that date, very minor points, such as the date of Antipas' martyrdom, can play a major role in swinging viewpoints one way or the other. The real message from John in this verse is that Antipas and his brethren held fast to their faith, even unto death, just as the Smyrna assembly was encouraged to do.

Unlike Smyrna, however, Jesus found the following faults with the people in Pergamum.

> *14 But I have a few things against you: you have some there who hold the teaching of Balaam, who taught Balak to put a stumbling block before the sons of Israel, so that they might eat food sacrificed to idols and practice sexual immorality. 15 So also you have some who hold the teaching of the Nicolaitans. (Rev 2:14-15)*

Unlike the Ephesians, who hated the works of the Nicolaitans, some in the church in Pergamum followed their practices. Likewise, some held to the teaching of Balaam. I discussed these teachings in the section on Ephesus, so I won't go into them again here.

How does that apply to us today? In Hindu and Buddhist cultures, as well as some animist cultures around the globe, animal or meat sacrifice is still their practice. However, in the western world, most of us don't make sacrifices to idols. Or do we? These might not be meat sacrifices, but might we enter into fellowship with demons in other ways when we compromise our faith, say, by accepting lifestyles that go against the teachings of Christ? Perhaps one accepts abortion as a woman's right to choose. In John's day, the sacrifice of children to the demons Molech and Chemosh was commonplace and condemned by Christ. Gehenna, a Biblical name for hell, was so named after the Valley of Hinnom in which the Canaanites and apostate Jews sacrificed their children to these demonic idols. Have some replaced the red-hot arms of a brass idol with the sterile inner chamber of the abortionist? Sadly, many self-proclaimed "Christians" today see no problem with this.

I just mentioned lifestyles that Jesus would call unacceptable. Yes, I'm holding back no punches. I mean LGBTQIA+ lifestyles. However, I also mean lifestyles considered "straight" by most in which couples are living outside the bond of marriage. Friends with benefits, cohabitation, conjoint marriage, polyamorous relationships, or whatever term you wish to give it, all fall into the category of sexual immorality. Morality is not a relative construct, changing with the whims of a culture or individual. God defined morality. It's clearly laid out in His Word. It's an absolute truth in a world that wants to reject absolutes. When eternal judgment comes, His truth is the only one that counts. On which side of that line do you want to be standing on that day?

Thyatira

Thyatira, now covered by the modern city of Akhisar, Turkey, was southeast of Pergamum and the northernmost city of the four inland churches in Revelation. Founded initially as a military outpost to guard the pass between the Hermus and Caicos river valleys, which carried the main trade and postal route between Pergamum and all points southeast, under the *Pax Romana* it, too, became a prominent trade center. Historically, it was one of the first cities to use minted coins as money, an invention accorded to the Lydian culture. The name means "odor of affliction."

During the Hellenistic and Roman eras, the city was known for its textiles, particularly "purple" cloth. Lydia, a merchant of purple goods mentioned in Acts 16:14, was a native of Thyatira. As a side note for your next trivia night, purple was used loosely in that era to mean a variety of diverse colors. The region around Thyatira was known for its madder-root, the Rubia plant, which produced a bright red color known today as Turkey red. Purple, as we know it today, at that time came from a shellfish native to the Phoenician and Spartan coasts, and Philippi, where Paul encountered Lydia, was nowhere near those coasts. As Lydia was a seller of "purple" goods, there's a strong likelihood that she maintained some sort of ties with the appropriate trade guild in Thyatira.

I bring that up because the trade guilds were strong in Thyatira. Archaeologists have found inscriptions naming more specific trade guilds here than in any of the other cities mentioned in Revelation: "wool-workers, linen-workers, makers of outer garments, dyers, leather-workers, tanners, potters, bakers, slave-dealers, and bronze-smiths."[21]

Considering the last one, it seems quite appropriate that Jesus would be introduced to this church as *"the Son of Man . . . whose feet are like burnished bronze."* (Revelation 2:18) The word for 'burnished bronze' is *chalkolibanon*, **χαλκολίβανον**, which, in the Bible, is found only in the Apocalypse. While Thyatira had bronze-smiths, we don't know exactly what metals they forged. Bronze, an alloy of copper and tin, was a valuable commodity of that era due to its hardness and lack of rust. Brass, an alloy of copper and zinc, was not common until the

---

[21] Ibid., pp. 244

post-medieval period because zinc was not recognized as a metal until then. Here, *chalkolibanon* has been translated to bronze but is defined as fine brass with a brilliant luster. However, the word also referred to an alloy of gold and silver, polished to such brilliance that some considered it more precious than gold alone. When we consider that gold is symbolic of God's kingship, glory, and holiness and that silver is symbolic of redemption, the description of "burnished bronze" takes on a new level of meaning.

Although Thyatira was not a city that the Romans would have great concern about, the letter to the church there would be seen as an affront to the empire. Just as Pergamum was associated with the sword, the power over life and death, Thyatira was associated with the *"rod of iron."* Rome ruled its empire with a rod of iron and smashed its opposition like potsherds, and yet, in this letter, the church in li'l ol' Thyatira was promised to be given authority over the nations and to rule them with the rod of iron. To the first-century mind, this was a clear insult to the emperor. Little wonder the Romans came down hard on Christians.

In this letter, the assembly in Thyatira was commended as follows:

> *"'I know your works, your love and faith and service and patient endurance, and that your latter works exceed the first. (Rev 2:19)*

Indeed, it sounds as if the church here had everything going for it. However, there's always that one troublemaker in every congregation.

> *But I have this against you, that you tolerate that woman Jezebel, who calls herself a prophetess and is teaching and seducing my servants to practice sexual immorality and to eat food sacrificed to idols. (Rev 2:20)*

Whether this woman's name was actually Jezebel, or this is simply a reference to the pagan, Sidonian wife of King Ahab in the OT (1 Kings 16-25), the woman was trouble. And she was about to face judgment:

> *21 I gave her time to repent, but she refuses to repent of her sexual immorality. 22 Behold, I will throw her onto a sickbed, and those who commit adultery with her I will throw into great tribulation, unless they repent of her works, 23 and I will strike her children dead. And all the churches will know that I am he who searches mind and heart, and I will give to each of you according to your works. (Rev 2:21-23)*

The reference to striking her children dead probably does not mean her biological offspring, since the Bible teaches that sons are not to be held accountable for the sins of their fathers and vice versa. These "children" are those who follow and spread her heresy and are guilty of the same sin. Fortunately, for those not following in her footsteps, Jesus gave them no other burden.

I mentioned the OT Jezebel earlier, but more should be said. As a Sidonian princess—from Tyre specifically—she worshiped Baʿal. Baʿal was the Semitic equivalent to Zeus—the Greek god of thunder and lightning who became the supreme god. Just as Zeus rose in stature from being a lustful tyrant to chief deity, Baʿal supplanted El as the leader of the gods in the Semitic pantheon. Jezebel brought her religion with her to Ahab's household and incited him to worship Baʿal with her. She was privileged and ruthless, killing Naboth for his vineyard as well as 400 priests of Yahweh. Following the Phoenician practice, she was likely the chief priestess of Astarte, the Greek counterpart to the Babylonian Ištar/Ishtar, goddess of love, beauty, sex, war, justice, and political power. Promiscuous sex was ingrained within their worship, as was great feasting with meat "sacrificed" to the goddess.

The mention of this woman in Thyatira brings up some interesting points. What did Jesus mean by giving his true followers no other "burden?" The two things for which this woman was condemned were two among the four restrictions that the Jerusalem Council had instructed Paul about in Acts 15:19-20:

> *19 Therefore my judgment is that we should not trouble*

> *those of the Gentiles who turn to God, 20 but should write to them to abstain from the things polluted by idols, and from sexual immorality, and from what has been strangled, and from blood.*

The council, now faced with converts from paganism, not just Judaism, no doubt pondered this question—how to deal with Gentile converts—in depth before listing these "burdens." Yet, that also points to a willingness to let other local customs, traditions, and the like continue. Did this woman simply misunderstand the freedom offered to them? Instead, was she being willfully disobedient to the apostolic teaching?

The former is a good possibility. Someone who was willfully disobedient would not have been readily tolerated, and yet, she must have been prominent in the assembly there to have been identified as a prophetess. As such, she likely had a significant following within the church, too. Note that the church was commended that its *"latter works exceed the first."* If she had a sizable following, did they contribute to these latter works? Perhaps they doubled down on their evangelism because they had a popular perspective: they could continue in their immorality, not be burdened by the restrictions listed by the apostolic council, and still be "Christians." Or perhaps Christ dealt with her/them and freed up the remaining body to do greater things.

Is this a message that today's more liberal congregations need to pay close attention to? Many of these congregations do great works feeding the hungry, helping the homeless, aiding the sick, and more. Yet, they also tolerate and even promote such a wide range of opinions and conduct that they might find themselves guilty of the same sin as this Jezebel. Antinomianism comes in a wide variety of colors and sizes. The warning is clear—His divine grace does not relieve us of all moral law or His Biblical standards. For us, today, this is His third and strongest warning to steer clear of idol worship—in whatever form that idol exists—and sexual immorality. Message received, loud and clear. Or is it?

Sardis

Sardis, meaning "red ones," was founded by the son of Hercules, according to Herodotus. In the 7th century B.C., it became the capital of the Lydian Empire. Sitting upon a 1,500-foot-high plateau with cliffs on three sides, its citadel was considered impregnable. However, the citadel, and the city below, were conquered by the Persians in 574 B.C. when soldiers, like thieves at some unknown time, took advantage of a cleft in the rocky cliffs to slip into the acropolis and take control of the gate. The cliffs they thought would protect them instead trapped the citizens. King Croesus went to bed feeling secure only to wake up a captive. In 213 B.C. history repeated itself when Antiochus the Great took the city the same way and claimed it for the Seleucid Empire.

I mentioned earlier that the Lydians were the first to use minted coins. Sardis sat on the gold-laden Pactolus River, which saw its gold come from nearby Mt. Tmolus. During the reign of Croesus, the last of the Lydian rulers, their metallurgists became the first to learn how to separate the gold and silver that were combined in the gold sands and nuggets of the river. As such, their pure gold and silver minted coins became trusted throughout the region and the name Croesus became associated with wealth.

While there were a few believers in Sardis who had not soiled their garments, the church there was one of two among the seven for which Jesus found nothing commendable.

> *1 "And to the angel of the church in Sardis write: 'The words of him who has the seven spirits of God and the seven stars. "'I know your works. You have the reputation of being alive, but you are dead. 2 Wake up, and strengthen what remains and is about to die, for I have not found your works complete in the sight of my God. 3 Remember, then, what you received and heard. Keep it, and repent. If you will not wake up, I will come like a thief, and you will not know at what hour I will come against you. (Rev 3:1-3)*

And evidently, they did not wake up. Actually, by the time of this letter, the city had grown along the western side of the plateau and the acropolis was largely unpopulated. As Byzantium (later renamed Constantinople) gained stature in the second century A.D., a new trade road was built and bypassed the city. It slowly diminished in importance, and in 615 A.D., the Persian Shahin sacked it during the Byzantine-Sasanian War. It was never fully repaired. Incursions by the Turks and the rising prominence of Constantinople continued its decline. Then, in 1402, the Mongol general Timur, aka Tamerlane, destroyed what remained of the city. Today, nothing remains of the city except a few Byzantine ruins. Nothing from its glorious ancient history is left. Even the gold sands that made the city rich have panned out.

The city relied much upon its history. In 26 A.D. when Rome considered which city in Asia to honor with a temple to Tiberius and his mother, Livia, nine were in contention. Most were dropped as unimportant or has already having great temples. Only Smyrna and Sardis remained on the list, and Sardis boasted of its grand Lydian past and of its being a royal city . . . in the past. At that point, the city was beginning to decay and offered little for the present. The temple was awarded to Smyrna. We, too, must continue moving forward in our faith and our works and not rely on things past.

What else might we learn from this city? The citadel fell on the two occasions mentioned because its leaders failed to post watchmen along the cliffs. They trusted in the fortifications they had placed along the southern access. Elsewhere in the NT, we are encouraged to keep the faith, to remain watchful, and that Christ's return will be like a thief in the night. If the city and history of Sardis teach us anything, it is to keep watch and not to misplace our faith.

Philadelphia

Philadelphia, the city "of one who loves his brother," was founded in 189 B.C. by Eumenes II, king of Pergamum, to honor his brother, Attalus II, who was known for his loyalty to Eumenes and had earned the nickname Philadelphus. Attalus later succeeded his brother on the

Pergamum throne. In 133 B.C., the city was among those cities bequeathed to Rome by Attalus III at his death. Situated on the Cogamus River—today, the Kuzuçay River and the city of Alaşehir— at the foot of Mt. Tmolus, it was known for its grapes, wine, textiles, and leather goods.

In Roman times, it was a large city and the administrative center for the district of Sardis. An earthquake in 17 A.D. severely damaged the city, along with 11 others in the great Lydian Valley, including Sardis. The emperor, Tiberius, helped by forgiving it of its taxes for five years. The city also saw favor under Caligula and Vespasian, so the imperial cult was prominent in the city.

The introduction to this letter holds an allusion to the OT that should be considered.

> *"And to the angel of the church in Philadelphia write: 'The words of the holy one, the true one, who has the key of David, who opens and no one will shut, who shuts and no one opens. (Rev 3:7)*

And again in v8 (below), we see reference to an open door that no one can shut. What is the key of David? We discussed the keys to Death and Hades in our review of chapter one. Are these similar? Different? Was Jesus just collecting a whole ring of keys to jangle in His pocket? Do white robes even have pockets? Wait, get back on track.

We see a parallel between Revelation 1:17-18 and Revelation 2:8 in which Jesus declares that He was dead but now lives, and died, but came to life. Is there a parallel between the keys of Death and Hades in Revelation 1:18 and the key of David in Revelation 3:7? Yes, but it's obscure and meant to be noticed by that obscurity. In Isaiah 22:15-25, we read of a shameful household servant named Shebna, who is replaced by Eliakim as the steward to his master's house, the house of David. Eliakim received the key to the house of David, which *"he shall open, and none shall shut, and he shall shut, and none shall open."* (Is 22:22) Interestingly, Eliakim means "God will raise up." In Revelation 3:7, John repurposed this scripture in substitution for "the keys of

Death and Hades" to point to Christ's ultimate and eternal sovereignty over His Father's kingdom. He alone decides our fates and has control over life and death. Both key allusions point to that.

Along with Smyrna, the church of Philadelphia was praised and found no disfavor with Jesus.

> 8 " 'I know your works. Behold, I have set before you an open door, which no one is able to shut. I know that you have but little power, and yet you have kept my word and have not denied my name. 9 Behold, I will make those of the synagogue of Satan who say that they are Jews and are not, but lie--behold, I will make them come and bow down before your feet, and they will learn that I have loved you. 10 Because you have kept my word about patient endurance, I will keep you from the hour of trial that is coming on the whole world, to try those who dwell on the earth. 11 I am coming soon. Hold fast what you have, so that no one may seize your crown. (Rev 3:8-11)

Unlike Smyrna, which was warned of coming tribulation, the assembly here was promised to be spared of the coming trial that the whole world would encounter. Again, as with Smyrna, we see the reference to the *"synagogue of Satan"* about the sham Jews who opposed the church. However, this time, with an allusion to scriptures in Isaiah (45:14 and 49:23, as cited earlier), we see these Jews bowing at the feet of the Christians as the true people of God, rather than Gentiles bowing at their feet.

Regarding these two churches—Smyrna and Philadelphia, history shows that these were the last holdouts against the Islamic takeover of Asia Minor. Philadelphia proclaimed itself a free and Christian city, holding out against Islam until the mid-14th century when the Turks finally conquered the city.

There are several traits of this city seen in this letter. Situated on a major east-west trade route between the port at Smyrna and Phrygia to the east, it controlled access to the difficult pass leading to the Phrygian plateau. In essence, it held the key, via its gates being open or closed, to trade moving along that road. After the earthquake of 17 A.D., its citizens lived in fear of another "hour of trial," to the point where many lived in huts outside the city, afraid to move back into their homes in the city. The aftershocks continued for years as described by Strabo in 20 A.D. when he wrote about their fear and the living conditions. In Revelation 3:12, Jesus promises the one who conquers will become "*a pillar in the temple of My God.*" Those who ventured to repair their homes within the city added a variety of structures to secure their walls and ceilings, including new pillars, which denote stability. Jesus also promised that the conqueror would never have to leave the temple, as these people had been forced to leave their city. Finally, in that verse, Jesus promises the conqueror a new name. Twice in the city's history, it briefly adopted new names—once to honor Tiberius for his assistance after the destruction (Neokaisareia) and again to honor Vespasian (Flavia).

For me, two other traits hold more meaning. Christ commends them for keeping his word, not denying His Name, and their patient endurance. I have little doubt that among their works they were known for their love of each other. That is, after all, one of His commandments (John 13:34, John 15:12,17) and they kept His word. Likewise, evangelism—making disciples of all nations—is among His commandments. Philadelphia was founded to become a center of the Greco-Asiatic civilization to spread the Greek language and manners into the eastern parts of Lydia and into Phrygia. So, in essence, it was a missionary city from the beginning. Paul's writings to the Corinthians and Colossians had established the "open door" phrase to mean good opportunity for missionary work. How fitting that the church in a city named after brotherly love and founded for missions work should be one of the two in which Jesus found no faults.

Laodicea

Laodicea ("justice of the people") sat at the crossroads of three major trade roads, almost due east of Ephesus (99 miles). The town was initially called Diospolis, the City of Zeus, but was built into a larger city (c.260 B.C.) by the Seleucid king Antiochus II Theos, who renamed it Laodicea in honor of his wife, Laodice. The location was roughly 11 miles west of Colossae and six miles south of Hierapolis.

The city was ruled by a series of kings, became part of the Pergamum kingdom after Rome conquered the Seleucids, and was ultimately bequeathed to Rome in 133 B.C. along with the other cities already mentioned. Like many of the cities, it began to prosper only when the *Pax Romana* provided the peace needed to allow such.

Perhaps no other letter among the seven is as strongly tied to the city like this one.

> *14 "And to the angel of the church in Laodicea write: 'The words of the Amen, the faithful and true witness, the beginning of God's creation. 15 "'I know your works: you are neither cold nor hot. Would that you were either cold or hot! 16 So, because you are lukewarm, and neither hot nor cold, I will spit you out of my mouth. 17 For you say, I am rich, I have prospered, and I need nothing, not realizing that you are wretched, pitiable, poor, blind, and naked. 18 I counsel you to buy from me gold refined by fire, so that you may be rich, and white garments so that you may clothe yourself and the shame of your nakedness may not be seen, and salve to anoint your eyes, so that you may see. (Rev 3:14-18)*

Laodicea's main problem was water. Its natural sources were full of lime. An underground aqueduct carried cold water from springs roughly six miles to the south, while hot spring water from near Hierapolis was brought in as well. By the time these waters reached Laodicea, they were lukewarm. Sitting on three major roads, the city became a center for banking and finance with their own minted coins and was so wealthy that when an earthquake in 60 A.D. completely destroyed it, the inhabitants refused imperial assistance and rebuilt it entirely from their personal wealth. They were known for a luxurious, glossy, soft black wool from which garments of high quality were made.

Their tunics, called *trimita*, were so famous that the city was called Trimitaria in some documents of the 4th and 5th centuries A.D. The city also had a medical school that followed the principles of Herophilos, who promoted a variety of compound medicines, some of which remained in medical formularies through the 19th century. Galen attributed an ear ointment made from the spice nard (spikenard) to this school. Also, a mineral powder made from "Phrygian stone"—first used in Laodicea and called "Phrygian powder" by Aristotle—was exported throughout the Greek and Roman world.[22] This powder, which came as a collyrium, not an ointment, was smeared upon the eyes to "strengthen" them.

From the beginning of the letter to the end, Jesus connects the church to its city. Just like their unsatisfying water, they were lukewarm. In the complacency of their wealth, they believed they needed nothing, yet Christ offered them *"gold refined by fire."* Instead of their famous black garments, He offered white to cover their shame. And for their blind eyes, He offered them an eye salve to let them see. However, where He is introduced as "faithful and true," they were not. Jesus offered them the solutions to their *"wretched, pitiable, poor, blind, and naked"* state but those solutions came with a cost that the Laodicean church appeared unwilling to pay in their self-sufficient, self-satisfied condition.

Out of all seven churches, in Laodicea He finds no commendable traits or even a remnant of those who are faithful. Also condemned, Sardis at least had a few faithful followers. Like Sardis, however, the city eventually disappeared totally. Today, the ruins are extensive and being restored, but the nearest city, Denizli, Turkey, is 24 miles away.

Seven Dispensations?

Since so many people in the U.S. believe in dispensationalism and that this viewpoint teaches that the seven churches relate to seven dispensations, or ages, I feel compelled to discuss this. Can we really

---

[22] Ibid., pg. 313-15.

look at these churches as being representative of seven dispensations in human history? First, to define a dispensation, the common definition would be "a certain order, system, or arrangement; administration or management."[23] The word can also refer to something dispensed or given out. In theological terms, dispensation has come to mean a divinely appointed order or age, but it can also point to the divine ordering of the affairs of the world.

So, with the theological definition in mind, many dispensational scholars have determined that human history is comprised of seven unequal dispensations, or divinely appointed ages. They are as follows:

1. The age of innocence — Adam and Eve in the garden before the fall
2. The age of conscience — from the fall to the flood, when man lived according to his conscience
3. The age of human government — from Noah to Abram, when human government was established
4. The age of promise — from Abram to Moses, when God established the Abraham Covenant and promises to His people
5. The age of law — Moses to Christ, when God's people were under the Law
6. The age of grace — from Christ until now, living under God's grace
7. The age of the millennial reign of Christ

For the dispensationalist, the seven churches of Revelation can be tied to these seven ages.

Where does this idea come from? In my previous book, *Still Here! Surviving the End Times*, I talked about the rise of dispensationalism with John Nelson Darby of the Plymouth Brethren in England in the early 19th century. He popularized the idea at the Powerscourt Prophecy Conferences in Ireland from 1827 to 1830 and then brought

---

[23] https://www.dictionary.com/browse/dispensation#

his ideas to America. C.I. Scofield picked up on his teachings and added them to the side notes of his study Bible. By 1910, over a million copies of that Bible were sold, and the dispensational teachings found root in the major seminaries of this country. You can find Scofield's teaching on this at http://www.biblerays.com/seven-7-dispensations.html.

Darby, and his successors, picked up on the word translated to "dispensation" in the KJV version of Ephesians 1:10 and 3:2.

> *"That in the dispensation of the fulness of times he might gather together in one all things in Christ, both which are in heaven, and which are on earth; (even) in him: (Eph 1:10 KJV)*

> *"If ye have heard of the dispensation of the grace of God which is given me to you-ward: (Eph 3:2 KJV)*

They interpreted this to mean "divinely appointed ages in history"—such as the age of grace—and went about looking to define these eras in the Word. The seven ages presented above are the result. However, the Greek word that is translated as 'dispensation' in the KJV is *oikonomia*, **οἰκονομία**, which has nothing to do with time. It refers to the management, stewardship, or oversight of another's affairs or household. The ESV translates Ephesians 1:10 as *". . . a plan for the fullness of time . . ."* and Ephesians 3:2 as *". . . the stewardship of God's grace . . ."* which give us that concept of management, not of a span of time.

Let's assume, though, that we are talking about periods in history. Does the dispensational teaching stand up to scrutiny? If you've made it this far in this book, you know the Bible says nothing about a millennial reign and that the 1,000-year number in Revelation 20 signifies a long time, not a literal span of time. So, for me, that knocks out the 7th dispensation right off the bat. What about the others? How in the world could the church of Ephesus be connected to an age of innocence in the Garden of Eden? Taken from Sir Robert Anderson's *The Lord from Heaven* (pgs. 86-87), here's what he wrote:

"In Ephesus, the 'overcomer' shares with unfallen Adam the right to 'the tree of life which is in the paradise of God.' In Smyrna, he shares with Noah immunity from 'the second death' – the judgment which brought the first 'dispensation' to a close. In Pergamos, he partakes with Moses of the hidden manna; and in Thyatira he exercises kingly rule with David. And Sardis speaks of the fellowship of the prophets and the reward for those who witness a good confession in days of apostasy.

"In Philadelphia, therefore, the 'overcomer' is called to share in the heavenly realities of which the temple that was the place of earthly worship, and the city, which was the center of earthly blessing, were but shadows. In Laodicea, which represents the 'dispensation' now drawing to a close, there is no reference to the past of Jewish symbolism or terminology; and the 'overcomer' is a follower of him who, as 'the faithful and true Witness,' has reached the throne by the path which led him to the cross."

Anderson, who taught with Darby and was a member of the Plymouth Brethren for a time, takes one phrase or idea out of each letter to make his connections. So, for Ephesus, they use the promise of "the tree of life" to tie it to Adam in the garden. Yet, Adam *had* fallen, and he *wasn't* entitled to the "tree of life." He was cast out of the garden so that he wouldn't eat of it. And to have the thoroughly condemned Laodicean church represent the reign of Christ because there's no mention of the Jews or Jewish symbolism in that letter is really stretching it.

I've mentioned before how each eschatological viewpoint has its inconsistencies or compromises with respect to the Word. If you reread the Anderson quote above, you'll find errors even within what he writes, when compared to Darby or Scofield. The first "dispensation" didn't end with Noah and the flood. The dispensation "now drawing to a close" would be that of grace, not Laodicea, which they teach as symbolizing the final, or Messianic, age of the 1,000-year reign.

True, on a superficial level these ages and the connections to these churches sound plausible, and yet, the relationships written of here are flimsy at best. Even the idea of specific ages is spurious. Did man stop living with his conscience at the flood? Did human government stop with the Abrahamic Covenant? An 'age' is a defined period of time. Man's conscience continues. Human government continues. (Maranatha!) For the Jews, the law of Moses continues. For believers, God's grace continues. These are not trapped in time.

On a different note, you may have also heard that the seven churches reflect upon seven stages of the church throughout the church age. That is, Ephesus represents the First Apostolic church; Smyrna, the Second Apostolic church through the reign of ten emperors; Pergamum, the Roman Imperial church; Thyatira is the Roman Catholic church; Sardis, the Reformation church; Philadelphia, the missionary church; and Laodicea is the final apostate church preceding the return of Christ.

The problem with these dispensational views is two-fold. First, they pick a short phrase or a single idea from one of the letters and assign that to one of their dispensations. They don't look at the letter to the church as a whole. Yes, the Philadelphia church is known today as the Missionary church, but can we truly say that the Roman Catholic church of history should be known for its works, love, faith, service, patient endurance, and latter works that exceeded the first? (Thyatira- Revelation 2:19) The acceptance of Jezebel might be a more appropriate link with the greed, corruption, immorality, false teaching, and hatred shown by the leadership of that church through history. In the same sense, the Reformation church can hardly be compared to the church in Sardis, which had a reputation for being alive but was dead.

Secondly, they appear to use generalizations that aren't applicable. Throughout the church age, there have been those who share the faults for which these churches were condemned, as well as those who have remained faithful and never lost their first love. In today's church, whether Roman Catholic, Protestant, or Eastern Orthodox, there are those in each congregation who fall into these two groups. The condemned will be shocked to hear Christ say, "I never knew you," and the praised will be welcomed home.

Indeed, the eschatological promises with the seven letters were made to the churches, plural. Let's look at those now.

Our Take-Away . . .

From the seven letters, we've learned what some of the people in those congregations did wrong. To summarize, they became loveless, worldly, spiritually dead; followed false doctrine; and allowed complacency to take over. They tolerated immorality, pagan cults, and idolatry while allowing "self" to control them. They were called on to remember their faith and first love, to repent for their shortcomings, and to repeat the works they did at first. This was emphasized in the first letter, to Ephesus, but held true for all of the churches. It still holds true for the universal church today.

Perhaps the biggest issue with the churches was their tolerance of immorality and their acceptance of the worldly ways surrounding them. These were mentioned in three of the seven letters—Ephesus, Pergamum, and Thyatira. Maybe for emphasis? They were *of* the world as well as in it. How does that apply today? When was the last time you heard a sermon denouncing the LGBTQIA+ lifestyles? Can't recall one? What about a sermon, or perhaps acclaimed books by prominent Christians, teaching tolerance and acceptance of those lifestyles? They abound on Amazon. Not to highlight those subcultures alone, what about the acceptance of divorce and remarrying among straight members of your church? Christ gave us only one acceptable reason for divorce—the unfaithfulness of one's partner. All others are living in adultery. Yet, the divorce rate among those claiming to be Christians is the same as that of non-believers.

One current hot-button topic is Critical Social Justice and its subsets: Critical Race Theory, Critical Gender Theory, and others. These ideas arose from the neo-Marxist worldview of the Frankfurt School and have a humanist base, not a Godly one. Once taught only in law schools, they are now being foisted upon elementary school children under a variety of program names in an effort to indoctrinate a new generation. And, perhaps more dangerously, they are making inroads into evangelical circles where these ideas and the politics involved become the basis for interpreting the Bible. Should you bend the Bible's teachings to support your lifestyle and politics, or should the Bible shape your lifestyle and politics? The church doesn't need to be Woke; it needs to wake up society around it. These things today are like the trade guilds of the first century.

On the other hand, the faithful believers were commended for their hard work, patient endurance, rejection of evil and immorality, perseverance, loyalty to Christ, and refusing to deny Him. Some endured poverty and great suffering but still kept the faith. These praiseworthy traits are ones we should strive for today.

His Eschatological Promises

As we look at the promises given to those who overcome—to *the one who conquers*, each letter includes the phrase *"He who has an ear, let him hear what the Spirit says to the churches."* Although the KJV translates *nikaō*, **νικάω**, to the word 'overcome,' it is more correctly translated to 'conquer' and for us, being victorious means holding fast to our faith even unto death against the power of our foes, temptations, and persecutions.

As for having an ear to hear, I looked at some OT allusions to this earlier but only mentioned the NT books that present this. Jesus would often end a parable by saying, *"He who has ears to hear, let him hear"* (Matthew 11:15) or some variation of that. He explained His use of parables this way:

> *13 This is why I speak to them in parables, because seeing they do not see, and hearing they do not hear, nor do they understand. 14 Indeed, in their case the prophecy of Isaiah is fulfilled that says: ""You will indeed hear but never understand, and you will indeed see but never perceive." 15 For this people's heart has grown dull, and with their ears*

they can barely hear, and their eyes they have closed, lest they should see with their eyes and hear with their ears and understand with their heart and turn, and I would heal them.' **16 But blessed are your eyes, for they see, and your ears, for they hear.** *17 For truly, I say to you, many prophets and righteous people longed to see what you see, and did not see it, and to hear what you hear, and did not hear it. (Matt 13:13-17)*

If you ever had a question about having the necessary ear to hear, take note of v16 in bold.

Many teachers list seven promises to overcomers, one for each letter. However, most of the letters offer more than one. So, listen up, here are the promises He's given us, in the order given in the letters:

> The grant to eat of the tree of life in the paradise of God
> To receive the crown of life
> To not be hurt by the second death (the lake of fire)
> To partake of some hidden manna
> To receive a white stone with a new name written on it that only you will know
> Authority over the nations to rule with a rod of iron
> The morning star
> To walk with Him in white garments
> To never have our name blotted out from the book of life
> To have Jesus confess our name before the Father and His angels
> To be kept from the hour of trial that is coming on the whole world
> To be a pillar in the temple of God
> To have the name of God, the new Jerusalem, and Christ's new name written on him
> To have Christ come in to and eat with him
> To sit with Christ on His throne

While these might seem straightforward, we need to take a look at them more closely.

Eternal Life

Several of these promises can be grouped together as references to eternal life. In Genesis 3:22 we read,

> *"Then the LORD God said, "Behold, the man has become like one of us in knowing good and evil. Now, lest he reach out his hand and take also of the tree of life and eat, and live forever--"*

The **tree of life** offers eternal life, and Adam was cast out from the garden and denied eating from it. Believers, on the other hand, will be given that opportunity by the grace of God. We will "put on" immortal bodies.

> *51 Behold! I tell you a mystery. We shall not all sleep, but we shall all be changed, 52 in a moment, in the twinkling of an eye, at the last trumpet. For the trumpet will sound, and the dead will be raised imperishable, and we shall be changed. 53 For this perishable body must put on the imperishable, and this mortal body must put on immortality. 54 When the perishable puts on the imperishable, and the mortal puts on immortality, then shall come to pass the saying that is written: "Death is swallowed up in victory." 55 "O death, where is your victory? O death, where is your sting?" (1Co 15:51-55)*

Sadly, for the unbeliever, that imperishable body will experience the second death, the lake of fire (Revelation 20:14-15), because all whose names are not found in the book of life will end up there. The conqueror, however, is promised **not to be hurt by the second death nor to have his name erased from the book of life**. (Note: the concept of a book of life is ancient and goes back to Mesopotamia's

Tablets of Destiny. I won't travel down this rabbit trail. Suffice it to say that the book of life, presented six times in Revelation, holds the names of Christ's loyal followers who will share eternity with Him.)

In mentioning the book of life, note that one's name can be *erased* from that book. One's name can also be *restored* to the book of life.

> *22 Note then the kindness and the severity of God: severity toward those who have fallen, but God's kindness to you, provided you continue in his kindness. Otherwise you too will be cut off. 23 And even they, if they do not continue in their unbelief, will be grafted in,* **for God has the power to graft them in again.** *(Rom 11:22-23)*

This would seem to fly in the face of many people's ideas about predestination, of which they believe that God has ordained everything in your life. So, if you sin—whatever form that sin might take, God set that up ahead of time and nothing you do can change your destiny. Too often it's taught that being God's elect means we're predestined to certain things. This goes back to "once saved, always saved." Yet, being God's elect does not guarantee your name to be in the book of life. Being God's chosen people didn't save Israel in the wilderness. Being God's elect requires a sustained, believing loyalty to Him. You can't call yourself a Christian because your parents did, or even because you were sprinkled in a church as a baby, and expect a "golden ticket" to eternity as a result. It requires faithfulness to Him. You can be a prominent pastor or Grammy Award-winning musician and have your name blotted out of the book of life by turning your back on and denying Christ. He gave you free will so that *you* get to make that choice. You won't be able to blame anybody else.

Tied into this theme of immortality and the book of life we have another promise—that Jesus would **confess our names before the Father and His angels**, which goes back to Matthew 10:32-33:

> *32 So everyone who acknowledges me before men, I also will acknowledge before my Father who is in heaven, 33 but*

> *whoever denies me before men, I also will deny before my Father who is in heaven.*

and Luke 12:8:

> *"And I tell you, everyone who acknowledges me before men, the Son of Man also will acknowledge before the angels of God,*

and Romans 10:9-10:

> *9 because, if you confess with your mouth that Jesus is Lord and believe in your heart that God raised him from the dead, you will be saved. 10 For with the heart one believes and is justified, and with the mouth one confesses and is saved.*

Another word for acknowledge is to 'confess'—*homologeō*, **ὁμολογέω**: to declare openly to others, to speak out freely, and to profess oneself as a worshiper of. If we confess our loyalty to Him and profess His name to others, He will acknowledge us before the Father and His angels. How do we connect this to having our names written in the book of life? That book is where the names of those who are saved are written.

One last promise is connected to this theme of eternal life: *"I will* **keep you from the hour of trial** *that is coming on the whole world, to try those who dwell on the earth."* (Revelation 3:10) What is that hour? In Daniel 12:1, we read:

> *"At that time shall arise Michael, the great prince who has charge of your people. And there shall be a time of trouble, such as never has been since there was a nation till that time. But at that time your people shall be delivered, everyone whose name shall be found written in the book."*

Many tie this verse to the fall of Jerusalem. However, the

destruction of the temple and its city had nothing to do with names being written in a book. Throughout the Word, we see reference to the Day of the Lord as that terrible time immediately preceding His return, or perhaps the very day of His return. The word translated to 'hour' is *hōra*, ὥρα, which means a moment or any definite time and can be a day, as in the 12 hours of daytime, or an hour of daytime. John takes this verse in Daniel to refer to that final time at the return of the Lord, and to John, the book is the book of life.

Will those whose names are written in the book of life will be spared from going through that time of turmoil? While we'd like to not have to go through that period of worsening tribulation, this promise of deliverance is not necessarily a physical one. It is certainly a spiritual one, but the word for 'keep,' *tēreō*, τηρέω, in combination with the phrase ἐκ τῆς ὥρας τοῦ πειρασμοῦ that is translated 'from the hour of testing' is perhaps better thought of as "not to leave" or as "to guard," as in He will not leave us during that hour of trial. He will guard us.

Our Reign with Christ

Another theme in these promises is that of ruling with Christ. The "**crown of life**" is promised, in both the letter to Smyrna and James 1:12. In the Bible, the crown is a sign of royalty. You'll never find angels wearing a crown in the Bible, but believers make up a royal priesthood to God. We will be rewarded with crowns as we share in the reign of Christ and **sit with Him on His throne**. Together we **will rule over the nations with a rod of iron**—as foretold in Psalm 2. Regarding the reign of the Messiah described in that psalm, we also have the promise of **the morning star**. The morning star is a reference to the Messiah and His rule.

Many pastors teach that the crown is a reward little different than winning a gold medal in a competition, but there's much more implied here. While the word *diadēma*, διάδημα—from which we get the word 'diadem'—denotes rulership and authority, here John uses the word *stephanos*, στέφανος, which denotes not just rulership but also victory, and metaphorically refers to the eternal blessings given to the genuine believers in God and Christ as a reward for righteousness.

The final promise of this group is that we are to be **pillars in the temple of God**. *Stylos*, στῦλος, is directly translated to 'pillar' or 'column.' However, there is an OT allusion here to the massive pillars of Solomon's temple—Jachin and Boaz. Jachin means "He will establish" and Boaz, in the context of 1 Kings 7:21, is thought to mean "in strength." So, we are to be established in strength. Indeed, when you look at Thayer's Greek lexicon, the word 'pillar' in Revelation 3:12 means "I will assign him a firm and abiding place in the everlasting kingdom of God."

The Marriage Supper of the Lamb

We are also promised **to eat of "the hidden manna."** Of course, we all recall that manna was "grain from heaven" and the "food of angels" (Psalm 78:24-25) which God provided to the Israelites in the wilderness. Its name means "what is it?" While there are many "meals" portrayed in the OT that point to the marriage supper of the lamb, the connection to manna means more.

> *31 Our fathers ate the manna in the wilderness; as it is written, 'He gave them bread from heaven to eat.'" 32 Jesus then said to them, "Truly, truly, I say to you, it was not Moses who gave you the bread from heaven, but my Father gives you the true bread from heaven. 33 For the bread of God is he who comes down from heaven and gives life to the world." 34 They said to him, "Sir, give us this bread always." 35 Jesus said to them, "I am the bread of life; whoever comes to me shall not hunger, and whoever believes in me shall never thirst. (Jhn 6:31-35)*

Here we see that the manna we're promised is related to Jesus, the bread of life. In conjunction with the manna, Christ **will come in and eat with us**. So, those who refused the feasts associated with pagan idols and demons were promised end-time fellowship and identification with Jesus, consummated in the marriage supper of the Lamb. Today, we have that promise, too.

The victorious in Pergamum were promised to receive "**a white stone, with a new name written on the stone that no one knows except the one who receives it.**" In that same vein, those who were loyal in Philadelphia were promised that Christ would "**write on him the name of my God, and the name of the city of my God, the new Jerusalem, which comes down from my God out of heaven, and my own new name.**" And in Sardis, those who had not soiled their garments "**will walk with me in white.**" Here we find several ideas wrapped around white and new names.

White in the Bible stands for righteousness, innocence, and purity. It is used 13 times in Revelation, always referring to righteousness. Angels are typically shown to be wearing shining white when their garments are mentioned in the Word. It is the color of heaven and we, too, will be clothed in it.

So, what is this white stone? The Greek for 'white stone,' *psēphos leukos,* **ψῆφος λευκός**, comes from root words that mean more than what you might envision as a white rock like you might pick up at the beach. *Leukos* means 'brilliant' or 'light,' so the term means a brilliant, almost shining stone of a white color much like the dazzling white robes ascribed to angels. Here the stone could be more like a gem in a ring or more specifically, a magical gem. In that era, magical amulets bearing the names and epithets of deities were used. During those times, stones were also used as tickets to events. More frequently, however, *psēphos* came to mean 'vote' after the white stones used in voting, and *leukos* would refer to a favorable vote. The custom of the time was to use stones for voting, whether in an election or in the verdict of a trial where the white stone meant acquittal, and the black one meant guilty. Our white stones show us acquitted.

Curiously, the white stone is also linked to the idea of the manna as a heavenly reward. Exodus 16:31 describes manna as resembling white bdellium stones. In the Septuagint, Numbers 11:7 compares manna to rock crystals. With manna alluding to the marriage supper of the Lamb, I am reminded of the parable of Matthew 22 in which the king prepared a wedding feast for his son. Many who were invited ignored the invitation, so the king sent his servants to invite any who would come. When the king arrived at the feast, he saw a man not dressed in wedding garments and cast him into outer darkness where there will be weeping and gnashing of teeth. When I think of such a feast, I think of tables adorned in fine white linens, and our traditions have the bride wearing a gown of white. In fact, in Revelation 19:8-9, we find this about the Bride at the marriage supper of the Lamb:

> *8 "it was granted her to clothe herself with fine linen, bright and pure"-- for the fine linen is the righteous deeds of the saints. 9 And the angel said to me, "Write this: Blessed are those who are invited to the marriage supper of the Lamb." And he said to me, "These are the true words of God."*

In v8, the word for 'bright' is *lampros*, $\lambda\alpha\mu\pi\rho\acute{o}\varsigma$, which means shining and brilliant, and in some instances, it is used for brilliant and glistening white. At that feast, we, the church, are the bride, and we all shall wear white.

What about the new names written on the stone and upon us? Once again, John grabs scripture from here and there to present his theology. In Isaiah 62:2 God speaks of Zion:

> *The nations shall see your righteousness, and all the kings your glory, and you shall be called by a new name that the mouth of the LORD will give.*

And in Isaiah 65:15, God speaks of His enemies:

> *You shall leave your name to my chosen for a curse, and the Lord GOD will put you to death, but his servants he will call by another name,*

and we see God putting His enemies to death, while in Revelation 2:11, the conquerors are promised not to be hurt by the second death. Yet, as

He puts His enemies to death, His servants will be called by another name. So, Revelation 2:17 and 3:12 parallel each other with the idea of a new name. These can be linked to Revelation 19:12 where Christ is shown as a conquering warrior who *"has a name written that no one knows but himself."* Dr. Aune combines the use of magical amulets carrying the names of deities, the early church's use of divine names in healings and exorcisms, and Christ's carrying a name only he knows to point to this name being inscribed on the stone and upon believers as the new name of Christ. Dr. Beale believes that this is what Revelation 3:12 refers to directly and that the name of Christ being inscribed on the white stone is like your ticket to the hidden manna, to the marriage supper.

In essence, this is John's updating of Name Theology, where God's people bear His name. In the OT, we see Israel called by God's Name. In Numbers 6:27 we read, *"So shall they put my name upon the people of Israel, and I will bless them"*—after Aaron and his sons were to bless the people (Numbers 6:22-26). Solomon goes on to build a temple for His Name. Later in the Apocalypse, we will see the reverse, where the beast puts his name and number on those who follow him.

In Summary . . .

I believe that we find the above three main themes within the promises made to those Christ calls conquerors. Maybe I've read too much into these. You can judge that for yourself, but it seems to make sense to me. And maybe there are papers out there that discuss this, but I never came across them.

To reiterate:

Eternal Life:
The grant to eat of the tree of life in the paradise of God
To not be hurt by the second death (the lake of fire)
To never have our name blotted out from the book of life
To have Jesus confess our name before the Father and His angels
To be kept from the hour of trial that is coming on the whole world

Reigning with Christ:
To receive the crown of life
Authority over the nations to rule with a rod of iron
To sit with Christ on His throne
The morning star
To be a pillar in the temple of God

Joining in the Marriage Supper of the Lamb:
To partake of some hidden manna
To have Christ come in to and eat with him
To receive a white stone with a new name written on it that only you will know
To have the name of God, the new Jerusalem, and Christ's new name written on him
To walk with Him in white garments

The letters to the seven churches are instructive to us in both positive and negative ways. On the negative side, we see how compromising our faith, joining with the world's immorality, or even simply tolerating those spreading false teachings can lead to failure. The shortcomings of these seven churches are also those of today's church, as well as those of the church throughout history.

Yet, on the positive side, we see in clear language the promises Christ makes to those who remain faithful. If your walk with Christ seems a bit shaky when you compare it to these churches, seek Him first. And, as He told the body in Ephesus, remember, repent, and repeat. If you need motivation, read the above list of promises one more time ... and repeat as needed.

The Court is in Session

Revelation 4 and 5

As we move further into the book, let's look at chapters four and five together. Here, John is not only given a glimpse of God's throne room and His council, but he is also given a commission to prophesy along the lines of Elijah, Daniel, and Ezekiel. Most of what he sees has been seen and foretold by those prophets as well. And yet John's purpose is to show these earlier prophecies in the light of the universal church, as opposed to the nation of Israel. Where chapter one highlighted the divine nature of Jesus and declared Him to be the God Most High, and chapters two and three looked at seven churches as representative of the universal church, chapter four begins the prophetic portion of the book dealing with nonbelievers.

God's Divine Council

I mentioned earlier that many scholars believe that the Book of Revelation is a long courtroom scene with God's Divine Council in session. This follows what is called the covenant lawsuit motif, which is fairly prominent in the OT.

What exactly is the covenant lawsuit motif? Throughout the OT, where God judged both Israel and the nations that persecuted it, His decisions weren't capricious. We see consistently where He examined Israel (or another nation), presented its shortcomings and how they failed to keep their covenant with Him (or persecuted His people), and issued His subsequent judgment, which was then carried out by the council (1 Kings 22:19-22). In each case, justice was dispensed fairly. Micah 6 is a good example:

> *1 Hear what the LORD says: Arise, plead your case before the mountains, and let the hills hear your voice. 2 Hear, you mountains, the indictment of the LORD, and you enduring foundations of the earth, for the LORD has an indictment against his people, and he will contend with Israel. 3 "O my people, what have I done to you? How have I wearied you? Answer me! 4 For I brought you up from the land of Egypt and redeemed you from the house of slavery, and I sent before you Moses, Aaron, and Miriam. 5 O my people, remember what Balak king of Moab devised, and what Balaam the son of Beor answered him, and what happened from Shittim to Gilgal, that you may know the righteous acts of the LORD." 6 "With what shall I come before the LORD, and bow myself before God on high? Shall I come before him with burnt offerings, with calves a year old? 7 Will the LORD be pleased with thousands of rams, with ten thousands of rivers of oil? Shall I give my firstborn for my transgression, the fruit of my body for the sin of my soul?" 8 He has told you, O man, what is good; and what does the LORD require of you but to do justice, and to love kindness, and to walk humbly with your God? 9 The voice of the LORD cries to the city-- and it is sound wisdom to fear your name: "Hear of the rod and of him who appointed it! 10 Can I forget any longer the treasures of wickedness in the house of the wicked, and the scant measure that is accursed? 11 Shall I acquit the man with wicked scales and with a bag of deceitful weights? 12 Your rich men are full of violence; your inhabitants speak lies, and their tongue is deceitful in their mouth. 13 Therefore I strike you with a grievous blow, making you desolate because of your sins. 14 You shall eat, but not be*

> *satisfied, and there shall be hunger within you; you shall put away, but not preserve, and what you preserve I will give to the sword. 15 You shall sow, but not reap; you shall tread olives, but not anoint yourselves with oil; you shall tread grapes, but not drink wine. 16 For you have kept the statutes of Omri, and all the works of the house of Ahab; and you have walked in their counsels, that I may make you a desolation, and your inhabitants a hissing; so you shall bear the scorn of my people." (Mic 6:1-16)*

Isaiah 1 is another example (which I won't copy here) and it even mentions God's courts in Isaiah 1:12:

> "When you come to appear before me, who has required of you this trampling of my courts?

In some cases, we see Israel's sin and God's judgment being pronounced directly by one of His prophets. In other cases, we see the prophet describing God's council room—His throne room—from which God pronounces judgment. In these Divine Council scenes, God acts as prosecutor and judge while the beings in attendance have different functions: attending to God, supporting His throne, praise and worship, and warriors who fight Yahweh's battles. They can also participate in the council proceedings (1 Kings 22:20, Isaiah 6:8), give counsel (Isaiah 44:26), or serve as watchers and guardians (Daniel 4:13,17 and Daniel 12:1). We also see one member of the council acting as the accuser in the prologue to Job, but I think he's been kicked out now.

As we saw in the previous chapter, the examination of the seven churches—i.e., the universal church—falls into this motif. Under the New Covenant, we see Christ condemn followers' failings and those who are Christians in name only. For those who don't repent and clean up their act, their judgment is pronounced. And for the faithful, their rewards are great. In chapters four and five, the court moves into judging the rest of the world.

In chapter four, John describes God's throne room and His council.

> *1 In the year that King Uzziah died I saw the Lord sitting upon a throne, high and lifted up; and the train of his robe filled the temple. 2 Above him stood the seraphim. Each had six wings: with two he covered his face, and with two he covered his feet, and with two he flew. 3 And one called to another and said: "Holy, holy, holy is the LORD of hosts; the whole earth is full of his glory!"*

and of Ezekiel 1:4-28 (only partially copied below):

> *4 As I looked, behold, a stormy wind came out of the north, and a great cloud, with brightness around it, and fire flashing forth continually, and in the midst of the fire, as it were gleaming metal. 5 And from the midst of it came the likeness of four living creatures. And this was their appearance: they had a human likeness, 6 but each had four faces, and each of them had four wings. . . . 10 As for the likeness of their faces, each had a human face. The four had the face of a lion on the right side, the four had the face of an ox on the left side, and the four had the face of an eagle. . . . 22 Over the heads of the living creatures there was the likeness of an expanse, shining like awe-inspiring crystal, spread out above their heads. . . .26 And above the expanse over their heads there was the likeness of a throne, in appearance like sapphire; and seated above the likeness of a throne was a likeness with a human appearance. 27 And upward from what had the appearance of his waist I saw as it were gleaming metal, like the appearance of fire enclosed all around. And downward from what had the appearance of his waist I saw as it were the appearance of fire, and there was brightness around him. 28 Like the appearance of the bow that is in the cloud on the day of rain, so was the appearance of the brightness all around. Such was the*

appearance of the likeness of the glory of the LORD. And when I saw it, I fell on my face, and I heard the voice of one speaking. (Eze 1:4-6, 10, 22, 26-28)

as well as of other heavenly scenes such as Daniel 7:9-14, Ezekiel 10:1-20, and more.

Yet, the scene is "updated" by John in a few ways. Here we see the seraphim of Isaiah blended with the cherubim of Ezekiel to become the living creatures in Revelation. Plus, we not only see God's throne surrounded by a rainbow, an expanse like a sea of crystal, and the four living creatures, we also see 24 thrones occupied by 24 elders dressed in white, wearing golden crowns, and worshiping God. Since angelic beings are never described as wearing crowns in the Bible, we can take these elders as representatives of righteous mankind—those who have overcome according to the previous two chapters. Do they specifically represent the 12 apostles and 12 tribes of Israel? Perhaps, but that's not spelled out, and at the time of John's writing this, not all of the apostles were dead and in heaven. If we accept the late date for this book, 96 A.D., at least one of those thrones would have been viewed as vacant—John's. We also know these are not martyrs because in Revelation 6:9 we see *"the souls of those slain for the Word of God and their witness"* under the altar. Other possibilities exist, but I think it's safe to say they represent God's loyal believers, whether righteous Israelis from OT times or Christians. However, as promised, by being in the council, they are put over the nations *"to rule with a rod of iron"* as well as over the angels (1 Corinthians 6:3).

Also, notice that the 24 thrones *circle* God's throne. From an astral perspective, this holds a different meaning, and John might very well have "seen" his visions in astral terms, as was common for that period.[24] While the zodiac had its origins in ancient Mesopotamia, all of the cultures in the Near East at that time used the zodiac to observe celestial happenings. This wasn't, and still isn't, using the objects of the sky to predict and control individual fate, as astrology is believed to do

---

[24] Malina, Bruce J and Pilch, John R. *The Social-Science Commentary on the*

these days.

The living creatures are described as "full of eyes," and the ancients called stars "eyes," believing they were living beings. These creatures in Ezekiel 1:16 are also described as being constructed "*as it were a wheel within a wheel.*" The combination of eyes and wheels was a way of detailing the course of constellations across the sky, so John appears to be describing constellations in the heavens. Constellations cycle through the sky and were used to map time. Decans, from the Greek word *deka* for ten, were groups of stars used to mark specific phases of the night sky. Ancient Egypt and Babylon divided the sky into 36 decans, while the Hellenists had moved to 24. By the first century A.D., the day was divided into 12 double-hour periods. Later, men went to 24 periods, or hours, to better track time. John, then, saw 24 thrones representing the 24 decans of the sky encircling God's throne. Why call them elders? At that time, a council of elders was called a *Gerousia* or *dekania* and individual members were *decanos* (in Greek). Perhaps all of the above is valid, and John is pointing out that God and His Divine Council—on which representatives of righteous believers sit—control the flow of time, history, and destiny.

I should note, too, that the four living creatures represent both His terrestrial creation—wild animals, domesticated animals, man, and birds—and the four cardinal points of a compass. As previously discussed, four is the number of the created order. We will see this again in the judgments to come.

The Investiture of Christ

The first order of business? Examining the "credentials," you might say, of Jesus. With the council seated, we move into chapter five where the council determines the worthiness of Christ both to redeem the righteous and to judge the unrighteous. In Revelation 5:1-2, we read:

> *1 Then I saw in the right hand of him who was seated on the*

Book of Revelation, (Augsburg Fortress Publishers, July 25, 2000)

> throne a scroll written within and on the back, sealed with seven seals. 2 And I saw a mighty angel proclaiming with a loud voice, "Who is worthy to open the scroll and break its seals?"

and only one is deemed worthy:

> 6 And between the throne and the four living creatures and among the elders I saw a Lamb standing, as though it had been slain, with seven horns and with seven eyes, which are the seven spirits of God sent out into all the earth. 7 And he went and took the scroll from the right hand of him who was seated on the throne. (Rev 5:6-7)

The Lamb Who was slain is worthy, but note where He is. At this point, He's not seated on a throne at the right hand of God. He's standing among the elders, as one of us. Reading on, we'll see that Jesus is not depicted as sitting on a throne until Revelation 22:1. Likewise, in Daniel 7, the "one like a son of man" is not seated on a throne either.

Dr. David Aune, in his commentary, sees this as an investiture scene. Christ is not enthroned here, nor is He commissioned to perform a task, as was Isaiah in Isaiah 6. Christ has fulfilled the three aspects of an Israeli becoming king: anointed or designated as a candidate for kingship, proven himself kingly by His acts, and being exalted to His throne. Yet, He cannot sit on the throne of His kingdom until all is finished—the world being reconciled back to God and the new Eden established. So, we see His investiture in Revelation, where He is formally raised to the position He holds "informally" as King of kings and finally takes His seat. The same is true of Daniel 7:9-14 where we see the "one like a son of man" invested as King. He is given His eternal kingship but can't yet sit on the throne.

The Scroll

What is the scroll? That's been the topic of much debate. I've read that land deeds of that time were sealed with seven seals, and the speculation was that this scroll is the title deed to the earth, held out by God in His right hand for someone worthy to reclaim. This concept gives us an image of a scroll with seven seals attached to the outside. If you think about the reality of a scroll this way, we can't see the contents of the scroll until the seventh and last seal is broken, allowing us finally to unroll the scroll. As such, we see the judgments depicted in Revelation 6 being unleashed by the breaking of the seals and not necessarily contained on the scroll itself.

A second consideration is based upon a scroll with seven seals found in a cache of Egyptian scrolls. Here, there was a single outer seal, which when broken allowed the unrolling of part of the scroll. Unrolling that part revealed a second seal that allowed a second part to be unrolled. This was repeated to find the final, seventh seal and roll. The first six rolls, upon being unrolled, were blank, but the seventh held a legal document believed to be a last will and testament. If we use this concept for the scroll in Revelation 5, we don't find blank rolls with the breaking of the seals, but instead the judgments from God. As such, this scroll appears to hold the judgments of God upon the world, and the seals imply a legal validity to it.

John appears to allude to Ezekiel 2:9-10:

> *9 And when I looked, behold, a hand was stretched out to me, and behold, a scroll of a book was in it. 10 And he spread it before me. And it had writing on the front and on the back, and there were written on it words of lamentation and mourning and woe.*

While Ezekiel 2 talks of judgment on the people of Israel, John universalizes it to the whole world, and this would seem to support the idea that God's judgments are written upon the scroll. In truth, we're never told explicitly what the scroll holds.

The Comparisons to Daniel

Perhaps the most crucial OT council scene with respect to Revelation 4 and 5 is Daniel 7:9-28. Beale and Carson, in their *Commentary on the New Testament Use of the Old Testament*,[25] point out that the scene in Revelation aligns with Daniel in 14 (2x7) ways:

1. Introductory phrasing of the vision (Dan 7:9 - Rev 4:1)
2. Setting up of multiple thrones (Dan 7:9a - Rev 4:2a)
3. God sitting upon His throne (Dan 7:9b - Rev 4:2b)
4. The description of God upon His throne (Dan 7:9c - Rev 4:3a)
5. Fire before the throne (Dan 7:9d-10a - Rev 4:5)
6. Heavenly servants surround the throne (Dan 7:10b - Rev 4:4b, 6b-10, 5:8, 11,14)
7. Book(s)/scroll before the throne (Dan 7:10c - Rev 5:1-7)
8. The opening of the book(s)/scroll (Dan 7:10d - Rev 5:2-5, 9)
9. A divine, messianic figure (Son of Man/Lamb who appeared slain) approaches God's throne to receive authority to reign forever over a kingdom (Dan 7:13-14a - Rev 5:5b-7, 9a, 12-13)
10. This kingdom includes all peoples, nations, and tongues (Dan 7:14a - Rev 5:9b)
11. Daniel/John gets emotionally upset over the vision (Dan 7:15 - Rev 5:4)
12. Daniel/John is given heavenly counsel about the vision from one of the divine beings (Dan 7:16 - Rev 5:5a)
13. The saints are granted authority to rule over the kingdom (Dan 7:18, 22, 27a - Rev 5:10)
14. Concludes with a statement about God's eternal reign (Dan 7:27b - Rev 5:13-14)

---

[25] Beale, G.K. and Carson, D.A., *Commentary on the New Testament Use of the Old Testament*, Baker Academic, Nov 2007.

Again, is John using Daniel's vision as an allusion that he expects the receivers of this book to understand and be comfortable with? Or is he seeing the same glimpse of Christ's assuming His reign that Daniel was given? I'd go with both. After all, both are visions of the End Times. Of note, the kingdom mentioned is one of all peoples, not just Israel, and the saints are given joint reign with the Messiah.

John also makes use of Daniel 12:1,4,9 and Isaiah 29:11.

1 "At that time shall arise Michael, the great prince who has charge of your people. And there shall be a time of trouble, such as never has been since there was a nation till that time. But at that time your people shall be delivered, everyone whose name shall be found written in the book. . . . 4 But you, Daniel, shut up the words and seal the book, until the time of the end. Many shall run to and fro, and knowledge shall increase." . . . 9 He said, "Go your way, Daniel, **for the words are shut up and sealed until the time of the end**. *(Dan 12:1, 4, 9)*

11 And the vision of all this has become to you like the words of a book that is sealed. When men give it to one who can read, saying, "Read this," he says, "I cannot, for it is sealed." (Isa 29:11)

Daniel 12 is a vision of the End Times, while Isaiah 29 is one of the sieges of Jerusalem, also possibly in the End Times, not 70 A.D. The word translated to 'book,' *sēp̄er*, סֵפֶר, is also used for 'scroll,' as is the Greek word, *biblion*, used by John. Scrolls were used per the custom of the day, and the first codex, like books we have today, was a late first century A.D. development. Note that, in both instances, the words have been sealed up. They're waiting for John to reveal and Christ to open.

Our Take-Away . . .

While we could investigate numerous other metaphors and OT references in these chapters, my goal was not to write another humongous commentary on Revelation. I've tried to hit the highlights. still, the page count keeps mounting. There's that much to understand about this book.

In these two chapters, John gives us a glimpse of God's throne room and his Divine Council, on which we are now members. This glimpse is like that which the Father gave Daniel, Ezekiel, and Isaiah, whose visions are incorporated into, blended, and universalized in John's depiction. We see God extending a scroll to one who is worthy to open it, and only Jesus is found worthy. The precise contents of that scroll are not given, but it appears that it might contain "words of lamentation and mourning and woe." God's judgments? These same words might have been given to Daniel, but he was instructed to seal up the words "until the time of the end." It is John who was tasked to reveal what Daniel had sealed up.

Most importantly, we see the investiture of Christ, who upon His death, resurrection, and ascension was given His eternal kingship. Yet, in another case of "already but not yet," He has His kingship but can't assume His throne until all things are done. Now we move prophetically into that period of history when God's judgment takes place, the earth is reconciled back to God, and Christ can take His rightful seat in the new Eden.

Release the Four Horsemen!

As we move into the judgments (Revelation 6) awaiting those who have not accepted Jesus as Lord and Savior, it might be helpful to first take a look at Leviticus 26:14-33. In the first part of that chapter, we find the blessings promised to those who obey and follow God's statutes. In these verses, we see a pattern designed by God for judging the unfaithful.

> 14 "But if you will not listen to me and will not do all these commandments, 15 if you spurn my statutes, and if your soul abhors my rules, so that you will not do all my commandments, but break my covenant, 16 then I will do this to you: I will visit you with panic, with wasting disease and fever that consume the eyes and make the heart ache. And you shall sow your seed in vain, for your enemies shall eat it. 17 I will set my face against you, and you shall be struck down before your enemies. Those who hate you shall rule over you, and you shall flee when none pursues you. 18 And if in spite of this you will not listen to me, then I will discipline you again sevenfold for your sins, 19 and I will break the pride of your power, and I will make your heavens like iron and your earth like bronze. 20 And your strength shall be spent in vain, for your land shall not yield its increase, and the trees of the land shall not yield their fruit. 21 "Then if you walk contrary to me and will not listen to me,

> *I will continue striking you, sevenfold for your sins. 22 And I will let loose the wild beasts against you, which shall bereave you of your children and destroy your livestock and make you few in number, so that your roads shall be deserted. 23 "And if by this discipline you are not turned to me but walk contrary to me, 24 then I also will walk contrary to you, and I myself will strike you sevenfold for your sins. 25 And I will bring a sword upon you, that shall execute vengeance for the covenant. And if you gather within your cities, I will send pestilence among you, and you shall be delivered into the hand of the enemy. 26 When I break your supply of bread, ten women shall bake your bread in a single oven and shall dole out your bread again by weight, and you shall eat and not be satisfied. 27 "But if in spite of this you will not listen to me, but walk contrary to me, 28 then I will walk contrary to you in fury, and I myself will discipline you sevenfold for your sins. 29 You shall eat the flesh of your sons, and you shall eat the flesh of your daughters. 30 And I will destroy your high places and cut down your incense altars and cast your dead bodies upon the dead bodies of your idols, and my soul will abhor you. 31 And I will lay your cities waste and will make your sanctuaries desolate, and I will not smell your pleasing aromas. 32 And I myself will devastate the land, so that your enemies who settle in it shall be appalled at it. 33 And I will scatter you among the nations, and I will unsheathe the sword after you, and your land shall be a desolation, and your cities shall be a waste. (Lev 26:14-33)*

What do we read first? God will send panic (unrest), wasting disease (pestilence), the sowing of seed in vain and enemies that eat of it (famine), being struck down by enemies (the sword), and those who hate you to rule over you (conquered). He sends these as warnings to urge His people to reconsider, humble themselves, and repent. We'll see these again as we discuss the four horsemen of the apocalypse in the next section.

However, what comes next? For those who don't repent at these first warnings, He ups the ante. Although we read of some of the same judgments—famine, wild beasts, the sword, and pestilence—this time God Himself will strike the unfaithful **sevenfold**. He strikes sevenfold **four** times with each judgment becoming more severe. What John is about to show us is three sets of seven judgments, known as the Seal, Trumpet, and Bowl Judgments. There was to be a fourth set of judgments—the seven thunders—but a voice from heaven told John to seal up what they said and not to write it down (Revelation 10:4). So, God set the pattern for Israel, and now, with John universalizing it to the entire world, God is consistent in using that same pattern.

After all, what's fair is fair, right? Well, choose your own metaphor. There are lots of those coming ahead, too.

The Four Horsemen of the Apocalypse

After the number '666' and the "antichrist," perhaps the second most widely known reference from Revelation in our modern culture is "the four horsemen of the Apocalypse." From graphic novels to cinema, you can find references to these carriers of destruction and death and their colored horses.

The idea of horses and horsemen roaming the world has roots in several OT passages. For example, in Zechariah 6:1-8 we find horses of four different colors pulling chariots and *"going out to the four winds of heaven."* These horses have a precedent in Zechariah 1 where we also see horses of red, sorrel, and white which *"patrol the earth."*

Plus, the concept of the judgments delivered by these horsemen is foreseen in Ezekiel 14:12-23 (and Leviticus 26, as already stated). Here, Ezekiel delivers a message about Jerusalem not being spared from judgment and that even Noah, Daniel, and Job could not get Him to spare the city from famine, wild beasts, the sword, and pestilence. They alone would be spared by their righteousness. Here are v21-23:

> *21 "For thus says the Lord GOD: How much more when I send upon Jerusalem* **my four disastrous acts of judgment,**

sword, famine, wild beasts, and pestilence, *to cut off from it man and beast! 22 But behold, some survivors will be left in it, sons and daughters who will be brought out; behold, when they come out to you, and you see their ways and their deeds, you will be consoled for the disaster that I have brought upon Jerusalem, for all that I have brought upon it. 23 They will console you, when you see their ways and their deeds, and you shall know that I have not done without cause all that I have done in it, declares the Lord GOD." (Eze 14:21-23)*

We see these four "*disastrous acts*" listed upon the breaking of the fourth seal. Is Jerusalem in these verses a type or foreshadowing of what's to come upon the whole earth? Like Ezekiel, we, too, will know that God has "*not done without cause all that (He) has done in it.*"

In Revelation 6:1-2 we read:

1 Now I watched when the Lamb opened one of the seven seals, and I heard one of the four living creatures say with a voice like thunder, "Come!" 2 And I looked, and behold, a white horse! And its rider had a bow, and a crown was given to him, and he came out conquering, and to conquer.

While some scholars debate what is meant by "the Lamb," I suspect most of us recognize this as Jesus. After all, with the subsequent seals, the scriptures say ". . . **He** opened . . ." and 28 of the 29 times the word 'Lamb' is used in Revelation, it refers to the Messiah. However, the metaphor of the lamb is interesting and multifaceted. In most Near Eastern cultures of the time, the sheep and lamb were used as symbols of deity, of their gods, as well as a symbol of something sacrificial—the sacrificial lamb. Going one step further, an Aramaic word for 'lamb,' *talyā'*, can also mean 'servant.' So, the metaphor of the Lamb brings with it the idea of deity, sacrifice, and servant.

There is also significant debate about just who the rider on the white horse is. Many have argued that this rider is Christ because of the white horse. However, note that it's the horse that's white, not that the rider is clothed in white. This is in line with the scriptures from Zechariah. The image is consistent with that of a Parthian king, riding his sacred white horse and armed with a bow. The Parthians were known for their conquests, their horsemanship, and their skills with the bow. For a period of time, they proved to be a formidable foe to the Roman Empire. The bow and crown have also been linked with Apollo, a prominent deity in Smyrna and Thyatira. That, too, would point to this rider being someone other than Christ. Dr. Beale's commentary lists the various pros and cons of this figure being Christ, and the cons outnumber the pros. For me, the unlikelihood that Jesus would break open a seal that would commission Himself to some action is the deal breaker. He's not going to go out conquering what's in reality already His.

More importantly, though, notice who utters the command, "*Come!*" Although Jesus breaks the seals on these four judgments, it's the four living creatures who give the commands—one for each of the judgments. As attendants to the Father Himself, their commands come directly from and with the authority of God, as noted by having a voice like thunder. God's voice is typically depicted as thunder, trumpets, or rushing waters. As I stated in the previous chapter, they also represent the four corners of the earth and God's terrestrial creation. As such, these horsemen have been released upon the entire world.

Notice that I said, "have been." It's been my belief that these judgments began upon Jesus' ascension and claiming of His kingship. The Lord led me to that conclusion as I researched my earlier book, and I wondered if I was reading more into these verses than was there. So, as I studied for this book, I was relieved to learn I'm not alone in that belief. Dr. Greg Beale says:

> The natural inference of this is that the events described in 6:1-8 are not reserved exclusively for a period of severe trial immediately preceding Christ's final coming. At least some of

these events began immediately after his ascension.[26]

In that same section, Dr. Beale also states that the judgments are unlikely to be sequential. Although there is a certain logic to thinking that conquest (horseman 1), together with civil unrest (horseman 2), can lead to famine (horseman 3), which leads to death (horseman 4), he says "but more probably the disasters are simultaneous." This idea seems validated by the description of the fourth seal, Death, in which a fourth of the earth suffers from **all** of these judgments—killed by the sword, with famine, with pestilence, and by wild beasts (Ezekiel 14:12-23, although in a different order).

The idea of wild beasts killing mankind should not be seen as literal. Jewish tradition associates wild beasts with persecuting nations. In particular, the four chariots of Zechariah are linked with the four beasts of Daniel 7, and the horsemen are seen as the evil, heavenly counterparts to those nations. In a similar vein, these four horsemen of Revelation are metaphors for global (four corners of the earth) persecution of the church.

Having said this, we should also note that the extent of these judgments is limited at the start. With the third seal, a voice from the midst of the living creatures limits the famine such that the essentials for life—wheat, barley, oil, and wine—are still available. Many people won't be able to afford them, but they'll be there. Likewise, Death on the fourth horse is given authority over only a quarter of the earth, not the entire planet.

Curiously, Islam is the group most involved in persecuting Christians and Jews today, and Muslims currently make up roughly 25% of the world's population. If you look at landmass, the predominantly Muslim nations make up 16% of the earth's landmass. However, when you add China and the Hindu nations where Christians are also persecuted, roughly 25% of the world is involved.[27]

---

[26] Beale, G.K. *The New International Greek Testament Commentary, the Book of Revelation*, William B. Eerdmans Publishing Co, Grand Rapids, MI, 1999, pg. 326

[27] worldpopulationreview.com/country-rankings/muslim-population-by-

So, we now have four judgments over a fourth of the earth. To me, these four afflictions always correlated well to the "beginning of birth pains" described by Jesus in His Olivet Discourse. Again, I found in studying for this book that many scholars agree. As such, they have been going on for over 2,000 years, affecting one part of the world and then another throughout the course of history. And as with any pregnancy's birth pangs, soon the real labor starts. As we'll see, "the time of trouble" will intensify according to the blueprint of Leviticus 26.

The Altar

In v9-11, we read of what transpires upon the breaking of the fifth seal.

> *9 When he opened the fifth seal, I saw under the altar the souls of those who had been slain for the word of God and for the witness they had borne. 10 They cried out with a loud voice, "O Sovereign Lord, holy and true, how long before you will judge and avenge our blood on those who dwell on the earth?" 11 Then they were each given a white robe and told to rest a little longer, until the number of their fellow servants and their brothers should be complete, who were to be killed as they themselves had been. (Rev 6:9-11)*

Which altar is John referring to? In both earthly temples, Solomon's and Herod's, there were two. The outer altar was the altar of burnt offering. Located in the "Court of Priests," this large bronze altar was where the Israelites burned their sacrifices to God. In the inner court, just outside the Holy of Holies, was the golden altar of incense. As the souls of these martyrs appear to be within the realm of the throne room, near to God, the golden altar of incense appears to be the logical candidate, as it is nearest to God and in front of His mercy seat. This

---

country
en.wikipedia.org/wiki/List_of_countries_and_dependencies_by_area

appears to be confirmed in Revelation 8:3:

> *3 And another angel came and stood at the altar with a golden censer, and he was given much incense to offer with the prayers of all the saints on the golden altar before the throne,*

This is also consistent with Revelation 5:8 where we read of the 24 elders holding *"golden bowls full of incense, which are the prayers of the saints."* (Also, Psalm 141:2) The incense ordained by God was to be used by no one else. While the Bible (Exodus 30:34-35) details only four ingredients explicitly—stacte (possibly storax gum), onycha (modern equivalent is unclear), galbanum, and frankincense—seasoned with salt to be pure and holy, the Temple Institute states that 11 herbs and spices are used, with the other seven *"sweet spices"* kept secret by one family, the Avtinas, from generation to generation. One of those herbs, *ma'aleh ashan*, was crucial to the formula. It allowed the smoke of the incense to rise in a straight column toward heaven before hitting the ceiling and billowing out across the room.[28]

But why *under* the altar? From what I've read, scholars speculate that God has them there as a place of protection. But that's all they offer, speculation. However, there is one group who believe they understand this description—the scholars who see validity to the idea of John using astral descriptions, as mentioned about the 24 elders. There is a constellation named The Altar in the southern sky within the Milky Way. Since stars were typically used to signify celestial beings and glorified believers, the stars of the Milky Way, seen under The Altar, could be metaphors for the souls of those *"slain for the word of God and for the witness they had borne."*

So, who are these saints? The juxtaposition of these verses, following the actions of the four horsemen, is consistent with these people being those persecuted and killed by said afflictions. Some believe these souls to be those of Christians alone since it appears these

---

[28] https://templeinstitute.org/the-incense/

judgments occur after Christ's ascension. However, the phrase *"slain for the word of God and for the witness they had borne"* (Revelation 6:9) leaves open the possibility that righteous Jews also have a place here.

We've looked at the symbolism of the color white before. These saints are rewarded with the white robes promised in Revelation 3:4 and told to wait a little longer. It would appear that more of us have a place waiting under the altar before Christ is finished.

Does that thought scare or bother you? Many scholars, Dr. Beale being one of them, believe that just as Christ won an "inverse victory," believers will become conquerors the same way. What's an "inverse victory?" Christ won by dying. Therefore, they believe, we, too, will conquer and achieve eternal life through death.

However, to me, that seems to go against a large body of scripture that shows God as our refuge, our defender. I made that argument in my earlier book, *Still Here! Surviving the End Times*, as I looked at Psalm 91 in detail and listed numerous other verses to support that. Even in Revelation, the promise made to believers in Philadelphia (Revelation 3:10) that they will be kept *"from the hour of trial that is coming on the whole world"* shows that we can trust Him for protection. Yet, that said, like the saints in Smyrna, we must be prepared to *"be faithful unto death"* (Revelation 2:10) because I have no doubt that some of us will indeed join the crowd under the altar. That is, after all, what v11 above reveals.

The Sixth Seal

12 When he opened the sixth seal, I looked, and behold, there was a great earthquake, and the sun became black as sackcloth, the full moon became like blood, 13 and the stars of the sky fell to the earth as the fig tree sheds its winter fruit when shaken by a gale. 14 The sky vanished like a scroll that is being rolled up, and every mountain and island was removed from its place. 15 Then the kings of the earth and the great ones and the generals and the rich and the powerful, and everyone, slave and free, hid themselves in the caves and among the rocks of the mountains, 16 calling to the mountains and rocks, "Fall on us and hide us from the face of him who is seated on the throne, and from the wrath of the Lamb, 17 for the great day of their wrath has come, and who can stand?" (Rev 6:12-17)

This verse has always been problematic for me. In the literal sense, I can easily see a strong earthquake triggering, or triggered by, a series of volcanic eruptions which, in turn, spew dust and gases into the atmosphere that would darken the sun and make the moon appear reddish. In chapter one, "Before Delving In . . .," I presented a chart displaying the rise in earthquake activity and mentioned the increase in volcanic activity. Could these be the prelude to the "Big One?"

Not according to the scholars. In these verses, John appears to combine imagery from numerous OT verses—Isaiah 13:10-13; 24:1-6, 19-23; 34:4; Ezekiel 32:6-8; Joel 2:10, 30-31; 3:15-16; and Habakkuk 3:6-11—with additional allusions to Amos 8:8-9; Jeremiah 4:23-28; and Psalm 68:7-8. Even the apocalyptic verses of the Olivet Discourse and Acts 2:19-20 can be seen in these sources. The upheaval depicted in these verses are considered stock-in-trade OT descriptions of cosmic disruption, and other Second Temple Jewish literature, such as 1 Enoch, use similar wording, particularly the idea of "falling stars."

Isaiah 34:4 appears to be a foreshadowing for this section:

4 All the host of heaven shall rot away, and the skies roll up like a scroll. All their host shall fall, as leaves fall from the vine, like leaves falling from the fig tree.

Notice the plural in v4b—"*All **their** host of heaven . . .*" We see it also in v2:

"For the Lord is enraged against all the nations, and furious against all their host."

We see here that it's not just the nations and unbelievers who have enraged God but also their heavenly host, the angelic beings who have led these people astray. While *tsâbâ*, צָבָא, means an 'army' or 'group organized for war' and can refer to angels or men, the plural form, *tsâbâ'am*, is used in the Hebrew Bible only for a celestial army, never an earthly one. This points to not just men but also angelic beings facing judgment while apocalyptic destruction consumes the earth.

There is no consensus as to when this judgment takes place. Is it throughout the church age? Is it during "the time of trouble" in the period *preceding* the *parousia*, the return of the Lord? Is it *at* the time of the Lord's return? After all, v17 does say the great day of their wrath has come, and there's a close correlation to Revelation 19:18-21 in that the same groups of people now face judgment: kings, captains (great ones), mighty men (rich and powerful), horses and their riders (generals), and all men, both free and slave, both small and great. These are the allies of the beast. These verses also show six aspects of creation being affected, if not destroyed: earth, sun, moon, stars, heaven (sky), and the mountains and islands. Some of this cataclysmic destruction is depicted again later in the book in conjunction with the day of wrath. Another point made by those who argue that this section points to the final judgment, the Day of the Lord, is that five of the OT segments mentioned above are related to the historical end of a sinful nation.

Still, I find the placement of these events within the context of the book at odds with the idea that this portrays *only* the great day of wrath when Christ returns. There is still a seventh seal to be broken and additional judgments. Because there is an intensification taking place, I don't believe the next judgments are simply the same ones seen from a different perspective. Just as the phrase *"beginning* of birth pains" implies a time sequence, so does seeing these judgments intensify. But that's *my* take.

As I stated, there is no consensus, including by this non-scholar. Some see this as part of the tribulation leading to the Day of the Lord. Some see this as a picture of that great day of wrath. Some see it as literal and some as figurative. However, all see it as bad news for sinful people. What we don't see are dispensational black helicopters and thermonuclear detonations.

Our Take-Away . . .

    For me, the lessons of this chapter are that global judgment began after the ascension of Christ and that conquest, war, famine, and pestilence have been ongoing in varying places across the globe throughout these latter days. "Wild beasts" also started early in the history of the church with both the Jews and Rome persecuting believers.

    Are we still seeing this today? There might not be many places to conquer in the sense of one nation taking over another, but we're seeing worldviews trying to conquer others, and civil unrest has become rampant across the globe. Famine, too, has become a major problem, thanks to locusts in Africa, floods in China and elsewhere, and more. Will the drought in the western U.S. (as I write this) bring the beginnings of food shortages or even famine to this country? And death by pestilence certainly accelerated with the onslaught of COVID-19. Even though the numbers being released by the CDC—or as I call them, the Centers for Disease Commercialization and Profits—for the U.S. can be questioned, there is no doubt about the rising number of deaths in China, India, and third-world nations where poor sanitation, nutrition, and healthcare, along with crowded living conditions make them more susceptible to "pestilence." Yes, these are, at the minimum, the *beginnings* of the birth pains. Perhaps we're already seeing the intensity growing.

    [Now, in 2023, I sincerely believe we're seeing the intensification. Drought has indeed led to food shortages in many places across the globe, including here in the U.S. and the cost of basic necessities has increased, with inflation further eroding the value of our currencies. Tribal warfare in Africa has increased, and, of course, there's the war in the Ukraine. With regard to pestilence, the death toll from the COVID "vaccines" makes that gene therapy one of the deadliest "cures" ever. We're seeing a 40+% increase in excess deaths, which is defined as the number of deaths in excess of the previous five years' average death rate. In addition, those excess deaths are occurring in younger age groups—groups that are typically healthier. We're also seeing SADS—Sudden Adult Death Syndrome—in celebrities, athletes, and others who are expected to be in top physical condition. Ten years ago, such death reports would have listed the cause of death. Today, the reports never state the cause, most likely because they're due to myocarditis and other COVID jab adverse events.]

Have we seen the sixth seal judgment yet? I can't say this with 100% assurance, but perhaps we have. If we're looking for a physical earthquake and the sun turning black, well, no, that clearly hasn't occurred. However, if we're dealing with political or cosmic upheaval and acceleration of judgment, that might have occurred early in 2021.

On the last Sunday of May in 2020, during a time of virtual praise and worship with our church, I was focused on the words of the song when I clearly, almost audibly heard the voice of the Lord. The word I received was "By this time next year, the earthquake of the sixth seal will occur." At that point in time, I had just begun my serious study of Revelation, and I fully expected a great, global, physical, cataclysmic shaking. When that didn't occur within the year, I questioned what I had heard. And yet, the voice was so clear, and the judgments of Revelation were nowhere in my thoughts at that time. What had I missed?

As I've studied the seal judgments, I've come to recognize that perhaps I've missed nothing. Instead, my understanding was incomplete. While there was no physical earthquake, we have had massive disruption. I don't know about you, but I sensed a tidal change in the world after the Biden administration came into power. So far in 2021, we've seen major political upheaval with a mammoth push toward totalitarianism and population control. In reality, not just population control but depopulation as outlined by The Great Reset (formerly known as UN Agenda 21). We've seen the onslaught of pestilence . . . of man's own making. Major flooding, historic droughts, earthquakes, hurricanes, economic inflation, and more have dominated the news cycles. The level of anger in men is unlike anything I've seen in my lifetime. And much of it started, or certainly accelerated, in the past year (2020-2021).

Is what man wants to call climate change actually the intensification of God's judgment that we'll find in the coming first four trumpets? Food for thought.

Yet, even as things intensify, we see in these verses Who is in control. It's the Lord opening those seals and God calling forth the afflictions through His attendants, directly from the throne room. These destructive events take place for both redemptive and judicial purposes. Even with the covenant community, they serve to help purify the faithful and punish those who are disloyal to Christ. And through all of this, He holds the keys to Death and Hades. So, should any of the righteous get caught up in this destruction, they can be assured that Christ has them covered . . . for eternity.

Signed, Sealed, and Delivered

The Seal of God

Revelation 7:1-3 states:

1 After this I saw four angels standing at the four corners of the earth, holding back the four winds of the earth, that no wind might blow on earth or sea or against any tree. 2 Then I saw another angel ascending from the rising of the sun, with the seal of the living God, and he called with a loud voice to the four angels who had been given power to harm earth and sea, 3 saying, "Do not harm the earth or the sea or the trees, until we have sealed the servants of our God on their foreheads."

While it's unclear whether these are four different angels or the four living beings previously described and associated with the four corners of the earth, it's clear that their goal is to cause damage to the earth and sea. Since the next four judgments afflict the earth and sea, it seems probable that these are the first four angels who will soon blow their trumpets to release these terrors.

However, the four horsemen of chapter 6 are associated with the four winds of the earth in Zechariah 6:5. So, some see these angels as holding back the four horsemen and these "upcoming" judgments as the same as those of Revelation 6 but in greater detail. As I've stated, I see an intensification rather than the same in greater detail. Either way, the fact that these angels are standing at the four corners of the earth signifies that they have global jurisdiction.

The more noteworthy aspect of these verses is the *"seal of the living God."* Just what is this seal? This isn't any type of visible mark, like some golden letter branded on our foreheads. In the same vein as the name of Christ being written upon us, this is a spiritual mark that protects us. Indeed, Paul tells us in Ephesians what this seal is:

> *13 In him you also, when you heard the word of truth, the gospel of your salvation, and believed in him, were sealed with the promised Holy Spirit, . . . 30 And do not grieve the Holy Spirit of God, by whom you were sealed for the day of redemption. (Eph 1:13, 30)*

Protection from what? Dr. Beale states it this way: "The main alternatives are: (1) for protection from physical harm, (2) for protection from demons, and (3) for protection from losing their faith and hence their salvation."[29] Dr. Steve Moyise does not agree with the first point stating that, at this point in Revelation, believers have suffered through the first six seal judgments already.[30]

However, we can look back into the OT for another series of events in which a seal from God protected His people from physical harm—the Exodus (Exodus 12:7,13, 23-28). As we'll see, the next two sets of judgments are reminiscent of the plagues of Egypt. On the night of Passover, the people were instructed to mark the lintel and two doorposts of the doors of their homes. That night the Lord passed over the homes so marked, and His people were protected from that final, awful judgment.

Yet, note that the Israelites were also instructed to stay inside. To disobey and leave the protection of their home made them vulnerable

---

[29] Beale, G.K. *The New International Greek Testament Commentary, the Book of Revelation*, William B. Eerdmans Publishing Co, Grand Rapids, MI, 1999, pg. 356

[30] Moyise, S., *The Old Testament in the Book of Revelation*, Sheffield Academic Press, 1995.

to the death being inflicted upon Egypt. When these later judgments arrive in our time, we, too, need to remain obedient.

Dr. Beale is unique in applying Ezekiel 9 to this question of protection, but it, too, is revealing. In v1-6 we read:

> 1 Then he cried in my ears with a loud voice, saying, "Bring near the executioners of the city, each with his destroying weapon in his hand." 2 And behold, six men came from the direction of the upper gate, which faces north, each with his weapon for slaughter in his hand, and with them was a man clothed in linen, with a writing case at his waist. And they went in and stood beside the bronze altar. 3 Now the glory of the God of Israel had gone up from the cherub on which it rested to the threshold of the house. And he called to the man clothed in linen, who had the writing case at his waist. 4 And the LORD said to him, "Pass through the city, through Jerusalem, and put a mark on the foreheads of the men who sigh and groan over all the abominations that are committed in it." 5 And to the others he said in my hearing, "Pass through the city after him, and strike. Your eye shall not spare, and you shall show no pity. 6 Kill old men outright, young men and maidens, little children and women, but touch no one on whom is the mark. And begin at my sanctuary." So they began with the elders who were before the house.

This is probably the closest OT type to what we're reading in Revelation 7. In this passage, the first man marked the faithful, while the other five killed those involved in idolatry. The latter did so without mercy—men and women of all ages. And they began with the so-called priests. What does that say about what's to come at the end of the age?

While being sealed definitely protects us spiritually, I want to believe that physical protection is also part of being sealed. Should that surprise us? Not if we hold Him to the promise He made to us via the church in Philadelphia to keep or guard us from the hour of trial that is coming. Then add in the dozens of scriptures about His being our refuge. Take another look at Psalm 91. Pestilence shall not come near our tents. We shall see violence only from afar. And more. Do we hold Him to His Word, or just gloss over verses such as those, perhaps thinking they were for another era?

That said, I don't mean to imply that we will live inside some kind of protective bubble. We will need to dig into His word, stay strong in prayer, and tightly hold on to His promises, or we might find ourselves straying outside the house at night. All of us will find our faith being tested. Yet, *He* is the author and perfecter of our faith.

Getting back to Dr. Moyise's perspective, it requires a belief that the sixth seal is opened sequentially and before the sealing of God's faithful. That might not be the case. As I discussed earlier, some see the sixth seal as representing the final judgment at the return of the Lord. And some don't, me included.

Is there a point where the sealing of God's people is complete and no one else will be added? That's not clear. Some scholars believe so. Some believe that there are people who are currently antagonistic toward God but have been sealed and will turn to God as the judgments worsen. Again, there's no consensus. We're still seeing "believers" falling away, whether prominent or not. Plus, there are still those who will join the souls under the altar. Yet, at that point in time when we will need His protection, He'll be ready with His spiritual Sharpie®. Oops, wrong metaphor.

The 144,000

Ahhh, the mysterious 144,000. Just who are they?

This is the first mention of the 144,000. We'll see them again in chapter 14. Clearly, though, we can't take this number literally. That quota would be filled in the blink of an eye. Oh. Wait. Blink of an eye? Where have I seen that before?

Seriously, we see 12,000 being sealed in each of 12 tribes to hit that total. The dispensational futurists see this list as proof that this period of tribulation will only affect the Jews and that the church is no longer there. However, their concept of a great tribulation is flawed to begin with. They impute that seven-year period of time from Daniel's 70 Weeks Prophecy even though the only mention of a "troubled time" is within the 62 weeks (Daniel 9:25), not the 70th week. The concept of a seven-year period of trouble appears nowhere in Daniel 9:24-27. In fact, the vocabulary for "tribulation" never occurs with the words for "seven" or "week" anywhere in the Bible. More on the "great tribulation" later.

Regarding the 144,000, we're again talking about a large number with 12 x 12 emphasizing the totality of perfection and then multiplying it by 1,000 to indicate large numbers. I believe this number symbolizes the completeness of God's people finally being realized. The number of souls to be added has been completed because now, in v9, we find *"a great multitude that no one could number, from every nation, from all tribes and peoples and languages, standing before the throne and before the Lamb, clothed in white robes, with palm branches in their hands."* They are no longer under the altar. Are these the same as the 144,000? Maybe, but the "great multitude" is in heaven while the 144,000 are on earth.

So, if this symbolizes the completed group of God's people, why the tribal relationships? First, the list of tribes is unique to Revelation. Only one other place in the Bible lists Judah first, and that's in Numbers 2:3 where we find the tribes encamped around the tabernacle in the military order by which Israel is called to move out. This military angle has some merit, but I don't believe it to be the main point here. We read in Revelation 14 that these are male virgins, but Israel's warriors, when called up, were only required to abstain from sex with their wives, not to be virgins. Also, the tribe of Levi was never conscripted into the army, although the priests often accompanied the army. The list is also different in that Joseph and his son Manasseh are listed but Ephraim and Dan are not.

Instead, the idea of the restoration of Israel seems to fit better. As Dr. Aune points out in his commentary,[31] "the eschatology of the late

---

[31] Aune, David E. *World Biblical Commentary 52B, Revelation 6-16*, Zondervan

OT and early Jewish periods emphasized the hope of the restoration of Israel," and he offers a dozen or so verses to support that idea (Deuteronomy 30:3-5; Isaiah 11:11-16, 27:12-13, 49:5-6, 54:7-10; Jeremiah 31:7-14; Ezekiel 37:15-23; Hosea 11:10-11, Matthew 19:28, and a number of Second Temple Period writings). I believe this restoration will have occurred by our being grafted into the people of promise. And having equal numbers in these tribes seems, to me, to point to an equality that wasn't there in the original 12 tribes, no matter who they are.

So, are these 144,000 ethnic Jews or not? That's been another topic of great debate. Some say 'yes,' some 'no.' Dispensationalists believe that these are unsaved ethnic Jews, who, by being sealed for God, will come to accept Christ by going through their great tribulation. Others believe these are Messianic Jews, a view supported by the further description of their standing with the Lamb in Revelation 14:1 and following Him in 14:4.

Some argue that the two groups of 144,000 are different, with one on earth and the other in heaven. They argue that the phrase *ho siōn oros*, τό Σιών ὄρος, in 14:1, has Mount Zion transferred to heaven and that the 144,000 were redeemed—*agorazō*, ἀγοράζω or 'purchased and removed'—*from* the earth. Others counter with the idea that there is no reason why the 144,000 can't be seen in both places since these are visions. However, everywhere in the Bible where the term *Mount Zion* is used, it refers to the earthly location.

I see a simpler answer: one group and they follow the Lamb *wherever* He goes. Perhaps this subset of believers function as Christ's personal attendants or are analogous to The Thirty of King David, his mighty men, his toughest military warriors (1 Chronicles 11:15, 12:4). That would fit the warrior theme. However, the list of David's mighty men included men from Ephraim and Dan, so I can't scripturally support this idea.

It's in Revelation 14—I know, we're getting ahead of ourselves—that we learn that these men follow the Lamb wherever he goes and that they *"have been redeemed from mankind as firstfruits for God and for the Lamb . . ."* (Revelation 14:4) Remember Exodus 13:13? The second part of that verse reads, *"Every firstborn of man among your sons you shall redeem."* Looking back at being sealed, when we see the 144,000 mentioned again in Revelation 14:1, we read *"on Mount Zion stood the Lamb, and with him 144,000 who had his name and his Father's name written on their foreheads."* Let's not forget that the high priest bore the name of God on his forehead. So, could these 144,000 be priestly figures?

Dr. Michael Heiser, in his book *Reversing Hermon*,[32] looks at work done by Terel Manikam and Jan A. DuRand, titled "The 144,000 Undefiled Levites of Revelation 14:1-5 and the link to the defiled watchers of 1 Enoch 1-36."[33] In their paper, they see the 144,000 "virgins" being shown in stark contrast to the defiled fallen angels known as the Watchers in 1 Enoch 1-36. These are the same fallen angels mentioned in Genesis 6:1-4 and Jude 1:6 as having engaged in sexual relationships with the daughters of men. In Revelation, they stand opposite to the followers of the beast from Revelation 13 as well. DuRand and Manikam go on to argue that these 144,000 symbolize the entire people of God, pointing to the OT idea of substitution where the Levites take the place of the firstborn. This sure fits in with 1 Peter 2:9:

> *9 But you are a chosen race, a royal priesthood, a holy nation, a people for his own possession, that you may proclaim the excellencies of him who called you out of darkness into his marvelous light.*

I think that rather than look to answers a), b), or c), I'm going with d) All of the Above. While the 144,000 represent all of us, as a royal priesthood with God's Name borne on our foreheads, they also fulfill the substitutionary role of the Levites. Isaiah 66:20-21 support this:

---

[32] Heiser, M. *Reversing Hermon*. Defender Publishing, Crane MO, May 22, 2017
[33] DuRand, JA and Manikam, T., "The 144,000 Undefiled Levites of Revelation 14:1-5 and the link to the defiled watchers of 1 Enoch 1-36.", Ekklesiastikos Pharos 94.1, 2012, pg. 123-136.

20 And they shall bring all your brothers from all the nations as an offering to the LORD, on horses and in chariots and in litters and on mules and on dromedaries, to my holy mountain Jerusalem, says the LORD, just as the Israelites bring their grain offering in a clean vessel to the house of the LORD. 21 And some of them also I will take for priests and for Levites, says the LORD.

As such, they are a select subset of believers with certain military aspects, *"who follow the Lamb wherever He goes"* while the rest of us, the multitude, stand before the throne. The number reflects the totality and completion of believers because in the next chapter we see judgment unleashed. Has the sealing been finished?

Where's Dan?

Earlier, I mentioned that Ephraim and Dan were missing from the list of tribes being sealed. The tribal lists within the Bible were often fudged in one way or another to achieve a count of 12. Here, with these two tribes being omitted, Joseph was likely added to make the count.

So, if we look at the 144,000 as representatives of God's people globally, does the absence of these tribes make a difference? Probably not, but it has been a point of debate among scholars which I found interesting. Please allow a moment of digression to explore this a bit.

If you recall the stories about Dan from the OT, they weren't among the most encouraging. Jacob/Israel's final "blessing" of his son in Genesis 49:16-17 says he will judge his people but goes on to call him a *"serpent in the way, a viper by the path, that bites the horse's heels so that his rider falls backward."* With a blessing like that, who needs to be cursed? In Deuteronomy 33:22, Moses "blesses" him by saying he's *"a lion's cub that leaps from Bashan."* Bashan was the region of King Og, a giant whose people God designated for total destruction by Moses and the Israelites. It was an area known for its idolatry and the worship of Ba'al. In the Canaanite language, Bashan was *"bathan"* which means serpent. This region sat at the foot of Mount Hermon, and, curiously, in 1 Enoch, Mount Hermon is attributed as being the point of descent of the fallen angels, the watchers.

The original territory granted to Dan was a small area west of the territory of Benjamin and northern Judah, bordering the Mediterranean. Joppa and Ekron—a city of the Philistines' Pentapolis: Ashdod, Ashkelon, Gaza, Ekron, and Gath—were within its boundaries. However, Dan was unable to conquer their territory (Joshua 19:47) and later, in Judges 18, we read of Dan migrating north, destroying the unsuspecting city of Laish and resettling there, in the region of Bashan. With them, they took a young Levite—Jonathan, the son of Gershom, the son of Moses—to set up their own tribal priesthood. They also took the idols of Micah and set them up as their gods. The city of Dan (Laish) became a cult center for the worship of Ba'al, and Dan is associated with the rebellion against God. For that reason alone, I can see that tribe being eliminated from the list in Revelation.

However, after the Assyrian invasion in which the northern tribes were removed from the land, Dan might have simply disappeared as a people from the land. Ephraim, it would seem, suffered that fate as well. Ephraim, too, was active in its rebellion against God. The capital of Ephraim became the city of Samaria, the home of King Ahab and Jezebel, as well as all of the other idolatrous kings of the house of Israel condemned by God. Later, their territory was repopulated by non-Israelis sent there by the Assyrians after Israel was conquered by Tiglath-Pileser III (Pul) in 740 B.C. It may be that these two tribes were eliminated as people groups because of their rebellion, and thus, they no longer exist to be included in the list in Revelation.

Another theory is one I explored in my 2016 novel *A Zealot's Destiny*. Prominent historians at the turn of the 19th century wrote that the Saxons were in reality Israeli "escapees" from the Assyrian deportation and that the name was derived from "Isaac's sons."[34] Likewise, the Scythians and Gauls were thought to have come out of the "lost tribes." While I offer much more detail in the afterword of that novel, the gist of it is that the western European nations and their monarchies developed from the "lost tribes" of Israel.

The similarities in royal crests and other symbols between these

---

[34] Turner, Mr. Sharon, *History of the Anglo-Saxons*, 1805

nations and the tribes lend support to this idea, but there is no historical proof that can be substantiated. Today, the idea of "British Israelism" is scoffed at by most scholars, and that concept is more in line with replacement theology. However, according to some British historians, Dan populated the Scandinavian area and parts of Germany. Thus, we have Scan-Dan-avia, the Danube River, Denmark (the mark of Dan), the Dnieper (Dan-ieper) River, and more. The heraldry of Ephraim—primarily the unicorn—can be seen in that of Great Britain, Scotland, and the Netherlands. Perhaps these two tribes became "Gentile" nations without a remnant in the Levant. Thus, the exclusion from the list in Revelation. Despite the scoffing, I find this idea interesting in light of Jesus' declaration to the Canaanite woman that He had come for *"the lost sheep of the house of Israel"* (Matthew 15:24). Not the house of Judah or the house of Jacob, but the house of Israel. And then these European nations became some of the primarily Christian nations of the world. I know, I know, I'm reading too much into it.

Anyway, the absence of Ephraim and Dan from the list in Revelation 7 is something of a minor point in the overall view of Revelation. Yet, it will be interesting to someday learn why.

The Great Tribulation

In Revelation 7:14 we read that the great multitude described in v9 are those who came out of the *"great tribulation."* I've already made mention of the dispensational view that this is the seven-year span preceding the return of our Lord and that there is no mention of such a period in the Bible.

In Matthew 24:21 and Revelation 2:22, 7:14 this time of trouble is called "great." Daniel 9:25 describes a "troubled time," but this takes place within the 62 weeks of that prophecy. In Jeremiah 30:7, we see it called *"the time of Jacob's trouble"*, and there it is also described at great. Daniel 12:1, which I've shown before, says *"there shall be a time of trouble, such as never was since there was a nation (even) to that same time."* The belief that even the ancient Israelis associated these verses with the apocalypse comes from such Second Temple writings as

Jubilees 23:11-21, 4 Ezra 13:16-19, and others.

So, what is this great tribulation? With God's judgments happening, we'll see the physical manifestations of such: famine, natural disasters, economic upheaval, pestilence, and more. These are going to worsen, not ebb and wane. But there's a more dangerous component to this time of trouble.

That element consists of pressure to compromise one's faith. How? Social pressure—what we see when prominent "believers" deny the faith and begin to pressure others to follow their lead, or when social media "friends" and/or media propaganda want you to act outside your faith, or when your family begins to ostracize you for belonging to "that cult" they keep warning you about. Economic pressure—what happens when your job requires you to do something outside your beliefs, or worse, in direct contradiction to your beliefs, or when you can't shop in a given store without an immunization passport or mask. Maybe it's also direct persecution, such as when you're arrested for leading a church service, or sued and/or charged with felonies for exposing something evil, or charged with hate speech for presenting the Biblical teaching about marriage being between a man and a woman.

The great tribulation doesn't require nuclear holocaust, meteors hitting the earth, or even war in the Middle East. It's likely to be more subtle, more natural—such as drought, heat, pestilence, locusts, and burning.[35] Wait a minute, that's pretty much what we're going to see in the upcoming trumpet judgments . . . and it seems to describe what the world is enduring today as I write this. Drought threatens Lake Mead and Lake Powell with their dams for power generation and supply of water to cities of the U.S. southwest. A heat dome over the U.S. southwest closed public playgrounds in Phoenix, AZ when the rubber mats on the ground hit surface temperatures of 150 degrees-F. COVID-19 and all the hype surrounding it have wreaked havoc on the world. Locusts decimate food production in Africa and elsewhere, and wildfires across the globe destroy large swaths of forests and produce

---

[35] Beale, G.K. *The New International Greek Testament Commentary, the Book of Revelation*, William B. Eerdmans Publishing Co, Grand Rapids, MI, 1999, pg. 355.

air quality alerts hundreds of miles away.

Jewish authors of the first and second century A.D. recognized the "great tribulation" as having already started (1 Maccabees 9:27, Midrash Psalm 119:31). We need to recognize that these "woes" are intensifying, and no longer affect only Israel, God's chosen people, but all peoples of the earth. Yet, there are no days, weeks, or years—no specific time frame—attributed to this time.

Our Take-Away . . .

As seen in Revelation 1:9, John states that he is a partner in the tribulation. Many see the tribulation of Revelation as being a future event, and yet, John says otherwise. And we see that the six seal judgments started after the ascension of Jesus. *That* was the beginning of the latter days and tribulation.

As we've moved into chapter 7, we see a progression. Believers are being sealed by God in preparation for what's to come. The number of those souls finding refuge under the altar now reaches the perfect total ordained by God, as symbolized by the 144,000. With the number completed, or near completion, there is now a great multitude standing before the throne, dressed in white, and worshiping God and Jesus. They will serve Him day and night, and in turn, He will shelter them with His presence. Plus,

> *16 They shall hunger no more, neither thirst anymore; the sun shall not strike them, nor any scorching heat. 17 For the Lamb in the midst of the throne will be their shepherd, and he will guide them to springs of living water, and God will wipe away every tear from their eyes." (Rev 7:16-17)*

For those whose mark comes from the beast, however, judgment has arrived. This time of transition is over. The first judgments came to encourage repentance. Now they come to exact judgment. In the next chapter, we see God, not Zeus, "release the Kraken," and the earth's devastation begins as He de-creates it to form His New Eden.

Not Your Typical Brass Section

The Sounds of Silence

With God's people sealed and secured, Jesus opens the final seal on the scroll.

> *1 When the Lamb opened the seventh seal, there was silence in heaven for about half an hour.*

While the old joke says this verse proves there are no women in heaven, we know that can't be true. So, it must be the lawyers who are missing, right?

In scholarly circles, there are numerous options, but only one stood out to me as likely, as it has good OT support. If you think back to our discussion about the construction of a scroll, there were two options. In one, the scroll could not be opened until all of its seals were broken. In the other, each seal opened another "page" with the most important being last. Either way, the crucial contents of the scroll are revealed with the breaking of the final seal.

This is the case now. The scroll is opened. Its subject matter is revealed for the first time. And those contents—His judgments—are so shocking that all of heaven is awed into silence.

Where do we see this in the OT? The OT associates silence with judgment. Psalm 115: 17 says, *"The dead do not praise the LORD, nor do* any who go down into silence." Similarly, Psalm 31:17 says, "... *let the wicked be put to shame; let them go silently to Sheol."* A closer allusion can be found in Habakkuk 2:20: *"But the LORD is in his holy temple; let all the earth keep silence before him"* as God announces judgment on Babylon. And again, in Zechariah 2:13, we read, *"Be silent, all flesh, before the LORD, for he has roused himself from his holy dwelling."*

Israel and Babylon both were silent because of God's judgments against them. See Amos 8:2-3 and Isaiah 47:5 respectively:

> *2 And he said, "Amos, what do you see?" And I said, "A basket of summer fruit." Then the LORD said to me, "The end has come upon my people Israel; I will never again pass by them. 3 The songs of the temple shall become wailings in that day," declares the Lord GOD. "So many dead bodies!" "They are thrown everywhere!" "Silence!" (Amo 8:2-3)*

> *5 Sit in silence, and go into darkness, O daughter of the Chaldeans; for you shall no more be called the mistress of kingdoms. (Isa 47:5)*

This latter reference to Babylon seems quite fitting, as John identifies the seductive, idolatrous culture as Babylon in Revelation.

Yet, Joshua 6 likely holds the best OT foreshadow. There we read of the siege of Jericho during which the Israelites marched around Jericho six times over six days in silence. Then, on the seventh day, they marched around the city seven times, the priests blew their trumpets seven times, and on the seventh long blast from the horns, the people shouted a great shout. An earthquake ensued and the walls of Jericho fell.

The Golden Censer

Next, we read of the *"seven angels who stand before God"* (Revelation 8:2) each being given a trumpet. Who are these seven angels? Although it's tempting to identify these as the seven angels of the churches, those divine beings are not shown standing before God, and their association with the churches makes it unlikely they would be meting out these judgments. However, there are seven who are well-known for standing before God—the archangels. Two of these are easily recognized from references in the Bible: Michael and Gabriel. The others are not named specifically in the Bible, but 1 Enoch 20:1-8 names them:

> *1,2 And these are the names of the holy angels who watch. Uriel, one of the holy angels, who is 3 over the world and over Tartarus. Raphael, one of the holy angels, who is over the spirits of men. 4,5 Raguel, one of the holy angels who takes vengeance on the world of the luminaries. Michael, one 6 of the holy angels, to wit, he that is set over the best part of mankind and over chaos. Saraqвкl, 7 one of the holy angels, who is set over the spirits, who sin in the spirit. Gabriel, one of the holy 8 angels, who is over Paradise and the serpents and the Cherubim. Remiel, one of the holy angels, whom God set over those who rise.*

Now, some of you might think, wait a minute, that's not the Bible. True. And we're to use scripture to evaluate scripture. However, there are many such books and writings from the Second Temple Period that were well read and studied by the writers of the NT, John being one of them. Besides 1 Enoch, there were 4 Ezra, the Book of Jubilees, books of the Apocrypha, large numbers of midrashim—rabbinic commentaries on the Jewish Bible, the OT—and other books that were the basis of education in those days. To understand how the NT writers might have thought, we need to look at what they read as well. Today's scholars do this all the time, so I think it's fair to use 1 Enoch as a source for these seven angels.

Prior to these archangels blowing their trumpets and releasing God's judgment on an unbelieving world, another angel comes and stands at the golden altar:

> *3 And another angel came and stood at the altar with a golden censer, and he was given much incense to offer with the prayers of all the saints on the golden altar before the throne, 4 and the smoke of the incense, with the prayers of the saints, rose before God from the hand of the angel. 5 Then the angel took the censer and filled it with fire from the altar and threw it on the earth, and there were peals of thunder, rumblings, flashes of lightning, and an earthquake. (Rev 8:3-5)*

These verses confirm the identification of the altar, as previously discussed, and within scripture, incense is associated with the prayers of the righteous. One example, Psalm 141:1-2 shows us this:

> *1 A Psalm of David. O LORD, I call upon you; hasten to me! Give ear to my voice when I call to you! 2 Let my prayer be counted as incense before you, and the lifting up of my hands as the evening sacrifice! (Psa 141:1-2)*

Indeed, incense was quite special to God. The recipe for His incense was a tightly kept secret, as mentioned earlier. Those who offered strange fire and incense, such as Aaron's sons Nadab and Abihu (Leviticus 10:1) and those of Korah's rebellion (Numbers 16), were killed. When the good kings of Judah reigned, among the first things they removed from the land were the unauthorized altars of incense. The lawful use of incense was important. Throughout both the OT and NT, incense was tied to sacrifices, as the burning of every sacrifice included incense to make it acceptable to God. Even the high priest had strict instructions for using it upon entering the Holy of Holies on the Day of Atonement:

> *12 And he shall take a censer full of coals of fire from the altar before the LORD, and two handfuls of sweet incense beaten small, and he shall bring it inside the veil 13 and put the incense on the fire before the LORD, that the cloud of the*

incense may cover the mercy seat that is over the testimony, so that he does not die. (Lev 16:12-13)

With incense closely tied to our prayers, isn't it good to know that those prayers are deemed so important by God? And its association with sacrifice seems to point to our having given ourselves to Him as living sacrifices (Romans 12:1). Some scholars point to these prayers in v3-4 are those of the souls under the altar and that v5 marks His answer: judgment poured out upon the earth. However, there seems to be no scriptural support for this, and these prayers are more likely to be those of *all* the saints.

As the angel throws the fire from the golden altar onto the earth *"there were peals of thunder, rumblings, flashes of lightning, and an earthquake."* Throughout the OT, these were the signs of a theophany, the appearance of God to men, as well as markers for coming judgment. In Exodus 19:16-18, we see these signs accompanying God's manifestation on Mt. Sinai. David spoke of these prophetically in Psalm 77:17-18. Isaiah sees these in 29:6 as he foretold of the siege of Jerusalem.

In Revelation, we see these signs again with the seventh trumpet and the seventh bowl. We also saw them in Revelation 4:5 but with a difference. In 4:5, we read of lightning, rumblings, and thunder. In 8:5, we read of *"thunder, rumblings, flashes of lightning, and an earthquake."* When we get to 11:19, we read of lightning, rumblings, thunder, an earthquake, and heavy hail. And in the grand finale, v16:18-21, we have lightning, rumblings, thunder, and an earthquake so great that cities fall, islands flee, and mountains collapse. That's topped off with 100-pound hailstones. Here, again, we find an escalation of events, just as these judgments first afflict a quarter of the earth and then a third, before affecting the entire globe. Sounds like the grand finale of an Independence Day fireworks show, letting it all loose, except that many believers will have gone home already.

The closest OT model for this is the Exodus passage mentioned a paragraph ago. This, and the fourfold nature of the signs, connects what's about to happen to God's judgment of the gods of Egypt. I say the gods of Egypt because, although the people of Egypt were afflicted directly by the plagues, those plagues were directly aimed at their gods. We'll look at that next.

Come, Blow Those Horns

It would seem appropriate that the first of the final judgments is announced by trumpets. The trumpet, after all, is associated with the voice of God in the OT. The pronouncement of this set of seven judgments with trumpets is as if God Himself is speaking them. Which, of course, He is.

> *6 Now the seven angels who had the seven trumpets prepared to blow them. 7 The first angel blew his trumpet, and there followed hail and fire, mixed with blood, and these were thrown upon the earth. And a third of the earth was burned up, and a third of the trees were burned up, and all green grass was burned up. 8 The second angel blew his trumpet, and something like a great mountain, burning with fire, was thrown into the sea, and a third of the sea became blood. 9 A third of the living creatures in the sea died, and a third of the ships were destroyed. 10 The third angel blew his trumpet, and a great star fell from heaven, blazing like a torch, and it fell on a third of the rivers and on the springs of water. 11 The name of the star is Wormwood. A third of the waters became wormwood, and many people died from the water, because it had been made bitter. 12 The fourth angel blew his trumpet, and a third of the sun was struck, and a third of the moon, and a third of the stars, so that a third of their light might be darkened, and a third of the day might be kept from shining, and likewise a third of the night. 13 Then I looked, and I heard an eagle crying with a loud voice as it flew directly overhead, "Woe, woe, woe to those who dwell on the earth, at the blasts of the other trumpets that the three angels are about to blow!" (Rev 8:6-13)*

Many believe these judgments are due to an asteroid or comet hitting the earth. I can see their point. In recent years the number of Near-Earth Objects being tracked by NASA has increased, with several of these NEOs coming quite close to our planet, in celestial terms. With the breakup of a large object, we might see smaller pieces striking first (hail and fire), followed by a larger piece (something like a great mountain), and then the devastating impact of the main asteroid (a great star).

While I once considered this a viable option because it's scientifically believable, I have to say my view has changed. The sequence I just mentioned would require a linear timeline, but these judgments are more likely to be seen together, overlapping, not one after the other. That said, it could still happen. Time will tell.

Also, since we see the foreshadowing of Revelation's events in the OT, we need to see what types might exist there. Throughout the OT, as well as other Jewish and apocalyptic literature, fire is associated with judgment. Likewise, mountains were symbolic of kingdoms. Jeremiah 51:25 is a good example:

> 25 "Behold, I am against you, O destroying mountain, declares the LORD, which destroys the whole earth; I will stretch out my hand against you, and roll you down from the crags, and make you a burnt mountain.

Here, Jeremiah is pronouncing judgment against Babylon. Babylon is not only metaphorically called a mountain, but it's to become a *burnt* mountain. As we'll see, John ties this latter-day kingdom, i.e., the world system, to Babylon of old in Revelation 18. Concerning the 3rd trumpet, in 1 Enoch 18:14 we find *"seven stars, like great blazing mountains, and like spirits entreating me"* and in 21:3, *"There, too, I beheld seven stars of heaven bound in it together, like great mountains, and like a blazing fire."* If we continue in 1 Enoch 21, we learn that these seven stars are fallen angels who have been bound *"in a desolate spot"* to be released at a later time. So, as we now see, there are ancient precedents to the concepts of a great mountain and a great star as metaphors and not a physical asteroid.

But, but . . . wormwood in Russian is Chernobyl, and the water is going to be poisoned by a huge nuclear disaster. Nope. An incorrect news report once misspelled the Ukrainian word "chornobyl" with an "e," and it stuck when the Russians named their ill-fated nuclear plant. The 12th-century Ukrainian town of Chornobyl was named after a common plant there, Artemisia vulgaris (mugwort in English). "Wormwood" is Artemisia absinthium, an ingredient in absinthe. Absinthe is extremely bitter because of the plant's oil, which was used as a vermifuge in past days. However, wormwood's bitterness is due to a chemical called thujone, which is toxic in high doses and is suspected to be the cause of psychedelic experiences reported by artists of the 19th century before absinthe liquor was banned in most Western countries. While absinthe is again available, it is regulated (by the FDA in the US) and thujone-free.

On a different note, wormwood was considered a sacred and magical plant associated with drunkenness and hallucinogenic behavior in the ritualistic worship of Artemis, the goddess of earth, fertility, life, and death. Thus, its botanical name, Artemisia. While John probably knew of its toxic potential, could Jesus, via John, also have been referring to the worship of Artemis and the death coming to those who participated in such worship or idolatry in general? While several scholars have linked wormwood to idolatry, I found no one making the link to Artemis.

[As we move forward two years into 2023, several events, or series of events, tie into these judgments. What the governments and media want you to believe is man-made climate change is what is described in these judgments. Wildfires (burning the trees of the earth) have been steadily increasing across the globe. As I write this, we just came off a week of the worst air quality alerts recorded in the U.S. Chicago was reported to have the worst air quality in the world just days ago. The cause? Since the beginning of the year, Canada has reported over 3,000 wildfires that have burned over 19 million acres of timber. The smoke reached Europe. Yet, Canada is not alone in seeing these catastrophes.

Drought continues across major parts of the globe. A recent study shows that so much water has been taken from underground aquifers that it has affected the tilt of the earth's axis.[36] In the U.S., drought has greatly affected the Plains States and Midwest and reduced the winter wheat crop despite an 11% increase in planted acreage.[37] Still, global production of grains is expected to hit an all-time high this season due to bumper crops of corn.[38]

Finally, regarding the burning mountain thrown into the sea and killing fish and poisoning the water, scientists are reporting record high water temperatures in the world's oceans.[39] While these temperature increases of a few degrees might not seem like much, when you consider the amount of water being heated by even 1-2 degrees, the amount of energy required is enormous. One atomic scientist equated that energy to 100 billion atomic bombs of the size dropped on Hiroshima in WWII. While most articles will blame climate change, numerous new thermal vents have been discovered opening along the oceans' floors.[40] And in January 2022, the Hunga Tonga-Hunga-Ha'apai undersea volcano erupted in the Pacific launching 40 trillion gallons of superheated water into the atmosphere.[41] Within a week, this water vapor had circled the Earth. Within three months, it had spread from

---

[36] https://www.livescience.com/climate-change-shifts-poles.html
[37] https://www.agweek.com/business/markets/drought-threatens-u-s-wheat-production-despite-acreage-bump
[38] https://farmpolicynews.illinois.edu/2023/05/global-grains-production-forecast-to-hit-an-all-time-high-as-drought-is-shrinking-u-s-winter-wheat-crop/
[39] https://blog.metoffice.gov.uk/2023/06/16/sea-surface-temperatures-breaking-records/

https://www.washingtonpost.com/weather/2023/06/14/record-warm-ocean-temperatures/
[40] https://phys.org/news/2023-04-scientists-hydrothermal-vent-fields-mid-atlantic.html
[41] https://agupubs.onlinelibrary.wiley.com/doi/full/10.1029/2023GL103855

pole to pole, and the atmospheric water vapor charts went "off the charts." Water vapor is much more effective in heating the atmosphere than carbon dioxide. These warm temperatures will affect aquatic life negatively. Don't be surprised at reports of major fish kills like the recent one along the Texas coast of the Gulf of Mexico.]

As mentioned, one of the first things you should notice in these verses is the similarities to the plagues of Egypt. The first plague was the turning of the Nile into blood so that the fish died, the water stunk, and they could not drink the water for a full seven days. The 7th plague was thunder, hail, and fire from heaven that destroyed their crops and trees and killed men and livestock who were outside. Only the land of Goshen was spared. With the 8th plague, God released locusts to finish destroying the Egyptian crops. In the 9th plague, the land of Egypt goes dark. All of these are seen in these trumpet judgments.

All ten of the plagues in Egypt were direct "attacks" on their gods, showing that Jehovah, the God of Israel, was superior to all of them and the one in control. Here are those gods and the respective plagues:

1. Hapi- Egyptian god of the Nile: the Nile River turned to blood, all the fish died, and the river stank
2. Heket- Egyptian goddess of fertility, water, & renewal (depicted as a frog): frogs came up from the river and were in their houses, in their food, in their clothing, in every place possible. From the greatest to the least, no one in Egypt escaped the plague of frog
3. Geb- Egyptian god of the earth, over the dust of the earth: the dust became lice throughout all the land, on both people and beasts. The very dust that was referred to in the creation process of man is now used to plague men
4. Khepri- Egyptian god of creation, movement of the sun, & rebirth (depicted with the head of a fly): swarms of flies filled Egypt, yet did not afflict the people of Israel
5. Hathor-Egyptian goddess of love & protection (depicted with the head of a cow): pestilence caused the death of cattle and livestock, but again the Israelites were spared

6. Isis- Egyptian goddess of medicine and peace: ashes cast into the wind by Moses settled on the Egyptians, causing boils and sores. Again, Israel is spared. This is the first plague to directly affect the people themselves.
7. Nut- Egyptian goddess of the sky: hail of unspeakable size and ability to destroy, rained down from the sky and turned to fire as it hit the ground
8. Seth/Set- Egyptian god of the desert, storms, and disorder (depicted with the head of the Set animal, something unlike known animals): while the flax and barley were destroyed by the hail, the wheat had been spared. Now, a plague of locusts devoured all of their remaining crops
9. Ra- The sun god; second only to Pharaoh as the most revered god (depicted with the head of a hawk): three days of total darkness engulfed Egypt
10. Pharaoh- the most worshiped god of Egypt and believed to be the son of Ra: God inflicts His most serious plague—the death of the firstborn

It's easy to see how each plague was aimed at "dethroning" a specific god. The first nine plagues were carried out by angelic beings (Psalm 78), but the 10th was conducted by God Himself.

However, here in Revelation, we see only four of the plagues repeated: hail and fire, the sea turning to blood, darkness, and locusts. Yet, the first three of these plagues—delivered by four judgments—affect *all* of material creation—land, sea, and the heavens. If you recall that the number "four" deals with the wholeness of the material universe, that's what we see here. Likewise, the first four bowl judgments still to come also affect the material creation. In many ways, God appears to be de-creating the earth in preparation for a new Eden—the new Jerusalem. (We'll get to the locusts in a moment.)

Can we consider these to be strictly metaphors? No. Just as Egypt experienced real afflictions, this world will face the same. The first three of the trumpets have been linked to famine. This makes sense since a third of the earth and trees and all of the grass have been burned up and the waters have been fouled.

The fourth trumpet echoes the darkness of Egypt, which placed very high stock in Ra, their sun god, and much of their theology was built around sun worship. Their greatest fear was of being exiled from their "true" god and becoming prisoners of darkness. Nonbelievers are already separated from God and prisoners of darkness through sin. But there's more to this. God created the sun, moon, and *"lights in the expanse of the heavens"* on day four of creation. Now, with the fourth trumpet, we see the "destruction" of these great lights. Again, He's de-creating the material universe in preparation for a new Eden.

Still, if we see the darkening of celestial lights, as noted by the effect on a third of the day and night, as diminished light reaching the earth, that, too, affects crop production. Scholars focus on the metaphor of darkness being associated with a judgment against idolatry, and that concept is certainly seen in the OT. However, Egypt experienced physical darkness. Shouldn't we expect a physical reality of this judgment as well?

Did you notice the number of "threes" in this chapter? The most obvious include the nominals of three—a third of the earth, the trees, the sea, the living sea creatures, the ships, and the rivers. We also see a third of the sun, moon, and stars going dark affecting a third of their light, a third of the day, and a third of the night. Can we take this literally? Probably not, but this, too, shows an escalation of God's judgment, since in the seal judgments only 25% of the world was involved.

We see this use of thirds in the OT in Zechariah 12-13. While this might seem to be a judgment of post-exile Judah and Jerusalem, this was an End Times prophecy. For example, in Zechariah 12:10, we find the verses about people looking on Him whom they pierced and mourning. In 13:7, we read of the shepherd being struck down and His people scattered. Then comes:

> *8 In the whole land, declares the LORD, two thirds shall be cut off and perish, and one third shall be left alive. 9 And I will put this third into the fire, and refine them as one refines*

silver, and test them as gold is tested. They will call upon my name, and I will answer them. I will say, 'They are my people'; and they will say, 'The LORD is my God.'" (Zec 13:8-9)

In this prophecy, we see that only a third of the people are saved and refined. Two-thirds perish. They've chosen the wide gate and easy path (Matthew 7:13-14). This does not bode well for the "all paths lead to heaven" crowd.

More importantly, believers are being tested by these events as well. Our faith is going to be tested like never before.

The Three Woes

13 Then I looked, and I heard an eagle crying with a loud voice as it flew directly overhead, "Woe, woe, woe to those who dwell on the earth, at the blasts of the other trumpets that the three angels are about to blow!" (Rev 8:13)

The eagle cries "woe" three times to foretell the coming three judgments. No longer do these afflictions affect creation. Now they affect those who have not been sealed by God. BTW, the eagle was known as the messenger of Zeus, and John now shows it as a messenger of the true God.

With the fifth trumpet, an angel descends to the abyss where he opens the shaft and releases smoke "like that of a great furnace" from which come locusts with power like that of scorpions. However, unlike the locust plague of Egypt, these creatures are not to affect green plants or trees. Instead, they target the people who are not sealed by God. The torment extends for five months, and people want to die but cannot (Revelation 9:1-11).

There is debate as to who this angel, a "star fallen from heaven," is. The options are that 1) he's a good angel and likely the same angel as in Revelation 20:1, 2) a good angel but not the same as in Revelation 20:1, or 3) he's an evil angel because of the term "fallen"—possibly Abaddon from 9:11 or Satan himself. Scholars land on all sides of this debate, but I opt for #1. While logic says that an evil angel is unlikely to do what the archangel blowing the trumpet says to do, the verse never says that the archangel commanded this angel to open the bottomless shaft, the abyss. The archangel simply blows the trumpet. This angel not only has the key but also seems to be acting independently as if fulfilling a God-given role or duty.

A more compelling argument is that since Christ holds the keys to Death and Hades, He's not likely to utilize a rebellious angel to unlock the abyss to inflict harm on the nonbelievers. That would be giving back what He took from Satan. This angel is also probably the same one as in Revelation 20:1 who proceeds to bind Satan. Thus, we're talking about a good angel.

According to 1 Enoch, this angel is likely Uriel, the archangel over Tartarus (the abyss) where the Watchers are imprisoned (Genesis 6 and 1 Enoch 21). In talking of these sinful angels, 2 Peter 2:4 uses the verb *tartaroō*, ταρταρόω, which means 'to commit to Tartarus,' the deepest abyss of hell. Also, in Luke 8:31, when Jesus casts out Legion from the "demoniac," the demons begged Jesus not to send them to the abyss. That makes this scene in Revelation one from the supernatural world, the three-tiered cosmology I talked of early in this book—the underworld, earth, and heavens. It doesn't fit into our scientific worldview where we can't "see" or prove the underworld, so what's released is not necessarily going to conform to something we'd expect in nature.

Indeed, the description of the locust creatures that are released is like something from a sci-fi horror flick—like horses prepared for battle, with human faces, women's hair, lion's teeth, iron breastplates, noise from their wings like that of horses and chariots rushing into battle, and tails that sting like scorpions. Gee, sounds like attack helicopters to me. Not!

[Is it just me or do you also believe that our culture has suddenly gone crazy with trans rights, drag queens in schools and libraries, riots by Antifa and BLM, and more? Much of France is in anarchy as I write this. To me, these things seem to have arisen in a very short order.

Could it be that these demonic creatures of the abyss have now been released? That could certainly account for the exponential rise in this activity. It could also account for the sudden pronoun craze. After all, there is a biblical reference to being called they/them. It was the demoniac called Legion.(Mark 5:9)]

The next woe also affects mankind directly. At the blowing of the sixth trumpet, a voice (God) signals the release of four angels whose special Crossfit program has prepared them for this hour, day, month, and year. They move to kill a third of mankind. How? Through troops numbering 200,000,000 mounted on horses that have fire, smoke, and sulfur coming from their mouths and tails like serpents with heads. Those three plagues—fire, smoke, and sulfur—kill a third of mankind. Yet, despite all of this turmoil, the rest of mankind still does not repent.

So, yes, apocalyptic literature of the first century was rife with fantastical beasts and monsters. These "locusts" and "horses" fit right into the genre. But what do they represent, since they aren't visions of modern weapons of warfare?

The "locusts," having been released from Tartarus, can only be demons, disembodied offspring of the fallen angels and daughters of man (the Nephilim) who have been imprisoned since before the great flood. Animal-like descriptions of demonic spirits were common in ancient classical and Jewish literature, and that is what we read here.

There is one OT foreshadow of this in Joel 1-2 where the sound of the trumpet both introduces a plague of locusts on Israel and later concludes that same judgment. Also, in Jeremiah 51:27, we read of the trumpet call for war and to *"bring up horses like bristling locusts."* While the former involved real insects and the latter reference talks of the nations going against Babylon, these "locusts" of Revelation are demonic spirits that are just as violent and nasty as their description, and they have now been released to torment nonbelievers.

We see the same thing with the sixth trumpet and the 200,000,000 troops on deadly horses snorting out fire, smoke, and sulfur. However, unlike the locusts that torment mankind, these demonic beings kill a third of the people on earth. The incredibly large number suggests that all of hell has been emptied, and the showdown between the sinful angels (and men) and God is about to take place.

The Angel and the Scroll

In Revelation 10, we continue:

> *1 Then I saw another mighty angel coming down from heaven, wrapped in a cloud, with a rainbow over his head, and his face was like the sun, and his legs like pillars of fire. 2 He had a little scroll open in his hand. And he set his right foot on the sea, and his left foot on the land, 3 and called out with a loud voice, like a lion roaring. When he called out, the seven thunders sounded. (Rev 10:1-3)*

These are the seven thunders mentioned earlier that John was told not to write down. They would have been the fourth set of seven judgments according to the template of Leviticus 26. As we read on, John is instructed to take the scroll and eat it. It's sweet in his mouth but turns his stomach bitter. He is then told he *"must again prophesy about many peoples and nations and languages and kings."* (Revelation 10:11)

So, first, who is this angel? The description provided is that of deity, and we've seen it earlier in Revelation. Angels in general are never described in such ways. In addition to the description above, He swears an oath *"by Him who lives forever and ever,"* the creator of all things. This must be Jesus, but why is He called an angel?

If you recall my earlier info on the Two Yahwehs, or Two Powers, theology of ancient Israel, you'll recall that God was manifested as spirit in heaven and also in physical form on earth. John combines three common OT motifs that described this. The first is God and the second is the Angel of Yahweh, aka the Angel of the Lord. There is also the "divine man" motif which we see as He met and ate with Abraham under the oak of Mamre (Genesis 18). We also see this in Daniel 8:16 when a man's voice commands Gabriel to explain the vision to Daniel, and again in Daniel 10:5-6 when Daniel sees:

> *5 I lifted up my eyes and looked, and behold, a man clothed in linen, with a belt of fine gold from Uphaz around his waist. 6 His body was like beryl, his face like the appearance of lightning, his eyes like flaming torches, his arms and legs like the gleam of burnished bronze, and the sound of his words like the sound of a multitude.*

Here God manifests as a man, described in terms of deity. He is superior to Gabriel (and to Michael) as He commands them to do His bidding.

We see the Angel of God motif in Genesis 48:15-16:

> *15 And he blessed Joseph and said, "The God before whom my fathers Abraham and Isaac walked, the God who has been my shepherd all my life long to this day, 16 the angel who has redeemed me from all evil, bless the boys; and in them let my name be carried on, and the name of my fathers Abraham and Isaac; and let them grow into a multitude in the midst of the earth."*

where Jacob calls God an angel, and also in Exodus 23:20-23:

> *20 "Behold, I send an angel before you to guard you on the way and to bring you to the place that I have prepared. 21 Pay careful attention to him and obey his voice; do not rebel against him, for he will not pardon your transgression, for my name is in him. 22 "But if you carefully obey his voice and do all that I say, then I will be an enemy to your enemies and an adversary to your adversaries. 23 "When my angel goes before you ...*

This isn't just any angel sent by God, it's *His* angel, in which His name resides. It's an earthly manifestation of God Himself going with the people. Thus, seeing Jesus called an angel in Revelation 10:1 is not out of line with scripture. In other scripture we find Him described as the Prince of princes (Daniel 8:25), the Angel of the Lord (used 63 times), and the Lord of hosts (used 232 times).

According to Richard Bauckham, an English Anglican theologian known for his work on NT Christology, it's likely that this angel is the same one noted in Revelation 1:1 where God sends *"his angel"* to John and in 22:16 where Jesus sends *"my angel"* to him. To John (and us) Jesus *is* God, so there is no inconsistency in this as John makes this co-identification clear.

As pointed out in any good police procedural, we must follow the chain of evidence. In Revelation 5:7, God gives the revelation to Jesus, the Lamb, who then opens the scroll. In Revelation 10, Jesus now gives the scroll to John who eats it as commanded. So, yes, it is widely accepted that this scroll is that which Jesus opened.

The OT foreshadow of eating the scroll is in Ezekiel 2:8-3:3 where the prophet is given a scroll to eat, and its taste is as sweet as honey (v3.3). Yet, written on this scroll were *"words of lamentation and mourning and woe"* (v2:10). Also, in Jeremiah 15:16-17, the prophet ate the words of God, and they became *"a joy and the delight of* (his) *heart,"* yet filled him with indignation. So, for John, eating the scroll was sweet because of the joyful and positive effect its words have on believers, yet became bitter due to the judgments about to befall nonbelievers.

Our Take-Away . . .

The trumpets announce the final judgments of an unbelieving world. God's people have been sealed, and now their prayers for the avenging of their blood are being answered. Trumpets, besides being associated with the voice of God, were also linked to warnings to repent, judgment coming, victory (salvation), the enthronement of a king, eschatological judgment or salvation, and the gathering of the people in the OT. In the NT, the trumpet sounds to point to the end-time coming of Christ and the gathering of His people.

As we see, God intends these afflictions to affect those both inside and outside the visible community of faith who do not have the seal of God to protect them. Ancient Israelites who failed to mark their doors with the blood of the lamb suffered the same fate as did their Egyptian oppressors.

How does God judge the earth and unbelievers? Dr. Beale says this:

> God typically fought Israel's holy wars from heaven by causing the elements of nature (inclement weather, etc.) to thwart the enemy. He defeated the Egyptians through the ten plagues and then the miracle at the Red Sea. Likewise, the sun, the moon, and hail were employed to defeat the Amorites (Josh. 10:10-15). "The stars fought from heaven" against the Canaanites, causing them to be defeated through a flood (Judg. 5:19-21). Some of the descriptions of victory in holy war are literal (Exodus 7-15), others figurative (Ps. 18:4-19), and still others a mixture of the two (as in Judges 5). Most are figurative (see on 6:12-14 and below). Against this background, the portrayal of the trumpet plagues in Revelation 8-9 with the same OT imagery enhances further the notion that the trumpets depict God conducting holy war.[42]

As we see in this, the judgments are very real.

As I've stated, I don't believe we'll see these events play out linearly, one after another. Many scholars see these judgments as recapitulation, the same afflictions seen from different perspectives. However, as I keep saying, there is a progression in severity. I see these as a "both . . . and" situation. My perspective is that the seal judgments have been occurring throughout history—the latter days—and represent the birth pangs. But now, with the possibility that we're seeing the start of the trumpet judgments, we're going to see God's final judgment on nonbelievers take place, while He has sealed His followers for protection. The upcoming bowl judgments will show these afflictions while also marking an increase in severity, as we'll see.

For most people, these judgments will be seen as "climate change"

---

[42] Beale, G.K. *The New International Greek Testament Commentary, the Book of Revelation*, William B. Eerdmans Publishing Co, Grand Rapids, MI, 1999, pg. 403

or pollution by man. Take a look around. We're already seeing famine in many parts of the world. Drought is affecting not just our western U.S.—to the point where agricultural water supplies have been cut off in major food production areas such as California's Central Valley—but Australia, Europe, Africa, and parts of Asia, too. Even in the southern hemisphere where it's winter now, freak weather is leading to expected crop shortages. A record cold snap has affected Brazil's corn production, and they project a 17% reduction for the upcoming season.[43] Their Arabica coffee bean crops have been severely affected, and coffee prices are already rising. Still, people won't recognize the food shortages and loss of water supply as being judgments from God.

Two days ago, as I write this, three volcanoes in Alaska erupted spewing ash into the atmosphere. For nearly a month, our skies in Wisconsin have been hazy and air quality alerts have been issued because of the wildfires in our western states . . . 1,500 miles away. Wildfires have been rampant in Greece, Turkey, Australia, Africa, South America, and elsewhere. Below is the July 2021 Aerosol Optical Thickness map of the globe from the NASA Earth Observation satellite. The darker the gray color (black means no data), the more particulate matter is in the air, which reduces sunlight reaching the earth as well as worsens air quality:[44]

---

[43] endtimeheadlines.org/2021/08/freak-weather-events-and-drought-are-now-devastating-agricultural-production-all-across-the-globe/

[44] https://neo.sci.gsfc.nasa.gov/view.php?datasetId=MODAL2_M_AER_OD

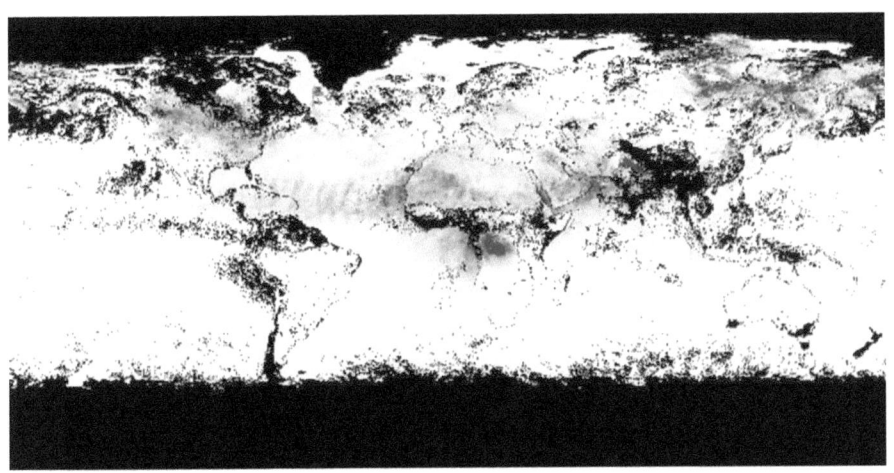

When our sunlight becomes diminished by a third because of the smoke from wildfires and other sources across the globe, they will again blame it on man and see no need to repent. Their focus is on man's science which they see as conflicting with the Bible. Yet, they choose to believe in that science rather than have faith in God.

Our Final Witness

As we continue into chapters 11 and 12, we come across even more controversial information. For the dispensationalist, these verses are to be taken literally, and they look for a physical return of two men who will prophesy for a literal three and a half years before being killed by a global despot and cause ethnic Jews to flee to a God-prepared refuge for protection. For the idealist, these chapters are more metaphors. We'll look at both, as well as one other intriguing aspect to chapter 12: the dating of the birth of Christ.

Which Temple?

While most people tend to skip past the first two verses of chapter 11, there is something in these verses we need to understand.

> *1 Then I was given a measuring rod like a staff, and I was told, "Rise and measure the temple of God and the altar and those who worship there, 2 but do not measure the court outside the temple; leave that out, for it is given over to the nations, and they will trample the holy city for forty-two months. (Rev 11:1-2)*

Here, reminiscent of Ezekiel measuring the temple in Ezekiel 40-48, John is given a measuring rod to measure the temple of God, its altar, and those who worship there. Yet, no measuring actually takes place.

Symbolically, in the OT, measuring something implied either its pending judgment and destruction (2 Samuel 8:2a, 2 Kings 21:13, and others) or its preservation (2 Samuel 8:2b, Ezekiel 40:1-6, 42:20, and Zechariah 2:1-5). So, do we have anything to point to a specific temple or outcome?

Before answering that, the temple reference does point to something interesting. The temple of John's time was the Herodian temple. Under this line of thinking, what is the outer court of the Herodian temple? According to the writings of Josephus, this temple consisted of a temple district enclosed by a high wall with gates in which was found the Holy of Holies, the holy place, the court of priests, the court of Israelites, and the court of women. Its outer court, the court of the Gentiles, was essentially a huge marketplace. That the court outside the temple district, a marketplace, *"is given over the nations"* appears fitting. What does the world today serve? Money, not God.

Back to the question. The dispensational view is that this is some future, third temple to be trampled by the Gentiles and Antichrist as they overrun a remnant of Jews worshiping there. That John is the one tasked to measure it seems to eliminate this possibility. The Preterist view insists that this temple is Herod's temple—again because John is the one tasked to measure it—and its existence places the writing of Revelation before its destruction. Another view points to the outer court as representing the apostate church which aligns itself with persecutors of the true Israel, God's people.

Yet, later in Revelation 11:19, we find the only other use in the book of the phrase **ναὸν τοῦ θεοῦ** for the temple of God. In that verse, the temple is explicitly described as "God's temple in heaven." So, another school of thought believes this verse further defines the temple in v1, rather than describing a second temple. Thus, both references seem to point to the heavenly temple. As such, John's measuring it reflects, once again, God's preservation of His people. This is best foretold in Zechariah 2:1-5 where a man measures Jerusalem while God declares He will be "a wall of fire all around . . . and I will be the glory in her midst." (Zechariah 2:5) Just as He protects us by sealing us with His Spirit, He will be a wall of fire surrounding and preserving us.

Remember my saying that every eschatological plan has its inconsistencies? Ironically, the partial Preterists, who interpret Revelation metaphorically, point to this being an earthly temple (Herod's), a literal view, so they can date Revelation to the mid-60s A.D. before the temple's destruction. And the futurists, who interpret Revelation literally, point to this being symbolic of a future third temple. Hmmm.

The OT foreshadowing of this temple occurs in length in Ezekiel 40-48. There we find Ezekiel has been taken to the top of a tall mountain and sees a man (an angel?) measuring the final eternal temple as well as its altar. As I pointed out in *Still Here! Surviving the End Times*, the temple district for this structure far exceeds the space available on the Temple Mount in Jerusalem, with or without the Dome of the Rock and the Al-Aqsa Mosque.

Later, in Revelation 21, it's John who is taken to a high mountain where he observes the descent of the New Jerusalem and an angel who measures it. In Ezekiel, the temple is the residence of the Prince. In Revelation 21, the Lord God Almighty and Lamb are the temple of the New Jerusalem. We see this also in Zechariah 2 where the Lord says He will be the glory in the midst of her (Jerusalem).

By Two or More . . .

The identity of the "two witnesses" can be a flashpoint in discussions of the End Times. Folks who look at Revelation literally see these two as real-life characters, but can we truly expect them to pour fire from their mouths to consume their enemies?

Could we be looking at real men whose their testimonies and warnings are the symbolic fire that spiritually consumes their enemies? For years, I've understood these verses to reflect just that. After all, the Bible says that it is appointed to man to die once, perhaps with the exception of many who survive the time of trouble prior to Christ's return. Some believe these two men to be Elijah and Moses based upon the judgments they issue during their forty-two months and the fact that it was Moses and Elijah who appeared on Mount Hermon at the transfiguration of Christ. However, my money was always on Elijah and Enoch, as they are the only two who have never tasted death. Also, it seems right to me that mankind from both before and after the great flood should be represented.

While I would not be shocked to see "breaking news" about two old guys preaching on the streets of Jerusalem, I'm no longer convinced that the two witnesses are two real, literal persons. If we look at the transfiguration, Moses and Elijah were there to be witnesses to God's declaration that Jesus is His son. There they stood for the law and the prophets. Jesus has now fulfilled the law and the prophets, so do these two need to return? Yep, it must be Enoch and Elijah.

Most scholars see the witnesses as representative of the universal church. Why number them at two? Well, the Word makes it clear that no one is to be put to death on the evidence of just one witness.

> *6 On the evidence of two witnesses or of three witnesses the one who is to die shall be put to death; a person shall not be put to death on the evidence of one witness. (Deu 17:6)*

> *28 Anyone who has set aside the law of Moses dies without mercy on the evidence of two or three witnesses. (Heb 10:28)*

And we are talking about the deaths of the multitude of nonbelievers. God's justice is fair.

Also, in looking at Hebrews 9:27, does it really say that all men are to die once?

> *27 And just as it is appointed for man to die once, and after that comes judgment, (Heb 9:27)*

The word translated as 'appointed to,' *apokeimai*, ἀπόκειμαι, means 'reserved for' or 'awaiting him,' while the word for 'die,' *apothnēskō*, ἀποθνήσκω, in the context of this verse, means 'of the punishment of death.' So, maybe a better way of looking at this is that the punishment of death is reserved for all men. But notice the comma at the end of v27.

There's a continuation of this thought:

> *28 so Christ, having been offered once to bear the sins of many, will appear a second time, not to deal with sin but to save those who are eagerly waiting for him. (Heb 9:28)*

So, while death is reserved for all men, the verse doesn't say that all men *will* die once. Plus, Christ is returning to save all who eagerly await Him. Hallelujah!

Is it so hard to think of the two witnesses as representative of God's people? In the OT, the prophets often represented the people. On some occasions, they spoke on behalf of God to the people and at other times they spoke to God on behalf of the people.

Let's look at the first handful of verses about the witnesses:

> *3 And I will grant authority to my two witnesses, and they will prophesy for 1,260 days, clothed in sackcloth." 4 These are the two olive trees and the two lampstands that stand before the Lord of the earth. 5 And if anyone would harm them, fire pours from their mouth and consumes their foes. If anyone would harm them, this is how he is doomed to be killed. 6 They have the power to shut the sky, that no rain may fall during the days of their prophesying, and they have power over the waters to turn them into blood and to strike the earth with every kind of plague, as often as they desire. (Rev 11:3-6)*

We'll look at the forty-two months and 1,260 days in the next section, so let's look at the two olive trees and lampstands.

Scholars point to Zechariah 4 when referencing the two olive trees. We've looked at Zechariah before with respect to eyes watching the earth and His divine council. Yet, in Zechariah 4:1-6 and 11-14, we again see reference to two olive trees, or *"anointed ones."* The story in Zechariah 4, however, begins in Hosea 1 where we see God forsake His people Israel while prophesying their restoration. It's that restoration through Zerubbabel and Joshua that we see in Zechariah where the two olives trees represent the *"word of the Lord to Zerubbabel: Not by might, nor by power, but by My Spirit, says the Lord of Hosts."* There, the two olive trees represented all of Judah, whereas now, in Revelation, the two witnesses represent all of God's people as we stand by the Lord, preserved by His Spirit.

However, for us, Zechariah 4 has another emphasis. In it, God was telling the prophet that Joshua and Zerubbabel had divine protection from their opponents and would complete the temple. Likewise, we have His divine protection against our foes.

The lampstand imagery is thought to point back to Revelation 1 in which the lampstands represent the churches. There we saw seven lampstands as a symbol of the completeness of the church. Now, only two are needed to testify against and witness to an unrepentant world. Some scholars point to the churches in Smyrna and Philadelphia, the only two for which Jesus found no faults. Indeed, if you look again at Revelation 3:10, Jesus promises not just that He will "keep" us from the hour of trial, but that He does so in order that we shall *"try those who dwell on the earth."*

What about the "superpowers" being displayed by the two witnesses? Note first that these "powers" apply to both witnesses, i.e., all of us. I look around our world, and I find it is oh so tempting to call down fire from heaven right about now. Zap! Sign me up for the Sons of Thunder fraternity. Oh wait, maybe Elijah could do that against the captains of fifty (2 Kings 1:8-15), but Jesus chastised James and John for wanting to imitate that prophet. (As a side note, Ahab sent three squads of fifty against Elijah and only one was spared. There's that one-third being saved again, as in Zechariah 13:8)

Of course, the literalists see these powers as an instant replay of the prophets' judgments in the OT. The idealists, however, see these as symbolic. Dr. Beale states:

> The purpose and effects of the "measuring" are explained further. Now the fire of the Spirit burning on the two lampstands is seen to be unquenchable, which makes the

> lampstands themselves spiritually invincible. The souls of the witnesses cannot be harmed because they are protected by the invisible sanctuary within which they dwell. "If anyone wishes to harm them" because of their prophetic witness, then such people themselves will be harmed by the witnesses. God's assured presence among his people guarantees that they will not be harmed in any ultimate, eternal sense. Therefore, the powers given to them in vv 5–6 do not demonstrate outwardly their prophetic legitimation but indicate rather God's protection of them. They may undergo bodily, economic, political, or social harm, but their eternal covenant status with God will not be affected. One reason they were measured was so that they would prosper in their prophetic witness despite persecution. Though they may suffer and even die, they will invincibly and successfully carry out the spiritual mission for which they have been "measured" and commissioned...[45]

Rats! Fire falling from heaven would be so much more impressive.

It should also be noted that those who would kill the witnesses will themselves be killed. This is Biblical, as it says in Deuteronomy 19:19 that *"then you shall do to him as he had meant to do to his brother. So you shall purge the evil from your midst."* By this point in the judgments, the events taking place are not meant to induce repentance but are punishments for those who have hardened their hearts, just as we saw with the plagues of Egypt.

When our testimony is complete, the *"beast who rises from the abyss makes war on,"* conquers, and perhaps kills us. Or so the beast believes. We'll discuss this beast later on but suffice it to say that it represents the governments of the world—the Deep State, as many would call it today. They will think that they've snuffed out the Christian witness for good. The three-and-a-half-year period of the witnesses' torment corresponds to Christ's three-and-a-half-year

---

[45] Beale, G.K. *The New International Greek Testament Commentary, the Book of Revelation*, William B. Eerdmans Publishing Co, Grand Rapids, MI, 1999, pg.

ministry on earth as well as Elijah's ministry during which the *"the heavens were shut up three years and six months."* (Luke 4:25, James 5:17) Elijah's ministry saw devastating famine, as we're beginning to see again. As with Christ's resurrection, three and a half days later, we're resurrected and ascend to the Father. For Elijah, *"Then he prayed again, and heaven gave rain, and the earth bore its fruit."* (James 5:18) *We* are that fruit.

It's unlikely that the "beast" literally kills the entire church. Instead, this appears to be hyperbole to indicate that the true church has been "defeated." The "great city" mentioned is the entire world, as every use of "the great city" in Revelation refers to Babylon the Great, not Jerusalem, Rome, or some other prominent city. As with "the beast" we'll take a look at Babylon the Great later.

At that point, a great earthquake rattles "the great city" such that a tenth of it is destroyed and 7,000 people die. For the idealist, this portrays a great upheaval that portends the immediate return of Christ. As with the seventh seal and seventh bowl, this group sees the upcoming seventh trumpet as symbolic of the final judgment that comes with the *parousia*, the Second Coming.

A Possible Timetable?

What's up with all of these three and a half years of this and forty-two months of that? Again, the literalist sees these as a timetable. The idealist sees them as figurative. I've already mentioned the relationship between three and a half years being reflective of Jesus' and Elijah's ministries, while the three and a half days relate to the duration of Jesus' burial. But what if there's more to this than meets the eye? [While there is sound reasoning to point to Jesus' walk on earth lasting only a little over a year, we'll continue using the more widely accepted period of 3.5 years for His ministry.]

We've seen these numbers before in Daniel 7 and 12. While many see these chapters as eschatological or End Times visions, they primarily applied to the reign of Antiochus IV Epiphanes (175-164 B.C.). In his first vision, Daniel saw four beasts arise from the sea, with the fourth beast being different from the others in that it had ten horns after which a smaller horn (Antiochus Epiphanes) emerged. In these verses we find the following:

> *25 He shall speak words against the Most High, and shall wear out the saints of the Most High, and shall think to change the times and the law; and they shall be given into his hand for a time, times, and half a time. (Dan 7:25)*

This is the first occurrence of this time sequence in the Bible.

Later, in Daniel 12, we find more information about the reign of terror of Antiochus IV. In this chapter, we find the following "timetables:"

> *11 And from the time that the regular burnt offering is taken away and the abomination that makes desolate is set up, there shall be 1,290 days. 12 Blessed is he who waits and arrives at the 1,335 days. (Dan 12:11-12)*

At the time of Antiochus IV, divisions between Hellenistic and Traditionalist Jews brewed to the point of civil war. Antiochus intervened on the side of Hellenists, invaded Israel, decreed the Jewish practices illegal, and killed the high priest Onias III in 170 B.C. In 167 B.C., three and a half years into a seven-year period, he defiled the temple by setting up an image of Zeus and having pigs sacrificed to Zeus on the altar. This led to the Maccabean Revolt. After three and a half years (163 B.C.), the Maccabeans won. Most scholars tie this to Daniel's Seventy Weeks prophecy, with these seven years being the final week, and the cessation of the daily offering and sacrifices (because of the defilement) being halfway through those seven years as foretold in Daniel 9:27.

One of the many things I've learned in this study is that everything about the Bible has its controversies. In this case, it's the calendar.

Today's Jewish calendar, which is also that of the Second Temple Period, is similar to our secular calendar in that it is a lunar calendar comprised of months of 29, 30, or 31 days, with various days thrown in for correction. For those of the Essene and Zadokite Jewish sects at Qumran that was considered apostate. Okay, I've heard of the Essenes and Qumran, but the Zado-who sect?

Zadok was a descendant of Aaron through his son Eleazar and was the High Priest during the reigns of David and Solomon. Indeed, he was instrumental in bringing Solomon to the throne and officiated at his coronation. In Ezekiel 44:15 we read:

> "But the Levitical priests, the sons of Zadok, who kept the charge of my sanctuary when the people of Israel went astray from me, shall come near to me to minister to me. And they shall stand before me to offer me the fat and the blood, declares the Lord GOD.

The Zadokites did not go astray, and their reward for staying true, they believed, was to remain the high priesthood, including for that final, purified temple of God at the end of time.

By the time of Christ, however, they had become a small sect isolated from Jerusalem as founders of the Qumran community, where many Essenes joined them. Why? The Hasmoneans had ousted them 150 years earlier during the Maccabean Revolt, its victory being celebrated ever since as Hanukkah. The Zadokites preserved the idea of a Davidic Messiah, while the Hasmoneans rejected it. Since Jesus presented Himself as the Davidic Messiah, the Hasmonean leaders rejected Him. Had the Zadokites been in power, it's speculated that they would *not* have rejected Jesus as their Messiah. (Think about that for a moment. Had they accepted Him, would He have died for our sins? God's hand in history is amazing.)

So, how does this play into the various spans of time? In two ways, actually. First, both the Zadokites and Essenes used a solar calendar of 12 months of 30 days each, not a lunar calendar. While the Essene, or Enochian, calendar differed slightly, the Zadokites acknowledged the equinoxes and solstices as special days that were not included in the calendar but separated the four seasons. The result was a 360+4-day year, but a calendar with 12 30-day months. This sabbatical calendar assured that Passover and the other feasts and festivals occurred at the same time each year.

As we look at the above numbers, we can quickly see that they work with a solar calendar using 30-day months—1,260 and 1,290 are equally divisible by 30. The 1,290-day span adds a month to the 1,260, while the 1,335 number adds another month and a half to the 1,290 number. From this, we see that Daniel used the Zadokite calendar in which the four days were not counted, and his numbers are consistent with history. That the Zadokite calendar was possibly based on the most ancient calendars is suggested by the flood account in which the flood lasted five months, counted as 150 days.

Before getting into the meaning of these numbers, I want to look at the second way in which the story of the Zadokites vs. Hasmoneans comes into play. Daniel 8 continues the prophecy regarding Antiochus IV Epiphanes. In Daniel 8:14 we find reference to "2,300 evenings and mornings" (not days) that are to take place between "the transgression that makes desolate" and the restoration of the sanctuary.

Dr. Gabriele Boccaccini is a professor of Second Temple Judaism and Early Rabbinic Literature at the University of Michigan. His paper, "The Solar Calendars of Daniel and Enoch," adds credence to the generally accepted belief that this prophecy was fulfilled by the events surrounding Antiochus IV. It was Antiochus IV whom Daniel blamed for changing *"the times and the law"* in v7:25. In other words, he changed the "times" from the longstanding solar calendar to the Hellenistic lunar calendar, as well as outlawed Jewish circumcision and other practices. According to Dr. Boccaccini's work, the 2,300 evenings and mornings (1,150 days) precisely fits the time between the defiling of the temple, which ended the daily sacrifices, and the 25th day of the month of Kislev when the Maccabeans stopped fighting and the eight-day restoration of the temple began. This day marks the first day of the miracle of lights or Hanukkah.[46]

Going further with this, Dr. Boccaccini goes to the end of the 1,260 days (and the death of Antiochus) and adds 30 days. That takes the calendar through the month of Passover. Adding another 45 days takes us to the Feast of Shavu'ot, the celebration of the harvest. How does that apply to Revelation? He postulates that at the end of the 1,260 days, believers will celebrate the Marriage Supper of the Lamb, reflective of the Passover supper, and at Shavu'ot, the final harvest of souls, along with judgment before the Great White Throne, will take place.

With the events of Antiochus IV foreshadowing the End Times, in Revelation 11:2 we see the holy city being trampled for "forty-two months" (three and a half years). Then, in Revelation 11:3, His witnesses are given 1,260 days (the same three and a half years?) to prophesy. The 1,260 days is repeated in Revelation 12:6, and this timespan ties back into Daniel 7:25 in Revelation 12:14:

> *14 But the woman was given the two wings of the great eagle so that she might fly from the serpent into the wilderness, to the place where she is to be nourished for a time, and times, and half a time. (Rev 12:14)*

From this, we see that John also used the Zadokite calendar. Fast forward to today, we can't look at those times from the perspective of our current Gregorian calendar. The Zadokite calendar must be considered.

For the idealist, this three-and-a-half-year period is symbolic of nothing more than an incomplete timespan, as opposed to seven years marking a complete one. Curiously, while the idealists look at the period as an undefined, incomplete period, they don't quite know what to do with the mention of 1,260 days. Dr. Beale, in his lengthy discussion of the forty-two months, says only this of the reference to days:

---

[46] Collins, J. And Flint, P., editors, *The Book of Daniel Composition and*

> "Twelve-hundred sixty days" has the same interpretative nuance, though the reason the period is named in terms of days is not clear.[47]

Not clear. It's my understanding that pretty much everywhere else in the Bible where a prophecy is given in terms of days, it means just that, a day or a portion thereof. This alone would seem to be strong evidence of a literal three-and-a-half-year period.

If we look at the events surrounding Antiochus IV and those of the Roman destruction of Jerusalem in 70 A.D. as foreshadows of the time preceding Christ's return, both occurred in fulfillment of specific timespan prophecies in Daniel. Should we not expect the same with John's prophecy in Revelation? When Revelation 20:3 talks of Satan being released for a little while, it's likely to be for this 42-month period. Our challenge is in recognizing when that three-and-a-half-year period begins.

The Seventh Trumpet

As we finish chapter eleven, we move to the final trumpet:

> *16 And the twenty-four elders who sit on their thrones before God fell on their faces and worshiped God, 17 saying, "We give thanks to you, Lord God Almighty, who is and who was, for you have taken your great power and begun to reign. 18 The nations raged, but your wrath came, and the time for the dead to be judged, and for rewarding your servants, the prophets and saints, and those who fear your name, both small and great, and for destroying the destroyers of the earth." 19 Then God's temple in heaven was opened, and the*

Reception, Vol 2, Brill Publishing, pgs. 311-328.
[47] Beale, G.K. *The New International Greek Testament Commentary, the Book of Revelation*, William B. Eerdmans Publishing Co, Grand Rapids, MI, 1999, pg. 468.

> *ark of his covenant was seen within his temple. There were flashes of lightning, rumblings, peals of thunder, an earthquake, and heavy hail. (Rev 11:16-19)*

This trumpet would seem to indicate that the final day of judgment has arrived. This is clearly what the idealists say, and with good reason. *"The nations raged"* refers to Psalm 2, and the remainder of v18 talks of God's wrath having arrived, the dead being judged, the saints being rewarded, and the destruction of the destroyers of the earth.

The other viewpoints all tend to have trouble with this section, for various reasons. I won't bother with the historicist view by moving yet again their 1,260-year goalpost. The futurists acknowledge that this is the Day of the Lord but have trouble explaining how this fits into their narrative of a 1,000-year reign of Christ with the judgment after that. The Preterists believe this refers to the fall of Jerusalem and that the *"dead to be judged"* refers only to the martyred dead. They tend to ignore the rest of that sentence, as well as what's missing in v17. Which, BTW, did you catch it? The *"Lord God Almighty, who is and who was..."* but not "who is to come." He has already come into His glory and power so that phrase is no longer valid, and if this is the time for the dead to be judged and His servants to be rewarded, how can this be 70 A.D.?

The juxtaposition of this trumpet's call with, but after, the 1,260 days of witnessing confirms, for me, not just that the period of witnessing consists of that three-and-a-half-years, but that this would be the 3.5 years just before the return of the Lord. It's also my take that since we have a timetable based upon God's judgments intensifying, these trumpet judgments, along with our witnessing, started with the seventh seal being opened. When might that have occurred?

I can't offer a clear opinion or understanding of when that might have happened, but I'm looking into something that keeps nagging at me about these verses, that maybe the clue is here in Revelation. If I get an answer to my queries that answers this question, this paragraph will be edited out. If you're reading this, I'm still losing sleep over this question.

So, what's nagging me? Most commentaries and scholars see

chapter 11 as ending one vision, while chapter 12 begins another as an interlude between chapters 11 and 13. However, 12:1 begins with the word καί. That's the Greek conjunction for 'and' or 'also.' The KJV, ESV, and a handful of other translations include this conjunction. The NIV, NASB, and some others seem to ignore it. However, it's there in the Greek, and as I read this, the seventh trumpet doesn't necessarily end with the *"flashes of lightning, rumblings, peals of thunder, an earthquake, and heavy hail."*

The seventh trumpet begins with another look at the 24 elders. We talked about the astral aspects of this earlier with the 24 elders being identified with the 24 decans of the celestial sky. In these verses, Revelation 11:16,19, we again have astral references. Besides the elders, we see *"God's temple in heaven"* opening up and the ark of the covenant being revealed. There is indeed a portion of the celestial map that is considered the opening to God's throne room, and there is a constellation associated with the ark.

While we don't have any ancient materials to corroborate that this was what John saw, we do have work from the Middle Ages to suggest this. The constellations of Crater (the cup) and Corvus (the raven), also known to some as the twin turtledoves, were also seen as the Ark of the Covenant when combined. Julius Schiller, a German lawyer, published a star atlas, *Coelum stellatum Christianum*, in 1620 in which pagan constellations were reorganized with Christian names.[48] His work was based upon earlier work by astronomer Johann Bayer, *Uranometria Omnium Asterismorum*.[49] In Schiller's work, Corvus and Crater were seen as the ark. Today, that would be the constellation Sagittarius.

Then we have that pesky "and." If we continue into chapter 12, we read:

> *1 And a great sign appeared in heaven: a woman clothed with the sun, with the moon under her feet, and on her head a crown of twelve stars. 2 She was pregnant and was crying*

---

[48] commons.wikimedia.org/wiki/Category:Coelum_Stellatum_Christianum
[49] en.wikipedia.org/wiki/Uranometria

> out in birth pains and the agony of giving birth. 3 And another sign appeared in heaven: behold, a great red dragon, with seven heads and ten horns, and on his heads seven diadems. 4 His tail swept down a third of the stars of heaven and cast them to the earth. And the dragon stood before the woman who was about to give birth, so that when she bore her child he might devour it. 5 She gave birth to a male child, one who is to rule all the nations with a rod of iron, but her child was caught up to God and to his throne, 6 and the woman fled into the wilderness, where she has a place prepared by God, in which she is to be nourished for 1,260 days. (Rev 12:1-6)

These verses encompass the constellations Virgo and Hydra (most likely), along with the paths of the sun and moon. We also see reference to 1,260 days again. As we'll see in the next section, these verses in chapter 12 (not including those in 11), have led to the discovery of an important birth date.

So, by including the verses in chapter 11, could these astral signs point to something else? After all, didn't He place the stars in the heavens as signs for us? (Genesis 1:14) Jesus chastised the Pharisees and Sadducees in Matthew 16:1-4 for not knowing the signs of the times, thus implying that we should be able to interpret them. Also, in Matthew 13:11, He says, *"To you it has been given to know the secrets of the kingdom of heaven, but to them it has not been given."*

As Solomon once said, *"It is the glory of God to conceal things, but the glory of kings is to search things out."* (Proverbs 25:2) I'm still searching for this answer.

The Woman and the Dragon

So, take a moment to reread the verses from Revelation 12 in the previous section. It would seem clear that the woman in these verses is Israel and that the child is Jesus. Curiously, the story takes Jesus directly from His birth to His ascension. After that, the woman flees to the wilderness to be nourished for a time, times, and half a time, or 1,260 days (Revelation 12:14). That she is carried by a great eagle is reminiscent of Exodus 19 where God bore Israel on eagle's wings away from the Egyptians, thus seeming to confirm that the woman here is Israel. However, this is the NT and John wrote this, with his penchant for changing metaphors. Here the woman is thought to be the church, which will find both testing and provision in the wilderness. Similarly, that the dragon's tail swept down *"a third of the stars of heaven"* is not believed to refer to fallen angels. Instead, two possible options exist. Those fallen could be angels and true saints with whom the devil has battled and who have seemingly died at his hand, just as Jesus appeared to die. The alternative is that these "stars" represent believers who have fallen away because of the devil's deceptions.

The dragon is a symbol of those nations that persecuted Israel throughout the OT. The word is also used to describe Leviathan, that sea monster that symbolically stands for the nations that persecuted God's people and represented chaos, the sea. In v12:3, the dragon represents Satan as the persecutor of God's people. Throughout the OT—in Isaiah, Ezekiel, Micah, Jeremiah, and more—we see this term, and similar ones, portraying Egypt, Assyria, and Babylon as the primary oppressors of Israel. We've been reading a lot of Exodus and plague imagery. Soon, we'll see that John uses Babylon to symbolize the world's humanistic culture that comes against the church.

The dragon goes after the woman, but the earth comes to the rescue of the woman. A flood was a common symbol of both Jewish and Gentile lore for persecution. And we've seen the earth swallow those who come against God before, in the story of Korah's rebellion. In his anger, the dragon goes to make war on the rest of her offspring. While futurists say that only ethnic Jews are going through this tribulation, v17 contradicts that idea by identifying those offspring:

> *17 Then the dragon became furious with the woman and went off to make war on the rest of her offspring, on those who keep the commandments of God and hold to the testimony of Jesus. And he stood on the sand of the sea.*

Ethnic Jews would not have held to the testimony of Jesus, and messianic Jews would have been raptured away under the futurist account. Of course, the futurist will counter by saying that these are Jews who have come to know the Lord during the tribulation. That might comprise a minuscule portion of believers but not *"the rest of her offspring."*

The idealist perspective, however, looks at the woman figuratively as the people of God. Israel was the people of God in the OT, and they produced the Messiah, but the church represents the people of God in the NT. Tying this back to chapter 11, there are several symbolic references to the church. As we believers are the temple of God (2 Corinthians 6:16), the reference to the Gentiles trampling the outer courts can also be seen as persecution of His people, us. The two witnesses, again representing the church, oppose that persecution but ultimately appear to succumb to it. And then we have the woman, who is borne on eagle's wings to a place of refuge, signifying a supernatural deliverance.

The Preterist view will say that all of this was fulfilled in 70 A.D. However, while there are historical reports of some supernatural happenings at that time, nowhere in historical writings (to my knowledge) are there reports of the Jews, the "people of God," being supernaturally delivered. In reality, the opposite seemed to occur. Yes, there are reports by Eusebius, Epiphanes, and Josephus that early Christians had left Jerusalem because of Christ's warning in Luke 21:20-24. They did so after the Roman governor, Cestius Gallus, ended his brief siege of the city in 66 A.D. They were not in the city when Vespasian started his siege a short while later. They reportedly fled to a town called Pella across the Jordan; however, modern-day archaeological digs at that site have not turned up any significant evidence to support an early Christian presence there.[50] Since they simply took heed to a prophetic warning, I'm not sure this qualifies as the supernatural deliverance spoken of in Revelation 12.

---

[50] Bourke, S. (2013). The Christian Flight to Pella: True or Tale? *Biblical*

The question remains. When? Dr. Boccaccini, previously mentioned, believes this three-and-a-half-year period ends the final seven years of this era, before the final judgment, using the Zadokite calendar. Going the extra 30 days takes us through Passover, or in our case, the Marriage Supper of the Lamb. The next 45 days take us to Shavu'ot, celebrating the final harvest and the Great White Throne judgment.

I'm still not convinced of this scenario. After all, weren't the spring feasts fulfilled by Christ's first advent? Aren't we waiting for the fulfillment of the fall feasts by His second coming? I made the argument in my previous book that Yom Teruah (now called by the Persian name Rosh Hashanah) seems likely to be the day of the *parousia*. By the nature of its timing, it is the feast where no one knows the day or hour of its coming since its beginning relies upon spotting the new moon. Only the High Priest (the Father) could announce its start. Plus, it's a feast that calls for the blowing of trumpets and celebration, requiring no sacrifices. I guess the panmillenialists will see how it pans out.

As we review all of this, we see that there is great persecution of the church for a three-and-a-half-year period, but that God miraculously delivers His people. During the exodus, God took His people into the wilderness where He provided water, manna, and quail. Should we be fearful that he would do less for us? In my earlier book, *Still Here! Surviving the End Times*, I wrote of Jehovah Machaçeh, the Lord our Refuge, and pointed to Psalm 91 in detail. I urge you to read that Psalm again and truly focus on what He said through David. And just as early Christians in Jerusalem trusted God's Word for guidance and deliverance, we must do the same.

Unto Us, a King is Born

Besides the word "and" found in Revelation 12:1, something else about the first five verses of the chapter leads me to suspect there's more to the story. The astral aspects of this description have led reliable researchers to pinpoint the birth date of Jesus.

I've mentioned before that some scholars believe that John's title as a seer points to his practice of watching the stars, the signs in the heavens. In fact, "astral theology" was a prominent aspect of the religious life of the Jews and early Christians. This is the belief that what was going on in the heavens were signs of God's will or His intent to do something. This had nothing to do with determining an individual's fate, as in astrology as we know it today.

In v12:1-5 we find the woman clothed with the sun, the moon under her feet, and a wearing a crown with twelve stars. The heavens also showed the dragon, with seven heads and ten horns, standing before the woman ready to devour her child upon her giving birth. In astral terms, the woman is the constellation Virgo, based upon Isaiah 7:14. John describes the dragon as red and says its tail swept away a third of the stars. The dragon is also said to be coming out of the abyss. Both the red color and the abyss (another constellation) point to a southern constellation. Draco is near the north pole, so Hydra is a better option. It sits in the southern sky, closer to Virgo than Draco, near the abyss, and there's a void of stars near its tail. Corvus and Crater sit above Hydra, and one has seven stars and the other ten. Of course, as mentioned, these two constellations together form the ark of the covenant as well. The virgin's crown would be Leo, which with its nine bright stars, plus the planets Mercury, Venus, and Mars, would appear to have 12 stars.

Astronomically, what does this mean? Virgo is a broad constellation that rises above the horizon in spring, traverses the heavens, and begins its descent to the horizon in late summer. The sun follows an imaginary path called the ecliptic, which holds its course 24/7. The ecliptic runs through the night sky as well, showing the sun's position on the other side of the earth. The ecliptic runs through every zodiacal constellation on a yearly schedule, which takes it through Virgo from roughly September 16 to October 30. However, to say she is clothed with the sun would imply its being in her midst, which only occurs for roughly 20 days during this timespan. Because the moon travels the ecliptic once every month, it passes to the east of Virgo (sits at her feet) more than once during those six weeks. However, for the moon to sit at her feet while the sun is in her midst takes us to a roughly 90-minute time window during that 20-day period. Taken as is, this combination isn't that unique and has occurred four times in the past 1,000 years, the most recent being September 23, 2017.[51]

However, the scripture gives us more information, and if we were Magi watching the skies for signs of the Messiah, we would be aware of other celestial pointers. The Magi were, after all, trained by Daniel who was chief of the Magi in his day. The Magi would no doubt associate Leo, the lion, with the tribe of Judah from which the Messiah would come. (Genesis 49:9-10). Leo is dominated by the star Regulus, known by astronomers as the "King star." Also, astronomers call Jupiter the "King planet."

At one unique point in history, the stars lined up and Jupiter went into conjunction with Regulus. That conjunction began on September 11th, 3 B.C. and continued through September 14th. Jupiter continued along its path until December 1, 3 B.C. when it appeared to stop for a while before beginning its retrograde path. On February 17, 2 B.C., it again joined in conjunction with Regulus. That conjunction on September 11th could account for the "star" of Bethlehem. The Magi would have seen this and ascertained that something wonderful had happened, particularly if they were aware of Isaiah's prophesies about the Messiah. Yet, they would require almost two years to prepare and to get to Jerusalem, thus Herod's decision to kill every male child two years old and under.

September 11th, 3 B.C. works as Jesus's birth date for other reasons. The timing perfectly fits with the birth of John the Baptist, calculated using his father's time of service in the temple. Also, September 11th was the Feast of Trumpets that year. Tishri 1, or Rosh Hashanah, the beginning of the Jewish new year, was the traditional day of Judean kings' inaugurations, as shown in the account of Solomon, as well as in Jeremiah and Ezra.[52] And per Jewish tradition, this

---

[51] earthsky.org/human-world/biblical-signs-in-the-sky-september-23-2017/
[52] Thiele, E. *Mysterious Numbers of the Hebrew Kings*, Zondervan Publishing House,Grand Rapids, MI, 1983, pgs. 28, 31, 161, and 163

celebrates the day on which the creation began, the first day of the human calendar. Finally, from the flood account, we find Noah opening the ark to discover the earth had dried. Jewish tradition also discerns from that account that Noah's birthday was Tishri 1, a belief celebrated by Jews. John likely included this celestial pointer to Christ's birthday because many Jews would believe that the Messiah would share a birthday with Noah.

Still, I have this nagging feeling that these celestial signs are there for more than that, for eschatological reasons. Why else was this account included here, in Revelation, and not in John's gospel?

So, Jesus was born on September 11th, 3 B.C. There's more to this story available in Earnest L. Martin's *The Star That Astonished the World*.

Our Take-Away

The span of three and a half years is prominent and consistent within the Book of Revelation. This is a period just before the return of our Lord during which the church is to take its stand and boldly witness to unbelievers. As we'll see, this is also likely the "little while" referenced in Revelation 20 in which Satan is released to once again deceive the nations at the end of 1,000 years (the church age). Satan is represented by the dragon in these chapters, and he will persecute the people of God and deceive many, fulfilling Jesus' prophecy of a great falling away.

Yet, God knows who His true believers are, and we have been sealed with His name by His Spirit. While bearing His name might protect us spiritually, that is not a guarantee against physical hardship, or even death, although I take Him at His word about being kept from the hour of trial. Our flight to the wilderness will be one of testing, as it was for ancient Israel, but as He did for them, He will provide for us.

Does God give a clue as to when this period will begin? I suspect it's in these verses, but I'm still working to uncover it.

The Beasts

The Beasts from the Sea and Land

The beasts! No, we're not talking about Marvel's co-founder of the X-Men riding the longest wooden roller coaster in the world. Which, BTW, is an awesome ride if you're ever in SW Ohio. And no, these beasts didn't inspire Paul Revere's famous 'one if by land, two if by sea' alert signal. But I'm getting closer to being on topic.

Chapter 13 brings us not one but two beasts. The first one we meet arises from the sea:

> 1 And I saw a beast rising out of the sea, with ten horns and seven heads, with ten diadems on its horns and blasphemous names on its heads. 2 And the beast that I saw was like a leopard; its feet were like a bear's, and its mouth was like a lion's mouth. And to it the dragon gave his power and his throne and great authority. 3 One of its heads seemed to have a mortal wound, but its mortal wound was healed, and the whole earth marveled as they followed the beast. (Rev 13:1-3)

Where have we seen this description before? Daniel 7, perhaps?

> 2 Daniel declared, "I saw in my vision by night, and behold, the four winds of heaven were stirring up the great sea. 3 And four great beasts came up out of the sea, different from

one another. 4 The first was like a lion and had eagles' wings. Then as I looked its wings were plucked off, and it was lifted up from the ground and made to stand on two feet like a man, and the mind of a man was given to it. 5 And behold, another beast, a second one, like a bear. It was raised up on one side. It had three ribs in its mouth between its teeth; and it was told, 'Arise, devour much flesh.' 6 After this I looked, and behold, another, like a leopard, with four wings of a bird on its back. And the beast had four heads, and dominion was given to it. 7 After this I saw in the night visions, and behold, a fourth beast, terrifying and dreadful and exceedingly strong. It had great iron teeth; it devoured and broke in pieces and stamped what was left with its feet. It was different from all the beasts that were before it, and it had ten horns. 8 I considered the horns, and behold, there came up among them another horn, a little one, before which three of the first horns were plucked up by the roots. And behold, in this horn were eyes like the eyes of a man, and a mouth speaking great things. (Dan 7:2-8)

John's beast from the sea appears to be an amalgamation of all four of the beasts in Daniel 7, which, when combined into one, would have seven heads and ten horns. This combination shows that the beast represents all empires past, present, and potentially the future. Its diadems point to its false claims of sovereignty. And like the beasts from Daniel, this one is given dominion and power, even though it is counterfeit.

Some scholars believe the seven heads might also come from ancient Near Eastern mythology that predated Daniel. In Ugaritic lore, Yam is Leviathan's equivalent, and surviving Ugaritic texts about the defeat of Yam describe it as having seven heads. Does this seem far-fetched or unBiblical? Actually, Psalm 74:13-14, Psalm 89:10, and Isaiah 27:1 use terminology consistent with that Ugaritic sea monster mythology.[53] Wow. Ugaritic sea monsters. Don't forget that one at your next Bible trivia night.

In addition to the similarities of the beasts in Daniel 7 and Revelation 13, we also see the same three-point structure (another use of three). First, an agent appears—all of the beasts in Daniel and the first beast in Revelation. Second, that agent is given authority over something. Third, and finally, the effect of that authority is described. We find this pattern twice in Revelation 13: in v1-8 and again in v11-17.

Regarding that second use of the pattern, John sees a second beast, this one arising from the land:

> *11 Then I saw another beast rising out of the earth. It had two horns like a lamb and it spoke like a dragon. 12 It exercises all the authority of the first beast in its presence, and makes the earth and its inhabitants worship the first beast, whose mortal wound was healed. 13 It performs great signs, even making fire come down from heaven to earth in front of people, 14 and by the signs that it is allowed to work in the presence of the beast it deceives those who dwell on earth, telling them to make an image for the beast that was wounded by the sword and yet lived. (Rev 13:11-14)*

We've seen this beast in Daniel as well. While it's not a separate beast in Daniel, its characteristics are those that we've already read about in Daniel 7. This beast is given the authority of the first beast and can perform great signs in order to deceive people. Some scholars associate these two beasts with the governing political and economic-religious powers of the earth, respectively. As with the dragon, the numbers seven and ten reflect the complete and worldwide oppressive power of the beast.

I find it interesting that the first beast—the government—gives its authority to the second beast—the corporate and religious powers—

---

[53] Beale, GK and Carson, DA, editors, *Commentary on the New Testament Use*

because that's pretty much what we're seeing happening today. As an example, the government can't mandate COVID vaccines, so it's encouraging corporations to do so and will use its power to fine those that don't. Government can't directly censor the free speech of those who argue against masks, and yet it has given that mandate to Big Tech which is more than happy to comply. Many "ecumenical" churches have been almost eager to accommodate the culture and government. Even in the Catholic church, a high-ranking Archbishop has recently (Sep 2021) accused the Pope of colluding with the Great Reset and Deep State to depopulate the world using COVID vaccines.[54] And of course, corporate Mainstream Media is doing all it can to accommodate the beast and make people believe in it.

Another example of today's world hit me as I read the following in Dr. Beale's commentary:

> Therefore, this imagery and background suggest deception within the covenant community itself. Whereas the first beast speaks loudly and defiantly against God, the second beast makes the first beast's claims sound plausible and persuasive. False teachers in the church are encouraging compromise with the culture's idolatrous institutions, which are all associated in some way with the Roman cult (cf. the Nicolaitans, false apostles, and Jezebel in ch. 2.) Therefore, it takes a discerning Christian to detect the evil inherent in the second beast.[55]

Isn't this exactly what we're seeing with the "Woke Movement?" Marxist ideology is being "repackaged" to sound plausible and persuasive and is leading many Christians astray. What speaks more loudly against God than the killing of the innocent, and yet, the killing of

---

of the Old Testament, Baker Academic, 2007.
[54] www.israel365news.com/199887/catholic-archbishop-accuses-pope-of-complicity-in-globalist-population-control/
[55] Beale, G.K. *The New International Greek Testament Commentary, the Book of Revelation*, William B. Eerdmans Publishing Co, Grand Rapids, MI, 1999, pg. 590.

the unborn is being idealized as a woman's right to choose and even necessary for a woman's good health. The U.S. Democrat Party is seeking to make abortion legal at all stages of pregnancy. Sadly, many "Christians" accept this. Is this another fulfillment of Daniel 11:30-37 where pagan forces attacked God's people on two fronts: directly persecuting those who would not compromise their faith and penetrating the covenant community with false teaching that caused some to defect from the true God?

What is that mortal wound by a sword? It isn't Mikhail Gorbachev's hemangioma birthmark on his forehead. Yes, the former Soviet Union premiere was a leading contender for the beast once upon a dispensational time. One view: the Word is a two-edged sword, and the wound is the spreading of the gospel. Had that wound been fatal, we might be living in that Postmillennial golden age of the church. And yet, that wound wasn't fatal, and the church has lost much, no, almost all of its influence over the past 50 years. The beast survived. The majority view, though, is that Christ's death and resurrection were the death stroke, and although the blow has been delivered, it's another "already but not yet" situation where the death of the beast is coming.

With the dominance of language similar to Daniel, the above interpretation of the beasts seems most likely. There is, however, another source for these two beasts: Job 40-41. In Job 40:15, we read of Behemoth, a beast of the land and the first of the works of God. Jewish tradition holds that Behemoth was the first thing created on the fifth day of creation. In Job 41 we read of Leviathan, a great beast from the sea. He is dreaded and uncontrollable, and *"he is king over all the sons of pride."* These verses are the only place in the Bible where these two are mentioned together. Both are individually mentioned in other verses, and more commonly Rahab is the name used for Behemoth. In Psalm 87:4 we find Rahab associated with Babylon, and in Isaiah 51:9, Rahab is identified as a dragon. In each case, the beast is personified as "he" not an "it," consistent with being symbolic of human endeavors against God.

Job is where we find these beasts characterized as being slain by God with a sword (40:19 in the Masoretic text), as waging war with his mouth (40:32 in the Septuagint, LXX), and as speaking great things against God (41:11,13 LXX). In Isaiah 27:1, we also read of God slaying Leviathan with His sword. With the demonic nature attributed to these beasts, these two have long been symbolic of chaos, with chaos being defined theologically as everything against God and His ways. The themes of chaos include death, decay, division of men, warring against God, being estranged from God, and so forth. Chapter 13 is all about the war of chaos against God and vice versa.

The beast has also been identified as "the Antichrist," a global tyrant believed by many to control the world at the end of days. While the Bible never says this will be an individual, this idea has also penetrated modern culture. Personally, while I acknowledge the possibility of such a world leader, I don't see scripture truly supporting such, and the events of Revelation can be fulfilled without such a world leader. The Deep State is bad enough.

The Mark

It's in chapter 13 that we first see all three members of the unholy trinity—the dragon (Satan), the great beast (from the sea), and the second beast—that is later called the false prophet, as he speaks for the beast. Again, for some, the great beast is the Antichrist. However, as I discussed in my other book, the NT doesn't speak of an individual as the Antichrist (capital A) but of a spirit of antichrist (small A), which is certainly more fitting of this beast representing the government powers.

Having been cast down from heaven, Satan now mimics the Father, Son, and Holy Spirit by endowing the beast with his power and throne and great authority, illegitimate though that authority is. The beast's survival from a fatal wound even imitates that of Christ, while the false prophet is also described in Christ-like terms as having horns like a lamb. Yet, the false prophet sports two horns, reminiscent of the evil ruler in Daniel 8, and speaks like a dragon, showing the ultimate deception. It looks innocent enough but beware of its words. Jesus prophesied about false prophets coming in sheep's clothing in Matthew

7:15. The prophet is also empowered with abilities such as raining down fire from heaven as well as speaking for the beast. Unbelievers the world over worship the beast in the sense that they praise it, rely upon it, follow it, give it their allegiance, and more.

As Moses had Aaron, the beast has his prophet to speak for him. Like Elijah, the false prophet calls down fire. That is where those similarities end and the deceptions begin.

For those whose names are not written in the Book of Life, they, too, bear a name on their foreheads and right hands. As believers, we bear the name of God, just as an ambassador bears the name of his country. In Exodus 13:9, God tells Israel that the Torah was to be worn on their hand as a sign and on their foreheads as a reminder. Here, the mark becomes a parody of that command. However, unlike bearing God's name and being spiritually protected, this name offers only allegiance to man's ways and eternal condemnation.

'The mark on the forehead and right hand could also be a reference to the ancient practice of branding or tattooing slaves, soldiers, and religious devotees. If thinking of slaves, the branding reflects them as property of the beast. In considering soldiers and religious devotees, they would be seen as faithful followers.

However, the mark is likely a spiritual one, not a physical mark, despite the verse stating that without it one cannot buy or sell—a reflection on the church of Smyrna where believers were materially poor because of not participating in the guilds' practices. That said, vaccine passports are unlikely to qualify as the mark despite what you might read in the news about New York City, Victoria (Australia), and other cities requiring or threatening to require such papers—or Bill Gates' digital tattoo—to be able to "participate in society." The time may come in our country when being identified as a Christian will be enough to have society shun you. That's already occurring in other parts of the world where believers meet "underground." This could play out in a variety of ways as persecution intensifies.

[Now, in 2023, I'm beginning to change my mind about vaccine passports. Not that they, per se, could become *the* mark, but that they, along with other "innovations" could merge to fulfill this prophetic word. The WHO and European Union recently agreed to develop and utilize the EU's Green Pass (vaccine passport) to limit travel in another pandemic. Recently, Aldi opened their latest store in the Netherlands in which you need the store's app to enter the store and buy groceries. Scanning the app gives you access to the store, records the items you select, and checks you out at the end. In the U.S., Sam's Club is pushing their app to scan items you wish to buy and will check you out at the end. In the U.K., a conservative leader of Brexit was recently "debanked." Nigel Farage had his bank accounts canceled and no banks would accept a new account from him. Travel, groceries, banking . . . how easy it has become to cancel a person's ability to buy and sell. Anyone who doesn't fall in line with the current Groupthink can get canceled with the push of a button.]

What about the beast's image? The word for 'image,' *eikōn*, εἰκών, is the word from which we get 'icon.' Although it is used to denote the image of God and Christ in the NT, as well as images of idols, it's also used in the Gospel accounts of Christ taking a denarius, asking whose image is on it, and telling His challengers to give to Caesar what is Caesar's and to give to God what is God's. I believe the image of the beast here refers to currency. Jesus also told us we can't serve both God and mammon (money). In the context of Revelation, if we aren't serving God, we're serving the beast, so money fits right into that situation. It also fits with those not having the mark of not being able to buy or sell. [There's a huge push for government issued and controlled digital currency. Should that ever happen, the government will have total control over your funds. Again, a push of a button and your savings are gone.]

That Famous Number

Finally. We get to *that* number.

> 17 so that no one can buy or sell unless he has the mark, that is, the name of the beast or the number of its name. 18 This calls for wisdom: let the one who has understanding

> *calculate the number of the beast, for it is the number of a man, and his number is 666. (Rev 13:18)*

Ignore the number for a moment and reread those verses. Most folks jump right to the number, but what is that number? It's the number of the name of the beast, and both the name and the number qualify as the mark of the beast.

V18 also says it's the number of "a man," and a lot of people have spent a lot of time trying to identify this individual. You'll hear Nero Caesar thrown around, but that gematria requires a corrupted spelling of his name, Neron, the Jewish alliteration to the Greek spelling. Other names have been suggested. However, if this is the number of a specific individual's name, we'll never know it in this lifetime. Too many options. Even Barney the dinosaur could qualify.

Irenaeus, who first proposed gematria for the number, discussed the number in *Against Heresies* (5, 30, 3) and never mentioned Nero once. Among his proposed names, however, he did suggest the Greek word for 'Titan' (spelled specifically as Τειτάν) as it isn't the name of a specific person but is an appropriate name for a king, or more specifically for a tyrant. That has been a favorite candidate among many scholars since.

As I hinted earlier, this also ties into 1 Enoch. In Greek mythology, the Titans were the children of Uranos (Heaven) and Gaia (Earth) who fought against Zeus and the gods and were ultimately imprisoned in Tartarus. Gaia was also the mother of the *gigantes*, who rose up against the Olympians in what is called the Gigantomachy. Recall that the bas reliefs of the Altar of Zeus in Pergamum depict the Gigantomachy. Does this sound familiar? Children of heaven and earth—the Nephilim, perhaps. Or maybe the giants, post-flood, following in those footsteps. Myth is typically founded in reality.

For the Second Temple Period Jew, this connection would resonate in another way: the titans were giants, Nimrod was a giant, and Nimrod founded Babylon. Hmmm. That's as good a yellow-brick road as any, I guess.

One of the things going against gematria is its complication. Are we to use the Greek or Jewish system? How would that apply to English? Do we use a name a certain way if that name has multiple variations in spelling? Would the average man know what numbers are assigned to what letters? Perhaps they did in John's day, but if the Book of Revelation was to be for all times, perhaps not in every period. Today, I couldn't do that, could you?

Others have suggested that the number is simply symbolic of man, and the Greek word *anthrōpos* can be used to refer to the nature of man. One option mentioned by Dr. Beale was that it's the number of humanity. Man's number is 6, as in being created on the sixth day and being just below the perfection of Christ. The nature of man would therefore be body (6), soul (6), and spirit (6)—666.

Some suggest that since the dragon, beast, and false prophet are a parody of the Godhead, that this number is also a parody. Six in the number for incompleteness. So, while the Godhead could be represented by 777, the unholy trinity would be represented by 666.

Yet others have suggested that the number 666 refers to Solomon's annual receipt of 666 talents of gold.[56] This author suggests that the number reflects Solomon's "wayward and unjust practices: his inordinate wealth, exploitation of his own people and eschewing of God's law."

Of the three OT references to "666," Solomon's gold receipts take up two. The third is a reference in Ezra 2:13 where a man named Adonikam is mentioned as having 666 sons (descendants). The meaning of Adonikam is "Lord of rising" and one source I stumbled upon suggested that this could refer to the beast rising from the abyss in Revelation 17:8.[57] Stretching it a bit in my opinion.

However, that same website made two comments that caught my attention. I had mentioned early on in the book that gematria arose from astrology and divination. The author of this web page asked a

---

[56] Bodner, K., & Strawn, B. (2020). Solomon and 666 (Revelation 13.18). *New Testament Studies, 66*(2), 299-312. doi:10.1017/S0028688519000523

[57] shalach.org/Antichrist/Number%20666%20and%20Name%20of%20the%20Beast.htm

simple question. Why would God use something occult in order for us to understand His prophetic word? Yes, why indeed. The second thing he pointed out was that the NT use of the word *arithmos*, ἀριθμός, used for 'number' in Revelation 3:18, always refers to the counting of people, as in a census.

That got me thinking—always a dangerous proposition according to my wife. I checked his references: Acts 4:4; 5:36; 6:7; 11:21; Romans 9:27; Revelation 5:11; 9:16; 13:18 (twice); and 20:8. Sure enough, in each case outside of 13:18, the word refers to the count of people. Why would the use of the word in 13:18 be different? Why does everyone jump to gematria when discussing this number? Did Irenaeus lead everyone down a long, twisting rabbit trail? Also in 13:18, we find the word *psēphizō*, ψηφίζω, for the word 'calculate.' Its only other use in the NT is in Luke 14:28 where Jesus asks if anyone would venture to build a tower without first counting or calculating its cost.

Look again at v18. John states "*it **is** the number*" of a man. The present tense shows that the meaning was intended to be something clear to John and his audience, not something unusual or in the far future. Maybe we're not talking about gematria. Could the answer be staring at us from nose length? Remember earlier in this book I mentioned Elijah sparing one of the three companies of men sent to kill him? That meant two-thirds were consumed by fire from heaven. Even earlier, I mentioned Zechariah 12-13 regarding a third. Here is Zechariah 13:8:

> *8 In the whole land, declares the LORD, two thirds shall be cut off and perish, and one third shall be left alive.*

We also see this idea in Ezekiel 5:2, 12:

> *2 A third part you shall burn in the fire in the midst of the city, when the days of the siege are completed. And a third part you shall take and strike with the sword all around the city. And a third part you shall scatter to the wind, and I will unsheathe the sword after them. ... 12 A third part of you*

shall die of pestilence and be consumed with famine in your midst; a third part shall fall by the sword all around you; and a third part I will scatter to all the winds and will unsheathe the sword after them.

One-third gets scattered and emptied out but are still alive. Two-thirds die. How else do we write two-thirds? Maybe, like, you know, 66.6%. Perhaps John's not trying to make us hunt down some unknown individual. Maybe he's telling us that two-thirds of the people will take the mark of the beast. Curiously, while I don't take any stock in Islam, it teaches that two-thirds of all people die shortly before the coming of their messiah, the Mahdi. Could it be that simple? Yes, it could be, and yet I've found this proposed solution to the 666 conundrum nowhere else.

Or I could simply be way off base. You know. Getting into trouble by thinking too much, as my wife says.

Our Take-Away

We've been introduced to the two beasts, but they aren't necessarily specific individuals. You can stop scanning the news portals for signs of a charismatic global leader rising on the world stage. These beasts are already here in the form of oppressive governmental power and the economic-religious factions that support it.

With the first beast having been given its authority from the dragon, it speaks against God and oppresses His people. It consists of the characteristics of the four beasts in Daniel 7, which were four empires: Babylon, Persia, Greece, and finally Rome. When John offers comparisons that directly point to Rome, he does so because the Roman Empire was the "Babylon" of his day, not because he expected some reincarnated version of the empire to come into power in the last days.

The second beast, later identified as the false prophet, also has characteristics of the beasts of Daniel 7. While the beast boasts of its power and speaks blasphemous words against God, the false prophet's role is that of making the beast's agenda plausible and persuading even the elect to follow the beast.

The beast will grow in power and begin to oppress God's people more directly. Its followers will "bear its name," which is symbolic of giving their allegiance to it. On the other hand, God's people will bear His name and be spiritually sealed, or protected, from the wiles of the beast and the persuasive lies of the false prophet.

One look at the news bears out my statement that this pair is already here. An ever-growing central government is overrunning local and state governments looking to take on their roles, restrict their constitutional rights, and mandate social behavior. Big Pharma, Big Tech, the Mainstream Media, and Big Ag all play critical roles in what our government does while at the same time doing the bidding of government leaders when those people find their hands tied by laws they haven't yet skirted or changed. The same is true of most governments of the world. Follow the money, which could very well represent the image of the beast. These people all serve mammon, not God.

Judgment Rains Down

As we enter chapter 14, we're in the middle of a vision that started in chapter 12. This seven-phase vision started with (1) the conflict between the serpent and the woman and her seed, moved on to (2) persecution from the beast from the sea, and continued with (3) persecution from the beast from the land. We're now at (4) with the Lamb and the 144,000 standing on Mount Zion. From there we'll read of (5) the proclamation of the gospel and judgment by three angels, (6) the Son of Man's harvest of the earth, and (7) the saints' victory over the sea beast and their celebratory song.

Remember my mention of the use of seven in the structure of several of the books of the Bible, as reflected by the logotechnical works of Schedl and Labuchagne? I mentioned that typically in that structure, the middle of a group of seven was there to give it prominence. Look who stands in point #4 above. Appropriate, right? But there's more. This vision is the fourth of the seven visions of John, so the sight of the Lamb and His 144,000 standing on Mount Zion occurs smack-dab in the middle of it all.

Three visions directly pertain to believers: the first (about the seven churches), this one, and the final vision of the New Jerusalem. The other four detail judgments on unbelievers. The vision of the seven churches details faults within the church, as well as promises to those who stay true. The final vision shows us the final reward. That this vision is in the middle is telling, as it has a stronger eschatological focus. As I pointed out in the last chapter, there is much about the beasts which we, today's believers, need to be aware of. We need to be alert to deception and be spiritually aware not just of what's going on around us in society, but also about what we're taught in church.

The End has Come

Whether or not we believe the Apocalypse has a "timeline" built into it, we've come to the Day of the Lord, as shown by the seventh trumpet. Christ, the Lamb, and the 144,000, sealed and representing God's people, are standing on Mount Zion. This is not a heavenly Zion but *Mount* Zion, the full name of which is used only of the earthly mountain of God in scripture. We've discussed the 144,000 already so I won't repeat that. The key here is that Christ has returned to earth.

Next, we see three angels delivering a message of good news (gospel):

> *6 Then I saw another angel flying directly overhead, with an eternal gospel to proclaim to those who dwell on earth, to every nation and tribe and language and people. 7 And he said with a loud voice, "Fear God and give him glory, because the hour of his judgment has come, and worship him who made heaven and earth, the sea and the springs of water." 8 Another angel, a second, followed, saying, "Fallen, fallen is Babylon the great, she who made all nations drink the wine of the passion of her sexual immorality." 9 And another angel, a third, followed them, saying with a loud voice, "If anyone worships the beast and its image and receives a mark on his forehead or on his hand, 10 he also will drink the wine of God's wrath, poured full strength into the cup of his anger, and he will be tormented with fire and sulfur in the presence of the holy angels and in the presence of the Lamb. 11 And the smoke of their torment goes up forever and ever, and they have no rest, day or night, these worshipers of the beast and its image, and whoever receives the mark of its name." 12 Here is a call for the endurance of the saints, those*

who keep the commandments of God and their faith in Jesus. 13 And I heard a voice from heaven saying, "Write this: Blessed are the dead who die in the Lord from now on." "Blessed indeed," says the Spirit, "that they may rest from their labors, for their deeds follow them!" (Rev 14:6-13)

We see this as the Day of the Lord because His *"hour of judgment has come."* And it's considered good news because Babylon, that symbol of chaos and evil, has fallen, and those who persecuted God's people are about to get what's coming to them.

Here again, Babylon stands for all of the evil empires in history, not a restored city in Iraq. Nor is it Rome, Jerusalem, or even New York—although Washington is looking like a good candidate these days. Throughout the OT, we see various empires opposed to Israel as foreshadows of all future opponents of God and His people. First came Egypt, then Assyria, Babylon, and Rome. Any inferences to Rome, the city or the empire, are believed simply to reflect on the main opponents to God's people in John's day, not to point to Rome in our day. The depiction of Babylon here is a mixing of Isaiah 21:9 and Daniel 4:30.

Curiously, the ESV translation above says, *"Here is **a call for** the endurance...,"* as if encouraging believers to remain faithful. You'll find this in other translations as well. However, the Greek of this verse simply says, "Here is the endurance..." as if presenting our faith as a done deal. Similarly, in v13, the phrase *"... from now on"* implies something for the future. The Greek *arti*, ἄρτι, means 'just now,' 'this moment,' 'at this very time,' or 'now at this time,' not 'from now on.' If you look elsewhere in the NT, *arti* is translated appropriately, and in over half a dozen NT scriptures it's translated as 'up to this time.' Why should it convey a future time in just this verse? It's as if the translators' personal, dispensational biases have tainted their translations. It happens.

The Fields Were White

As we continue in chapter 14:

14 Then I looked, and behold, a white cloud, and seated on the cloud one like a son of man, with a golden crown on his head, and a sharp sickle in his hand. 15 And another angel came out of the temple, calling with a loud voice to him who sat on the cloud, "Put in your sickle, and reap, for the hour to reap has come, for the harvest of the earth is fully ripe." 16 So he who sat on the cloud swung his sickle across the earth, and the earth was reaped. 17 Then another angel came out of the temple in heaven, and he too had a sharp sickle. 18 And another angel came out from the altar, the angel who has authority over the fire, and he called with a loud voice to the one who had the sharp sickle, "Put in your sickle and gather the clusters from the vine of the earth, for its grapes are ripe." 19 So the angel swung his sickle across the earth and gathered the grape harvest of the earth and threw it into the great winepress of the wrath of God. 20 And the winepress was trodden outside the city, and blood flowed from the winepress, as high as a horse's bridle, for 1,600 stadia. (Rev 14:14-20)

The "one like a son of man," wearing a golden crown and seated on a cloud, is Christ, not an angel. As previously stated, nowhere in scripture are angels depicted as wearing crowns. His coming on the clouds is also foretold in the synoptic gospels (Matthew 24:30, and so on). That He is described as seated on the cloud does not imply He has returned to heaven, after having just been shown on Mount Zion. For one thing, should you want to read this literally, clouds are part of the earthly realm, not heaven. Both the crown and white cloud are symbols of deity, also previously mentioned. Being seated on a cloud points to His deity.

As for "another angel" in v16, we've seen multiple angels coming from the temple, so saying "another" does not imply that the figure in v15 is an angel. Some would argue that an angel wouldn't be giving Christ a command to put in His sickle and reap. Yet, this angel is coming from the temple, from God's throne. It is the Father giving the command, and yes, Christ does what the Father instructs Him to do. The Father is saying, "It's time!" That day and hour of which no one knows except the Father has arrived.

Yes, these verses point to the Day of the Lord. As such, the harvest is taking place. Christ puts in His sickle to reap His followers and gather them to Himself. The second harvester, an angel, reaps those destined to wrath. The angel in charge of fire stands by to test their works by fire. The imagery of wine pouring out at the unleashing of God's wrath has numerous OT references: Psalm 60:3, 75:8, Isaiah 51:17, 21-23, Jeremiah 25:15-18, and Job 21:20. Specifically, Isaiah 63:6 speaks of:

> *"I trampled down the peoples in my anger; I made them drunk in my wrath, and I poured out their lifeblood on the earth."*

That the blood coming from *"the great winepress of the wrath of God"* flows as high as a horse's bridle for 1,600 stadia is clearly a metaphor. With a stadion measuring about 607 feet or 185 meters, this calls for blood roughly five feet deep for 184 miles. Hard to take that as literal, but it does point to a massive death toll.

There is symbolism in the number 1600, too. It is (4x4) x (10x10) which shows the completeness of this judgment. Others see it as 40x40, where 40 is a traditional number for punishment, as in 40 lashes.

The sickle imagery has OT and NT roots. Jeremiah 50:16 talks of Babylon, the sower, and the one who wields the sickle. Mark 4:29 speaks of the grain being ripe and putting in the sickle because the harvest has come. Joel 3:13-16 is perhaps the most relevant:

> *13 Put in the sickle, for the harvest is ripe. Go in, tread, for the winepress is full. The vats overflow, for their evil is great. 14 Multitudes, multitudes, in the valley of decision! For the day of the LORD is near in the valley of decision. 15 The sun and the moon are darkened, and the stars withdraw their shining. 16 The LORD roars from Zion, and utters his voice*

from Jerusalem, and the heavens and the earth quake. But the LORD is a refuge to his people, a stronghold to the people of Israel.

Joel is prophesying about the Day of the Lord in much the same language as John. I am particularly encouraged by the last sentence. He *is* our refuge.

Celebrate!

As we move into chapter 15, we begin another vision.

1 Then I saw another sign in heaven, great and amazing, seven angels with seven plagues, which are the last, for with them the wrath of God is finished. 2 And I saw what appeared to be a sea of glass mingled with fire--and also those who had conquered the beast and its image and the number of its name, standing beside the sea of glass with harps of God in their hands. (Rev 15:1-2)

As we see the final seven angels preparing to unleash the final seven plagues, which will again reflect upon the plagues of Egypt, we see *"a sea of glass."* There are several interpretations of the sea of glass, but if the sea is symbolic of chaos and corruption, its being as smooth as glass points to God's stilling of that chaos with the fire of His judgment.

John also sees God's people in heaven, those who have conquered the beast, its image, and the number of its name. For those who equate the beast with an Antichrist and try to identify that person using the number of its name, why are these three—beast, image, and number—separated here as if three different entities that need to be conquered? Perhaps they are, if we look at the beast as being the state, its image being money, and its number pointing to those who side with the beast. All three must be conquered. In terms of defeating those who side with the beast, it's likely not so much about physically defeating these people as it is about overcoming peer pressure and their opinions of us.

Jesus said we would be hated because He was hated. We can't let that sway us.

And I love what John sees all of us doing—singing. Nothing like a good praise and worship session. Plus, I can't wait to see my friend, heavy rock musician John Cooper of Skillet, playing a harp. Should be epic. (Yes, John laughingly approved this paragraph.)

Yet, while we're celebrating, God has prepared the final judgment on nonbelievers. The seven bowls full of God's wrath are handed to the seven angels who will release them. These bowls hold the final judgment of man to be dispensed on the Day of the Lord.

The Bowls of God's Wrath

1 Then I heard a loud voice from the temple telling the seven angels, "Go and pour out on the earth the seven bowls of the wrath of God." (Rev 16:1)

God now commands these angels to pour out the bowls of wrath upon the earth. Bowls were used for service within the temple. The word for 'bowl,' *phialē*, φιάλη, is understood to be a "cultic" utensil, which means one used in ritual or priestly service. Also of note, these bowls are mentioned 12 times in the Book of Revelation. One of the priestly uses of bowls was to carry out the ashes and fat from sacrifices. In context, the bowls could symbolize the removal of defilement from the earth.

Let's take a look at these plagues:

2 So the first angel went and poured out his bowl on the earth, and harmful and painful sores came upon the people who bore the mark of the beast and worshiped its image. 3 The second angel poured out his bowl into the sea, and it became like the blood of a corpse, and every living thing died that was in the sea. 4 The third angel poured out his bowl into the rivers and the springs of water, and they became blood. . . . 8 The fourth angel poured out his bowl on the sun,

> *and it was allowed to scorch people with fire. 9 They were scorched by the fierce heat, and they cursed the name of God who had power over these plagues. They did not repent and give him glory. 10 The fifth angel poured out his bowl on the throne of the beast, and its kingdom was plunged into darkness. People gnawed their tongues in anguish 11 and cursed the God of heaven for their pain and sores. They did not repent of their deeds. 12 The sixth angel poured out his bowl on the great river Euphrates, and its water was dried up, to prepare the way for the kings from the east. ... 17 The seventh angel poured out his bowl into the air, and a loud voice came out of the temple, from the throne, saying, "It is done!" 18 And there were flashes of lightning, rumblings, peals of thunder, and a great earthquake such as there had never been since man was on the earth, so great was that earthquake. ... 21 And great hailstones, about one hundred pounds each, fell from heaven on people; and they cursed God for the plague of the hail, because the plague was so severe. (Rev 16:2-4, 8-12, 17-18, 21)*

We can see that these plagues are like those of Egypt and similar to those of the trumpet judgments. Dr. Beale has the following to say:

> Both trumpets and bowls present the plagues in the same order: plagues striking (1) the earth, (2) the sea, (3) rivers, (4) the sun, (5) the realm of the wicked with darkness, (6) the Euphrates (together with influencing the wicked by demons), and (7) the world with the final judgment (with the same imagery of "lightning, sounds, thunders, and earthquake" and "great hail"). The overwhelming likeness of the trumpets and the bowls is a result of both being modeled on the exodus plagues.[58]

---

[58] Beale, G.K. *The New International Greek Testament Commentary, the Book of Revelation*, William B. Eerdmans Publishing Co, Grand Rapids, MI, 1999, pg. 669.

While Dr. Beale believes the two sets of plagues to be the same judgments from different perspectives, I deferentially disagree, as do others. The plagues of the seven trumpets affect a third of creation (earth, sea, sun, etc.) while these bowl judgments now affect not only creation but also nonbelievers globally. The trumpet judgments affect men and women indirectly through damage to the environment and serve as warnings, but these plagues affect people directly and function as their final judgment. Dr. Beale and others believe this all occurs before Christ's *parousia*, but nothing in what I've read supports that belief (IMO). I think these judgments come as a final barrage of sorts on nonbelievers in a very short time, the Day of the Lord, *at* His return, not before it.

That we're seeing these plagues poured upon the sun and air in the fourth and seventh bowls isn't contradictory to the command in v1 to pour out the bowls upon the earth. This reflects the Hellenistic understanding of the cosmos and the earth, where everything was composed of the four known "elements:" earth, water, fire, and air. With all four elements involved, John is showing the completeness of the destruction that is occurring. We also can't take these depictions literally since believers would also be affected by changes in the earth, water, sun, and air. These judgments are clearly for the nonbelievers.

The sixth bowl of wrath includes an interesting "event"—the drying up of the Euphrates. Can this be taken literally? With the severe droughts occurring across the globe, this wouldn't shock me. Indeed, this year, through August 2021, Iraq, with the Euphrates and Tigris Rivers, is having its worst drought in 70 years, and it now threatens the lives of 12 million people.[59] The Euphrates is at record low levels. In **70 years**? Hmmm.

However, the modified idealists, as represented by Dr. Beale, have an interesting take on this picture of that river:

> Therefore, the drying up of the Euphrates' waters is a

---

[59] www.msn.com/en-us/news/world/water-crisis-and-drought-threaten-12-million-in-syria-iraq/ar-AANCvAm

picture of how the multitudes of Babylon's religious adherents throughout the world become disloyal to Babylon. Disenchantment with Babylon is a prelude to Babylon's judgment and the final judgment itself. 17:16–18 states that "the kings of the earth," the political arm of the wicked world system, will turn against the economic-religious arm and destroy it. The same text implies that Babylon's destruction begins with "the kings of the earth" dissuading Babylon's innumerable economic-religious followers from remaining loyal to her.[60]

Might we be seeing the very early stages of the government turning on its corporate allies? While the corporate powers-that-be are accommodating the government with vaccine mandates, the US Congress is trying to push through a $3.5 TRILLION (more like $5+ trillion) spending package that includes incredible tax increases on business and wealthy corporate execs (as well as the working stiffs of the middle class).

Other than the futurists who take these passages literally, no one else seems to venture an opinion on just how these plagues will manifest. Although the shared imagery with the trumpets suggests ongoing and worsening drought, heat, famine, and the like—things we're seeing globally now—how might the human affliction present?

Could the COVID-19 "vaccine" play a role? As a form of gene therapy—not a traditional vaccine—it is a biological device that has never been used before, never underwent animal testing, was rushed to the "market" under false claims, and has already injured hundreds of thousands of people and killed over 6,000 per the Centers for Disease Commercialization and Profit's own stats on VAERS at the end of August 2021. In reality, the Medicare database at CMS shows nearly 50,000 deaths due to the vaccine as of the end of September 2021.

It is man's tinkering with our God-created DNA. What could

---

[60] Beale, G.K. *The New International Greek Testament Commentary, the Book of Revelation*, William B. Eerdmans Publishing Co, Grand Rapids, MI, 1999, pg. 674.

possibly go wrong? The Great Reset, aka UN Agenda 21 in the 90s and 2000s, calls for depopulation of the planet. Many believe this vaccine is the tool for this genocide.

We read the term "false prophet" for the first time in Revelation 16:13, although he has been described earlier as the second beast arising from the land. And this "vaccine" gives us a great example of the beast and the false prophet at work. The government's intense push to vaccinate, its mandates, and its vilification of the "unvaccinated" are being promoted by the false prophet's powers of persuasion and "deification" of the beast. Yet, the throne of the beast, representing his sovereignty, is about to go dark, i.e., lose its power.

Where do we end up in chapter 16? Armageddon. Since I believe that there is a sequence of events noted by the intensification of judgment, I see these bowls being poured out by God as Jesus stands on Mount Zion. The battle of Armageddon is taking place. *Har-megiddon*, transliterated as Armageddon, is unlikely to be a battle for Megiddo, as there has never been a Mount Megiddo and Megiddo is a broad plain. Many scholars contend that the term was derived from *magēdô*, where *magēd* means 'a place of gathering in troops' and adding the ô makes it 'his place of gathering in troops.'[61] *Har-magēdô* would then be the mount where He gathers His troops. In this case, Mount Zion, in a final battle at Jerusalem.

Other scholars argue that the word is derived from *har-mô`ēd*, which means 'mount of assembly.' The result would be the same: Mount Zion.

As for the kings of the east, don't think of China, as so many literalists do today. In John's day, there was only one kingdom associated with the east, and that was Babylon. We'll discuss Babylon as a metaphor shortly.

So, the dragon gathers his nations together for one last stand, and God's great wrath falls from heaven, 100-pound hailstones and more, all around Christ and the 144,000, His troops. If it wasn't going to be the reality for billions of people, you might say that image has a great

---

[61] Ibid., pg. 683.

cinematic touch. Sadly, it won't be a Marvel movie for them.

Our Take-Away

As we come to the end of the judgments of God, His people have been "harvested." Whether that means those of us remaining on earth are physically gathered to Him on Mount Zion, or whether it's a symbolic harvest, the great Day of the Lord has arrived. The final battle of *Har-magēdô* looms directly ahead.

However, we must understand that this apocalyptic battle isn't simply over some earthly real estate, Jerusalem. This is the battle for cosmic control. Satan, the dragon, and his forces are gathered to take on God spiritually. This goes back to the Deuteronomy 32 worldview that I mentioned earlier in the book. At Babel, God divided mankind into 70 nations and gave control of each to members of His Divine Council, the *elohim*, or sons of God. These are the powers and principalities against which we've battled throughout the church age. And now, they've come together in their final rebellion against God, with Satan hoping to claim the throne and title of Most High God.

God's desire all along has been for the return of Eden, with His human family populating it. For six "days"—or 6,000 years since a day is like a thousand years—He has been working and moving toward that goal. He has shown us His plan throughout the prophets and psalms, He gave us His Son to redeem His people, and it all culminates here. He's preparing to rest on the seventh day.

For the nonbeliever, he or she will share in the fate of the rebellious *elohim*. The bowl judgments might be physical, in which case great destruction and cataclysm appear to be close at hand. Or they might just be spiritual. Either way, the death toll will be massive. If you have family or friends who aren't on the narrow path right now, don't delay in trying to reach them.

The Prostitute and Babylon

A New Player

Revelation 17 introduces a new player to the scene, who, in reality, is one of the oldest.

> *1 Then one of the seven angels who had the seven bowls came and said to me, "Come, I will show you the judgment of the great prostitute who is seated on many waters, 2 with whom the kings of the earth have committed sexual immorality, and with the wine of whose sexual immorality the dwellers on earth have become drunk." 3 And he carried me away in the Spirit into a wilderness, and I saw a woman sitting on a scarlet beast that was full of blasphemous names, and it had seven heads and ten horns. 4 The woman was arrayed in purple and scarlet, and adorned with gold and jewels and pearls, holding in her hand a golden cup full of abominations and the impurities of her sexual immorality. 5 And on her forehead was written a name of mystery: "Babylon the great, mother of prostitutes and of earth's abominations." 6 And I saw the woman, drunk with the blood of the saints, the blood of the martyrs of Jesus. When I saw her, I marveled greatly. (Rev 17:1-6)*

Many pastors teach that the prostitute image is used in opposition to the bride of Christ—the immoral versus the righteous. That's true, but actually, the prostitute and her sexual immorality are symbolic of more. Throughout the OT, sexual immorality points to idolatry, the worship of the gods of the world who have been arrayed against God and His people for millennia. These are the gods who rebelled against God Most High at Babel.

Where the false prophet stands for the economic and religious establishments, the prostitute symbolizes the god-less culture, *"adorned with gold and jewels and pearls"* and astride the beast, with its blasphemous names, seven heads, and ten horns. Unlike an unfaithful wife who is seduced by a lover, the prostitute is the seducer. She goes out of her way to lure her victims into her lair using persuasive words, the finest things of life, riches, and more to gain their loyalty. Her seductive nature even penetrates the church and draws people away from Christ.

In the OT, Israel, Judah, and Jerusalem were often compared to an unfaithful wife, while Nineveh and Tyre were shown as seducers—the former with her idolatry and witchcraft (Nahum 3:4), and the latter with her wealth (Ezekiel 28). And in Isaiah 23:17, we read of Tyre, *"she will return to her wages and will prostitute herself with all the kingdoms of the world on the face of the earth."* The idea of using wealth and security to lure nations into idolatrous relationships is part of what's happening in this chapter of Revelation—selling themselves to the devil, as the saying goes.

And again, we have the reference to Babylon "the great" as the mother of prostitutes and earth's abominations. Babel is where it began after the great flood. Babel saw the beginning of chaos, and Babylon was one of the major empires that oppressed the Jews.

When John sees the woman, *"drunk with the blood of the saints, the blood of the martyrs of Jesus,"* the verse says he marveled. The drinking of blood in the ancient Near East was associated with oppression, so here John sees that persecution by the woman. Did he marvel as we define it today, that is, looking at it in astonishment and wonder, with admiration? No, this phrasing ties back to Daniel 4:17, 19, where, in the Aramaic, the term more closely denotes being appalled.

There are significant parallels between the prostitute and Jezebel of the OT, further linking the Jezebel of the church of Thyatira to the prostitute of Revelation 17. The OT Jezebel colors her eyes and adorns her head prior to her death in 2 Kings 9:30. Additional comparisons include: both are queens, both seduce people, both commit fornication (idolatry), both deceive by sorceries, both are greedy, both persecute and kill the saints, there's a remnant that refuses to follow the harlot's ways, and their destructions come quickly. In both cases, God avenges the blood of His people who died at her hands and God judges the followers of both.[62]

Much attention was paid to the beasts in the previous chapter because the nature of the prostitute cannot be known without understanding the relationship between her and the beast. That she **sits** on many waters shows her confidence and comfort. Indeed, v18:7 says "... *I sit as a queen, I am no widow, and mourning I shall never see.*" And the many waters are defined in v17:15 as *"peoples and multitudes and nations and languages."* In other words, the whole world. She, the nations, cooperates with Babylon, the beast, to guarantee her security and safety, and the beast's promise of economic prosperity is a temptation too great to resist.

What do we see around us today? In the Western world, people are giving up freedoms long taken for granted in return for a sense of security. And yet, like masks against a virus, or vaccines that don't really work, the security gained is a false one. And when people realize that, it will be too late to regain their freedom. The beast, government, won't give it back just as it never relinquishes power once it has taken it. Never in U.S. history have we seen the federal government shrink in size, spending, or power. This is likely true elsewhere, too. This is the beast consuming more and more, and, in time, it will turn on the people. I take that back. It already has.

[The seduction of "wealth" can be even more subtle. How many have yielded to Marxist ideology, which is godless and leads to totalitarianism, in order to keep their jobs and feed their families? With a syncretic worldview being dominant, it's easy to see why people are

---

[62] Beale, G.K. *The New International Greek Testament Commentary, the Book of Revelation*, William B. Eerdmans Publishing Co, Grand Rapids, MI, 1999, pg. 719.

reluctant to trust in God for their provision, and yet, He promises just that. He *is* Jehovah Jireh, the God who sees our needs.]

And an Old Player

Revelation 17:8 holds some interesting wording:

8 The beast that you saw was, and is not, and is about to rise from the bottomless pit and go to destruction. And the dwellers on earth whose names have not been written in the book of life from the foundation of the world will marvel to see the beast, because it was and is not and is to come.

While a mockery of Christ's title of "who was, who is, and who is to come," here we read, who was and **is not**. In John's time, the fallen angels were bound in the abyss, the bottomless pit. Yet, we've read that the angel in charge of the pit has opened its "doors" and these beings were released. These are the beings behind the beast of today, the spiritual version of the Deep State. I contend that they've already come back.

The description of the beast in v17:3, 7, 9-10 is the same as in Revelation 13:1 with the seven heads and ten horns and blasphemous names. This is the same beast, the worldwide governmental powers, or Deep State. The scarlet color further relates the beast to the dragon, while also denoting royal attire. Many today think of purple as the color of royalty but that was not the case in the ancient Near East. (I mentioned earlier in the book that the purple of that day was what we call Turkey red today.)

That the woman rides the beast shows their close collaboration—the social, economic, cultural, and religious aspects of culture working together with the state. This was reflected in John's day by the trade guilds in which you had to participate in worshiping their patron deity or else you were prevented from practicing your trade, enforced by the state. It was a direct connection between idolatry and one's economic survival. We see the same thing developing today as Big Media, Big Pharma, Big Ag, and corporate entities collude with the government to take away freedoms and move toward global totalitarianism.

Going on to v10, many find it confusing:

> 10 they are also seven kings, five of whom have fallen, one is, the other has not yet come, and when he does come he must remain only a little while.

Many spend great effort trying to ascertain who this must refer to in modern times, but that's a waste of time. The seven kings, as well as the seven mountains (metaphors for kingdoms or authority) in v17:9, represent the fullness of oppression that believers will face. The description here also points to the transtemporal nature of the beast throughout history. The one who had not yet come refers to the beast who was bound in the abyss. I suspect that beast is now on the scene. That he must remain only a short while will be seen again in Revelation 20 when speaking of Satan.

We also see in v12, that the ten horns are ten kings. Again, many commentators spend much effort trying to figure out who these kings are, but the number ten refers to government and law and cannot be used literally. The use of the number here likely refers to the complete power of these confederates of the beast, as well as the multiplicity of sovereignties involved. And the fact that they arise from the seventh head, the kingdom of the final days, shows that these "kings" are End Times powers.

They are given authority for only an hour. This was foreshadowed in Daniel 4:17. The timespan indicates a very brief period. The word for 'hour,' *hōra*, ὥρα, shows the smallest increment of time used by men of that day.[63] Time had not yet been broken down into minutes or other fractions of an hour. Truly, if these are the "kings" coming against Christ at *Har-magēdô*, they won't last long.

---

[63] Ibid, pg. 715.

Fallen, Fallen . . .

As we finish chapter 17, we see the beast turning on the prostitute.

> *16 And the ten horns that you saw, they and the beast will hate the prostitute. They will make her desolate and naked, and devour her flesh and burn her up with fire, 17 for God has put it into their hearts to carry out his purpose by being of one mind and handing over their royal power to the beast, until the words of God are fulfilled. 18 And the woman that you saw is the great city that has dominion over the kings of the earth." (Rev 17:16-18)*

The desolation of the woman was foreshadowed in Ezekiel 23:31-34 when he prophesied about the ruin of Jerusalem by Babylon. What's happening here is that the political side of the world system arouses the multitudes to turn against the socio-economic-religious aspects of the culture. The people become dependent upon the state for food, housing, education, and all that they own. The totalitarian state will eventually knock out capitalism, dictate the education of children, and take away private land/property ownership (all part of The Great Reset, BTW). It will become its own religion. And Christ will come against this.

Chapter 18 now shows us in more detail the indictment against Babylon, the culture.

> *1 After this I saw another angel coming down from heaven, having great authority, and the earth was made bright with his glory. 2 And he called out with a mighty voice, "Fallen, fallen is Babylon the great! She has become a dwelling place for demons, a haunt for every unclean spirit, a haunt for every unclean bird, a haunt for every unclean and detestable beast. 3 For all nations have drunk the wine of the passion of her sexual immorality, and the kings of the earth have committed immorality with her, and the merchants of the*

earth have grown rich from the power of her luxurious living." (Rev 18:1-3)

A place of demons and unclean spirits. A haunt for unclean birds and animals. All of mankind (the nonbelievers) have committed idolatry with her. And the merchants have grown rich.

In the next verse, a voice from heaven commands God's people to *"Come out of her, my people, lest you take part in her sins, lest you share in her plagues;"* lest we share in her indictment. The rest of the chapter adds more detail. Just as in a court of justice—in this case, the Divine Council's court of justice—the charges against her are reread as her judgment continues. And with that judgment, the kings of the earth, the merchants, and shipmasters (sea merchants) all mourn her sentence.

Note, however, that this final judgment does not occur over a long, drawn-out period. In v8 we read that *"her plagues come will come in a* **single day***,"* which is foreshadowed in Isaiah 47. Both in v10 and v17 we read that her judgment has come and her wealth laid waste in a **single hour**. Even though the modified idealists will say these simply symbolize a short timespan, it's from verses such as these that I believe that the "Day of the Lord" is aptly named. Christ has returned and is standing on Mount Zion. The Day of the Lord has arrived, and judgment rains down from heaven.

Our Take-Away

While I called the prostitute a "new player" in that section's title, I did so only because chapter 17 is where we're introduced to her "character." She's been around since time immemorial. Standing for the idolatrous culture, she uses every wile at her disposal to seduce believers to her ways. Want to succeed in big business? Do it "our" way. Want to be a movie star whose name is known worldwide? Sleep with "me" and push this agenda, and "we'll" make it happen. Want your records to go platinum? Stop talking about Christianity on your YouTube channel. Want to keep your job? Get vaccinated against a virus that has a 99.7% recovery rate without medical intervention. The seduction is everywhere and often subtle.

Also, in recognizing the courtroom (Divine Council) nature of the Book of Revelation, we see these two chapters as the final indictment against the world's system. Where we find the two beasts mentioned in chapter 13 embodying the state (government) and its economic-religious accomplice, here we find the godless culture itself personified. The sins of all three have been presented to the court, judgment has been made, and the penalty is meted out. The angel's promise in v17:1 is fulfilled in detail in chapter 18. And in understanding that a host of divine beings is spiritually behind these three, we see the fulfillment of Psalm 82 taking place, too.

The apostate church supports the beast and the prostitute and meets the same fate. For John, this focus on her and her ways is needed to warn the believing church against compromise with the system so that it doesn't share in its judgment.

It is Finished

Heaven Rejoices

The idolatrous, non-believing culture has now been judged and God's people, with all of heaven, are encouraged to rejoice.

> *20 Rejoice over her, O heaven, and you saints and apostles and prophets, for God has given judgment for you against her!" (Rev 18:20)*

And in chapter 19, we see that rejoicing, an affirmation that God's judgments are true and just:

> *1 After this I heard what seemed to be the loud voice of a great multitude in heaven, crying out, "Hallelujah! Salvation and glory and power belong to our God, 2 for his judgments are true and just; for he has judged the great prostitute who corrupted the earth with her immorality, and has avenged on her the blood of his servants." 3 Once more they cried out, "Hallelujah! The smoke from her goes up forever and ever." 4 And the twenty-four elders and the four living creatures fell down and worshiped God who was seated on the throne, saying, "Amen. Hallelujah!" (Rev 19:1-4)*

The sound of exultation comes from the *"great multitude in heaven"* and is the answer to the cry for justice we read in Revelation 6:10.

The phrase, *"the smoke from her goes up forever and ever,"* brings up debate about whether those being thrown into the lake of fire (fallen angels, Death, Hades, the beasts, Satan, and nonbelievers) are eternally punished or annihilated to exist no more. There are prominent scholarly voices on both sides of that debate, and I mention it only to make you aware that such a debate exists. There is strong scriptural support for both sides, and we'll not have the definitive answer until that time arrives.

The Marriage Supper

Once again, the multitudes sing out:

7 Let us rejoice and exult and give him the glory, for the marriage of the Lamb has come, and his Bride has made herself ready; (Rev 19:7)

The church—His Bride—is granted the right *"to clothe herself with fine linen, bright and pure"*— for the fine linen is the righteous deeds of the saints." (v8)

The marriage supper of the Lamb has been reserved for the faithful. It has also been foreshadowed in several places in scripture. In Exodus 24:9-11, we read of Moses, Aaron, and the elders of Israel ascending Mount Sinai to have a meal with God. In the NT, Jesus shares meals with the disciples, the 5,000, the 4,000, the Last Supper, and with the disciples on the road to Emmaus. I'm sure you can think of other examples of God, in human form in the OT, or of Jesus, in the NT, sharing a meal with men. With regards to the Lord's Supper (communion), in early Christian writings, it was typically accompanied by a feast. Yet, the most explicit foreshadow is found in Isaiah's 'mini apocalypse,'

6 On this mountain the LORD of hosts will make for all peoples a feast of rich food, a feast of well-aged wine, of rich food full of marrow, of aged wine well refined. (Isa 25:6)

With the mountain being Mount Zion and the feast being for *"all peoples"*—not simply ethnic Israel. All in all, it's a celebration of redemption.

Jesus, too, foretells this in Matthew 8:11-12 and 22:2-14. From these verses, it's clear that being an ethnic Jew was not a guarantee of being at the feast.

> *11 I tell you, many will come from east and west and recline at table with Abraham, Isaac, and Jacob in the kingdom of heaven, 12 while the sons of the kingdom will be thrown into the outer darkness. In that place there will be weeping and gnashing of teeth." (Mat 8:11-12)*

The other verses from Matthew contain the parable of the wedding feast, where many gave their excuses for not attending, the king reached out to all people, and one unfortunate attendee was cast into outer darkness.

For the Second Temple Period Jew, this feast also reflected the consumption of Leviathan and Behemoth (Psalm 74:14, Isaiah 27:1). In fact, according to the Second Temple Period scroll, 2 Baruch, we read:

> *And it will happen that when all that which should come to pass in these parts has been accomplished, the Messiah will begin to be revealed. And Behemoth will reveal itself from its place, and Leviathan will come from the sea, the two great monsters which I created on the fifth day of creation and which I shall have kept until that time. And they will be nourishment for all who are left. The earth will also yield fruits ten thousandfold. And on one vine will be a thousand branches, and one branch will produce a thousand clusters, and one cluster will produce a thousand grapes, and one grape will produce a cor of wine. And those who are hungry will enjoy themselves and they will, moreover, see marvels every day. For winds will go out in front of me every morning*

to bring the fragrance of aromatic fruits and clouds at the end of the day to distill the dew of health. And it will happen at that time that the treasury of manna will come down again from on high and they will eat of it in those years because these are they who will have arrived at the consummation of time. And it will happen after these things when the time of the appearance of the Anointed One has been fulfilled and he returns with glory, that then all who sleep in hope of him will rise. And it will happen at that time that those treasuries will be opened in which the number of the souls of the righteous were kept, and they will go out and the multitudes of the souls will appear together, in one assemblage, of one mind. And the first ones will enjoy themselves and the last ones will not be sad. For they know that the time has come of which it is said that it is the end of times. But the souls of the wicked, when they behold all these things, shall then waste away the more. For they shall know that their torment has come and their perdition has arrived (2 Bar. 29:3–30:5)[64]

The Jews of that time saw this as not only an eschatological event but as a daily one. And Leviathan and Behemoth are to be nourishment for those who are left. Imagine those steaks. Actually, don't. It's not literal, but rather a metaphor for the defeat of chaos.

The Supper of God

On the flip side of the Day of the Lord, another type of supper takes place. Christ and His heavenly army appear for that final, great battle, and the dragon, beast, and the kings of the earth have gathered to make war, whether that's a spiritual and legal battle or ends up being literal. The beast and false prophet are captured and thrown into the lake of fire. Those who followed them are slain as well. Here is the second

---

[64] www.yahweswordarchives.org/books-of-baruch/book-2-of-Baruch.pdf

meal:

> 17 Then I saw an angel standing in the sun, and with a loud voice he called to all the birds that fly directly overhead, "Come, gather for the great supper of God, 18 to eat the flesh of kings, the flesh of captains, the flesh of mighty men, the flesh of horses and their riders, and the flesh of all men, both free and slave, both small and great." ... 21 And the rest were slain by the sword that came from the mouth of him who was sitting on the horse, and all the birds were gorged with their flesh. (Rev 19:17-18, 21)

We have here another look at the battle of Armageddon. Earlier, we saw the blood of the dead reaching the horses' bridles for 1,600 stadia. Now, we see the birds picking on their flesh. Again, this, too, is a metaphor for the consumption of chaos.

History Revisited

Chapter 20 is like the lead-in to a TV series: "In previous episodes, we saw ..." Yes, while futurists want to use this as proof of a separate 1,000-year reign on Christ, it appears to be a recap of history, shown from the supernatural side.

The chapter opens with an angel (Uriel perhaps) coming down from heaven with the key to the abyss. The angel seizes and binds the dragon—identified now as Satan—for "a thousand" years. The NT shows that this decisive defeat of Satan occurred at Christ's death and resurrection: Matthew 12:29, Mark 3:27, Luke 10:17-19, John 12:31-33, Colossians 2:15, and Hebrews 2:14.

As said before, this timespan is not likely to be literal but to symbolize a long period, the church age. During that time Satan is not allowed to deceive the nations, and more specifically, the church. This binding allowed the church to flourish, even though his demons continue to wreak havoc. After that long period, he is released for a short while, which I've discussed as being the three-and-a-half years during which we must act as witnesses. Dr. Beale argues for the short time of Revelation 12:12 being the 42 months, and the "little while" of 20:3 being a very brief period right before Christ's return. Whichever, he is released shortly before the *parousia* to gather his forces against the church. He will deceive some of the church, try to stop the church from spreading the Gospel, and physically kill many believers. In a way, this is a final, refining test of believers.

In v4, we again see the heavenly throne room and thrones, plural. Not 24 or just one. Thrones, plural. As conquerors, we're all promised one. Wonder if it's assigned seating or we get to pick one.

John again sees the souls of those martyred for Christ, and they came to life to reign with Christ. Since Christ's reign began with His resurrection and ascension, this points to ruling in the heavenly places, not on earth. It's that "already but not yet" aspect of Revelation that we've seen before.

And then in this recap, Satan is released and again begins to deceive the nations, focusing on those within the church. He gathers his "army"—Gog and Magog—for the final battle. The number of those gathered *"is like the sand of the sea."* But they are consumed by fire from heaven and Satan is thrown into the lake of fire along with the beast, false prophet, and those who followed them.

The best OT foreshadowing of Armageddon is the war of Gog of Magog in Ezekiel 38-39. While futurists see this war as preceding the millennial reign of Christ, most scholars see this as the war for Zion, or *Har-magēdô*. This becomes clear in Revelation 20:8 where Gog and Magog are named. Most scholars believe that Ezekiel 39 is a recap of the battle of Gog and Magog described in Ezekiel 38 and that John follows this pattern where v20:8-10 are likely to be a recapitulation of 19:17-21.

We also see similarities of language in Revelation 16:12-16, 19:19-20, and 20:8 in the gathering together of forces for war. Likewise, these verses express the idea that deception is involved in getting the nations' participation. This reinforces the idea of Satan deceiving the nations.

The identity of Gog of Magog, chief prince of Rosh, Meshech, and

Tubal, has been yet another source of debate and has posed a vexing problem for those who study the OT. Any link to *ro'sh* being Russia—a dispensational favorite—isn't supported exegetically or by Hebrew grammar. Even the Septuagint and Masoretic texts don't agree on the identity of Gog. There is, however, a possible link to the Watchers of 1 Enoch. Typhon—a Titan who opposed Zeus and all the gods and became linked to the Egyptian god Seth in the sixth century B.C.—has textual and conceptual connections to Daniel 7-12, from which the antichrist typology arose. As we know, Daniel 7 is seen throughout Revelation.

What are the connections? Typhon spoke insolent words against Zeus, while the little horn in Daniel 11:36-37 spoke them against God. Typhon warred against Zeus and his entourage, and the little horn battled against God and His holy ones (Daniel 7:21-27; 11:36-37). Both showed mutual contempt for existing laws. Typhon, like the eleventh horn, has both human and animal features (Daniel 7:8, 20-21; 8:5-9,21). These similarities point to Gog as an End Times, supernatural opponent to God, not a human foe. This fits with the title of "chief prince," just as Michael is called a "chief prince" in Daniel 10:13.

The Great White Throne

The final judgment of man is shown in v11:15:

> *11 Then I saw a great white throne and him who was seated on it. From his presence earth and sky fled away, and no place was found for them. 12 And I saw the dead, great and small, standing before the throne, and books were opened. Then another book was opened, which is the book of life. And the dead were judged by what was written in the books, according to what they had done. 13 And the sea gave up the dead who were in it, Death and Hades gave up the dead who were in them, and they were judged, each one of them, according to what they had done. 14 Then Death and Hades were thrown into the lake of fire. This is the second death,*

> *the lake of fire. 15 And if anyone's name was not found written in the book of life, he was thrown into the lake of fire. (Rev 20:10-15)*

The One seated on the throne is not clearly identified. God the Father is the one seated on the throne in the previous sections of Revelation, while Christ stands among His people. Yet, Christ will be seated at the right hand of the Father (Matthew 26:64, Mark 14:62, Luke 22:69, Colossians 3:1, Hebrews 8:1, and 12:2), so this could be Christ. Indeed, when we get to chapter 21, we find that it is. In 21:5, the One seated on the throne speaks, and in 21:6, He is identified as *"the Alpha and Omega, the beginning and the end,"* titles given to Christ.

Of note here is that those given up by the sea, Death, and Hades are the nonbelievers, who are then judged *"according to what they had done."* They are judged and then, in the end, Death and Hades are thrown into the lake of fire. V15 does not imply that additional nonbelievers are judged after Death and Hades are vanquished but simply that their destiny was based upon being written in the book of life. After all, if Death and Hades have been disposed of, death no longer exists. By the way, this second death is a spiritual one, just as the lake of fire exists only in the spiritual realm, and the dragon, beasts, and prostitute represent spiritual entities behind their earthly ones.

Our Take-Away

In these chapters (19 & 20), we see the consummation of history. The dragon (Satan), who has been locked away and not allowed to deceive the peoples, so that the church could flourish, has been released and his deceptions resumed. That leads to members of the body falling away, persecution of those who stand strong, and the gathering of the kings and peoples to make war against Christ and His body. Yet, they do not prevail. Instead, they are judged and cast into the lake of fire, the second (spiritual) death.

As we look around us today, do we see such deception? I'd say yes. As I've pointed out before, once prominent believers such as musicians and pastors make the news by denouncing Christ, whom they say they once followed. Woke Christianity has allowed basic Marxist tenets and idolatry to penetrate churches. Once stalwart groups such as the Southern Baptist Convention are being split by such teachings. Other denominations have appointed openly gay pastors to lead major churches. Christians in the Middle East and elsewhere are attacked and killed or denied access to basic economic resources, such as the ability to earn a living or buy essentials. Churches are being burned or padlocked, and that's in places such as Canada. In the U.S., evangelicals are being blamed and targeted for spreading vaccine misinformation even though many evangelicals have accepted the COVID vaccines.

Satan knows that his time is short. His anger and thirst for vengeance must be mounting daily.

Eden Returns

The Final Vision

In John's final vision, we read of the new creation, the new Eden, which has been the endpoint of God's plan to restore what He had created millennia ago.

> 1 Then I saw a new heaven and a new earth, for the first heaven and the first earth had passed away, and the sea was no more. 2 And I saw the holy city, new Jerusalem, coming down out of heaven from God, prepared as a bride adorned for her husband. (Rev 21:1-2)

We see a new heaven and earth because the old ones have passed away (Revelation 20:11). Here, the word for 'new,' *kainos*, **καινός**, holds a qualitative meaning, not a temporal one. So, it's likely we're looking at a distinctly different cosmos with a transformation of its fundamental structure. Whether or not this means the literal destruction of our current cosmos awaits to be seen. As for the reference to the sea, this more likely refers to the sea as a symbol for chaos, rebellious peoples, and idolatry, not just a literal body of water.

And with the new creation, we read of the greatest of all rewards for those who remained faithful.

> 3 And I heard a loud voice from the throne saying, "Behold, the dwelling place of God is with man. He will dwell with

them, and they will be his people, and God himself will be with them as their God. 4 He will wipe away every tear from their eyes, and death shall be no more, neither shall there be mourning, nor crying, nor pain anymore, for the former things have passed away." (Rev 21:3-4)

V3 is the fulfillment of numerous OT prophecies about God being a tabernacle in the midst of Israel, of their being His people, and of His being their God. That said, to think that there will be no more tears, death, mourning, crying, nor pain is amazing, but the ultimate reward is that God Himself will dwell with us. We see this in the next two verses:

6 And he said to me, "It is done! I am the Alpha and the Omega, the beginning and the end. To the thirsty I will give from the spring of the water of life without payment. 7 The one who conquers will have this heritage, and I will be his God and he will be my son. (Rev 21:6-7)

Of course, *"the spring of water of life"* refers back to His encounter with the woman at the well in Samaria (John 4:5-26). That conversation included the first time that He openly stated that He was the Messiah. And now we hear those words again at the end. Plus, instead of referencing "my peoples," we are referred to as "my son." While Christ remains God's only begotten, divine son, we have inherited the privileges of sonship.

The idea of a new creation was prophesied in Isaiah 65:17 and 66:22.

17 "For behold, I create new heavens and a new earth, and the former things shall not be remembered or come into mind. (Isa 65:17)

22 "For as the new heavens and the new earth that I make shall remain before me, says the LORD, so shall your offspring and your name remain. (Isa 66:22)

The foreshadowing in Isaiah 35:10 and 51:11 also comes into play here.

> *And the ransomed of the LORD shall return and come to Zion with singing; everlasting joy shall be upon their heads; they shall obtain gladness and joy, and sorrow and sighing shall flee away. (Isa 35:10, also 51:11)*

The main focus of chapters 21 & 22 is to contrast the imperfect church (chapters 1-3) with the perfect church. In the first three chapters, we read of the failures of those who faced the threat or reality of persecution. And yet, for those who overcome the reward is great. In Revelation 21:8, however, we read of the fate of the cowardly "Christians" who fail to show courageous faith, as well as a list of such vices. This list is also secondarily applicable to nonbelievers. Also, we will read a similar list in 22:15.

The New Jerusalem

Revelation 21:9 - 22:5 offers us a look at the new Jerusalem. We find five general thematic sections: the initial appearance and overview of the city, its measurements, its materials, its internal features, and the symbols of God's presence there. Much of this has been seen before by Ezekiel in chapters 40-48 of his book, but John collapses those views of the temple, city, and land into one broad picture.

While many interpret this picture literally as a cube city of nearly 1,400 miles in each dimension, there are many aspects of this image that lend credence to its being symbolic. For one, the city is equated with the Bride of Christ. Some symbols are explicit, such as the 12 gates representing the sons of Israel and the wall's foundations named for the 12 apostles. Note that the foundations are the apostles, not the tribes of Israel, despite the tribes coming first in history. The true Israel, the church, has the apostles as its base.

The numbers used are important in understanding the symbols. Recall that four stands for the wholeness of the cosmos, and a cube viewed from any direction is seen with four sides. Twelve stands for completeness, and we see the number 12 in the 12,000 stadia, the gates, and the foundation. Even the height of the wall is 12x12 cubits. Although that's drastically out of proportion if this is a city that's literally 1,400 miles high, the *"great, high wall"* shows the inviolable nature of our relationship with God. That there is only one wall—compared to multiple walls and courts of previous earthly temples—shows unity.

The materials mentioned also hold symbolism. The gold intensifies the reflection of God's glory, as it did lining the inside of Solomon's temple. Likewise with the precious stones. Jasper in particular represents His glory, as it is one of the two stones—along with carnelian—used to describe His glory in Revelation 4:3. The twelve stones, which are the same—either identical or semantically the same—as those of the twelve tribes on the high priest's breastplate symbolize all of Israel, or in this case, all of *true* Israel.

Other symbols are less obvious. Revelation 17:1,3 has wording almost identical to 21:9, but the former talks of the whore of Babylon in contrast to the Bride of Christ in the latter. In the former, the prostitute's adornment—also gold, precious stones, and pearls—is symbolic of the economic powers that cooperate with the state in persecuting believers. The Bride's adornment represents her faithful works and vindication (see also 1 Corinthians 3:5-15 and 1 Peter 2:4-7). Ezekiel 28:11-29 also comes to mind, with the king of Tyre being described as

> *13 You were in Eden, the garden of God; every precious stone was your covering, sardius, topaz, and diamond, beryl, onyx, and jasper, sapphire, emerald, and carbuncle; and crafted in gold were your settings and your engravings. On the day that you were created they were prepared. (Eze 28:13)*

While I've heard some teach that this king is Satan, the above verse (and others) points to it being Adam. These precious stones were prepared for Adam in Eden, and now the new Eden is built with them.

That the city has no sun or moon (v21:23) points to an eternity in which there is no timeline. Both celestial orbs were created as markers of time, and now they're gone. God alone is our light, and there is no night, as night was always symbolic of evil, terror, and such. Also, a sun or moon would pale in comparison to the light of God's glory. This was foreshadowed in Isaiah 60:19.

We see the further foreshadowing of the new Jerusalem in Isaiah 60. Revelation 21:24 speaks of nations walking by her light and kings bringing their wealth to her. That's Isaiah 60:3,5. And Isaiah 60:11 foretells of her gates being open continually to allow the kings to bring the wealth of the nations to her. That's Revelation 21:25-26. Here, the idea of wealth holds the connotation of glory in the form of praise, and the prophecy of Isaiah 60 describes the nations coming to the eternal Jerusalem to worship Yahweh.

I should note here that the final verse of chapter 21 does not imply that there are those who are unclean who remain and who will live outside the city, not allowed to enter it. This is a continuance of Isaiah's prophecy (60:18,21) and is used here for contrast.

The River of Life

V1-5 in chapter 22 conclude the image of the new Jerusalem.

1 Then the angel showed me the river of the water of life, bright as crystal, flowing from the throne of God and of the Lamb 2 through the middle of the street of the city; also, on either side of the river, the tree of life with its twelve kinds of fruit, yielding its fruit each month. The leaves of the tree were for the healing of the nations. 3 No longer will there be anything accursed, but the throne of God and of the Lamb will be in it, and his servants will worship him. 4 They will see his face, and his name will be on their foreheads. 5 And night will be no more. They will need no light of lamp or sun, for the Lord God will be their light, and they will reign forever and ever. (Rev 22:1-5)

Here we see the river of the water of life, those living waters that Jesus spoke of when He first revealed Himself to be the Messiah. Joel 3:18 speaks of the spring of life going out from the house of the Lord. Yet, the allusion goes back even further, to Genesis 2:10 which tells us of the river going forth from Eden. Yes, the new Eden has arrived.

Water and the Holy Spirit are closely connected in scripture. In Ezekiel 36:25-27, we read of being cleansed by water and filled with His Spirit. John 3:5 speaks of being born of water and of the Spirit. Baptism, of course, involves immersion and emerging as a new creation led by His Spirit. 1 John 5:6-8 speaks of Jesus coming by both water and the blood and of the Spirit's testifying and being the truth, and that those three—Spirit, water, and blood—agree. With this background, many see the river of the water of life as symbolic of the Holy Spirit.

We also see the tree of life, the very thing that God protected from Adam and Eve by exiling them from Eden. Ezekiel foretold of these trees and their healing fruits in 47:12. Now, we have full access to its fruits, all twelve of them. Kind of like a fruit of the month club. In reality, scholars believe that the reference to a monthly yield shows that John had trouble expressing the realities of eternity. He fell back to his earthly understanding and Ezekiel's description because he could not comprehend eternity. Time is no more. Only eternity looms ahead. I can identify with John here. Try wrapping your head around the concept of no time, just eternity. Whoosh. Brain freeze.

Also of note in the above verses, we will see His face, and His name shall be on our foreheads. This denotes an intimacy with God that we can't begin to imagine. In Exodus 33:20, Moses was told that no man might see God's face and live. Likewise, Talmudic tradition held that speaking God's name—the tetragrammaton, יהוה, transliterated as YHWH—meant that the speaker had no place in the world to come. Even today, Orthodox Jews use the name HaShem when speaking of God. But in the new Eden, we not only have His name on our foreheads, but we also see Him face to face. Makes you want to sing, "I can onnnly imagine..."

In Closing

I mentioned early on in this book that it held certain characteristics of an epistle. Chapter one opens with an epistolary greeting. And now, in the remainder of chapter 22, we find a typical epistolary closing.

I like what Dr. Beale wrote about the ending:

> This final vision of the book concerning these same five themes — new covenant, new temple, new Israel, new Jerusalem, and new creation — is also the climax and the expression of the main point of the Apocalypse thus far. But it is not the main point of the whole book. Why is this vision placed at the end of the book? It is here to underscore the ultimate basis for John's final goal and purpose in writing: to exhort God's people to remain faithful. This is why the book concludes with an epilogue of repeated exhortations, promises, affirmations of Christ's imminent coming, and warnings to the saints (22:6-21).[65]

In this closing, that is precisely what we find. John is exhorted to write down in words what he saw because the time is near (v22:10). We are blessed by keeping the words of this prophecy (v22:7). We find affirmation that Christ's return is imminent (v22:12-13, 20). We are promised the water of life without price (v22:17) and the right to the tree of life and entry into new Jerusalem (v22:14). And yet, there are warnings as well—not to add or subtract from these words (v22:18-19).

Let me just close this section with this:

> *20 He who testifies to these things says, "Surely I am coming soon." Amen. Come, Lord Jesus! (Rev 22:20)*

---

[65] Beale, G.K. *The New International Greek Testament Commentary, the Book of Revelation*, William B. Eerdmans Publishing Co, Grand Rapids, MI, 1999, pg. 907.

Some Final Words

Where are we now?

This book started as a project for developing a personal understanding of the Book of Revelation. For me, studying, researching, and then putting what I've learned into words is the best way of solidifying my understanding of complex issues or ideas. I never suspected it would become the length of a novel, as I wanted simply to touch on the "highlights" and possibly have a book that could make the Apocalypse comprehensible to others as well.

Too many people think of Revelation as some mysterious codebook, full of confusing images awaiting to be deciphered by only the smartest of people. I'm pretty sure that's not what God, through John, had in mind. After all, the recipients of this book in John's day were not usually the elites and highly educated.

In an interview with Dr. Michael Heiser, Dr. Alan Bandy said, ". . . eschatology is not a detached fortune cookie of this crystal ball of how things are all going to unfold in the future. Eschatology is not about the future, it's about the now in light of the future."[66] Despite the mixed metaphors of fortune cookies and crystal balls, he's right. In the letters to the seven churches, Christ shows us the shortcomings, the errors, the idolatry, and threats to the body not just in first-century Asia Minor but today, too—the now. He also shows us the promises that await if we stay faithful . . . faithful unto death if need be.

---

[66] https://nakedbiblepodcast.com/?s=207

And that is the main goal of the Apocalypse, to exhort God's people to remain faithful. The main theological point is that we are to glorify God for His consummate plan for salvation and the judgment that awaits. We see this in the final chapters of the book. We are to *"rejoice and exult and give him the glory, for the marriage of the Lamb has come, and his Bride has made herself ready;"* (Revelation 19:7)

As you can see by making it to the end of this (my) book, understanding Revelation requires a knowledge of the OT. As I've previously pointed out, there is more OT in Revelation than in the rest of the NT combined. I hope that by looking at the OT references I've given you, you have a deeper appreciation for the Apocalypse. Trust me when I say there's a ton of OT references and symbols I didn't get into, both in an attempt to hit the "highlights" and to shorten this book. The tomes I used as references were hundreds of pages long. Dr. Beale's commentary alone hits almost 1,200 pages. I was not out to replicate that.

Honestly, prior to wading through those pages, my connection between Revelation and the OT was, well, zilch. I had read several commentaries that approached the Apocalypse from a purely eschatological perspective, but they still left me wondering who will fill that role and what might fill this role.

Which brings me to the question, where are we now? Isn't that what many of us want to know? I've already made some references to current times in some of the chapters. Bear with me if I repeat myself here.

I think we all have a pretty clear idea of who Satan is and that the dragon of Revelation represents him. Historically, he was the original deceiver who led Eve and Adam astray. He was bound in the abyss and forbidden from deceiving the nations, which allowed the church to flourish. Think about that for a moment. Had he not been bound, would there even be a church today? At the end of the church age, he will be released for a short while, which many scholars (and myself) see as the 3.5 years shown in Revelation.

Once we understand that the beast from the sea, to which Satan gives his false authority, is the state—ie., government—and that the beast from the land, or false prophet, consists of the religious-economic supporters of the state, events happening in the world around us suddenly begin to make sense. The light bulb clicks on over our heads. There is no need for an individual antichrist or an individual false prophet, although such individuals might arise. Those roles are being well fulfilled by the state and by a combination of ecumenical religious groups, corporations, and the media who promote the state and do its bidding. Add in an idolatrous, unbelieving culture—the whore—and all of the pieces are on the board to persecute God's people.

And we're seeing that persecution rising. I've mentioned the direct physical attacks on Christians in areas such as the Middle East, India, and China. The progressive government of Canada is shutting down churches and jailing pastors, some on pseudo-public health grounds but others for simply preaching the Bible (ex, marriage between a man and a woman). Whoda ever thunk the easy-going, friendly Can-nooks would accept such tyranny? The U.K. is also jailing and/or fining people for preaching the Word, which the state finds discriminatory and hate speech. For those who say it would never happen in the U.S., look around. Churches nationwide were shut down over this alleged health crisis called COVID, a "crisis" purely manufactured by the state. (I'll resist putting on my white coat and climbing the medical soapbox on this one.) And the media directly attacks the evangelical church—not the progressive, Woke "church"—for being hateful, homophobic, against women who seek abortions, and for spreading "misinformation" about COVID and the so-called vaccine. (Hmmm . . .Where's that soapbox?)

Similarly, anti-Semitism and direct physical attacks on Jews are increasing. A recent poll showed anti-Semitism at an all-time high on U.S. college campuses. The U.S. government not long ago attempted to pull all of its advanced air defense batteries—the Patriot missiles—from Israel just as Iran's missile program is gaining new advances and is believed to be within weeks of obtaining nuclear capability. Terror attacks within the state of Israel are a weekly occurrence, if not more frequent. This could be the beginning of a time of ultimate testing for ethnic Jews. Will they call upon the name of the Lord and become part of the true Israel, or not? Time will tell, but scripture seems to point that way.

I don't know about you, but I sensed a big change in our culture after the last election. In my other book, I mentioned that the Trump administration was likely just a short reprieve before God's judgment on the U.S. intensified. It would appear I was right. Hatred, violence, division, greed, and more all seemed to have ramped up several notches with the election of Joseph Biden. To paraphrase the Word, a house divided will cannot stand, and our fall will be a steep one because our collective sins have been great.

Yet, it's not simply the Biden administration. Look around the world. Government worldwide is pushing to remove freedoms, to advance the Great Reset (aka UN Agenda 21), and to become totalitarian. Marxist thought wrapped up in Critical Race Theory, Critical Gender Theory, and more have taken over public universities, militaries, and school boards. Australia has returned to its penal colony roots with its current draconian home quarantine policies. If you don't reply to a government text with your photo and location, they send the police to your door. Citizens are required to have tracking apps on their phones and facial recognition is being implemented everywhere to track the populace. And don't dare criticize. One woman was arrested and dragged from her home in front of her children for simply posting on her Facebook page about a planned protest. I guess gulags in the Outback are next.

Earlier, I mentioned the May 2020 survey released by George Barna for the Center for Biblical Worldview at the Family Research Council. Despite 51% of American adults claiming to hold a Biblical worldview, after answering 51 basic worldview questions, only 6% of American adults truly hold a Biblical viewpoint. Of those self-proclaimed believers, only 31% felt that their faith was important in influencing every aspect of their lives. And within that 31%, less than a third felt they were effective in integrating their faith into their lives.[67] [And now, in 2023, the latest survey shows a further drop in those

---

[67] https://downloads.frc.org/EF/EF21E41.pdf

holding a biblical worldview, to 4%.]

While those results point more to a failure of the church, are we seeing deception on the rise? I'd say so. The prime example of this is, again, the so-called pandemic. It has been an amazingly successful PsyOps program using fear to deceive the public and get people to turn on one another. Also, why are people so easily turned against neighbors, churches, and once-respected institutions, such as the police, unless they are being deceived?

I think I've made it clear that I see a timeline in Revelation, one inferred by the intensification of judgment. Many scholars won't agree with me, but here's my take on this idea. In the seals, we see God's judgments in a general sense, afflicting various peoples and places across the globe throughout history since Christ's resurrection and ascension. These events occur as warnings to prod people into repentance, but most don't recognize them as such. To most, it's just "mother nature" or human nature that's causing the problems.

Yet, we see a gradual intensification of these occurrences leading into the trumpets, where now a third of the earth, plus men, are plagued. Again, these are warnings, but most men are blind to that. They see man as the problem—global warming aka climate change— and continue on their way. The culture gets more and more idolatrous and sinful, but now it's called plurality, political correctness, or being Woke. The trumpets take place in the final three and a half years.

Satan is released and things go down the drain in a rapid whirlpool. He has 42 months to rally his troops and take down as many of God's people as he can. At the end of that time, Christ returns to Mount Zion with the 144,000. The Day of the Lord has come. Satan and the kings of the earth come against him, but He unleashes the most severe judgments, the bowls, against all of the earth. Satan, his cohorts, and nonbelievers face their final judgment and are cast into the lake of fire, while God's people join in at the Marriage Supper of the Lamb. Finally, we move to the new Eden.

Has Satan been released? Are we inside that 42-month time window? I believe we are. And, yes, I recognize that some in every generation for the past 2,000 years have believed theirs was the generation of His return. Yet, in those past generations, there remained a beacon of freedom and God's Word, first in Europe, then the British Empire, and ultimately, the United States. Where will people find freedom based upon the Word once the United States falls?

In *Still Here! Surviving the End Times*, I mentioned a Bible chronologist friend, William Struse. His work has shown that there were 41 jubilee cycles between Adam and Abraham, 41 cycles between Abraham and Jesus' first advent, and we're now near the end of the 41st cycle since Jesus. Due to the Sanhedrin messing with the calendar in the first century BC, precise dating is not possible, but Bill has used the Masoretic text to try to accommodate those discrepancies, and he believes he has a +/- four-year window around his calculation.

Given that range, I believe we're within the window not just because of the deceptions going on in general but because of all that's going on in the church, Satan's primary target. Prominent pastors leaving the faith. Popular musicians leaving the faith. Woke Christianity taking over entire denominations and splitting others.

In my nearly 70 years in this world, I've never seen it like this. It has accelerated in the past year, but even more so since the beginning of 2021. The "progressives"—and I use that term loosely—regaining power in the U.S. launched a global push toward what they'd like to believe is a New World Order. It's anything but new, but no one ever claimed these people learn from history. Plus, the increase in major wildfires, the extensive drought conditions facing much of the world, worsening hurricanes, and more all point to an intensification of judgment as portrayed by the trumpet judgments.

I could be wrong. My discernment could be way off. We could be closer to Armageddon than I think, or we might have many years to go. The way the world has changed, I pray it's not the latter.

Finally, if you've read this and it's caused doubts to arise inside, specifically doubt as to where you stand in eternity, it's important that you understand that it is God's will that all men be saved (1 Timothy 2:3-4).

Yet, the persuasive powers of the enemy can be intense. Have you allowed those convincing words to lure you away from a belief in God's

Word? I mentioned earlier in this book the research done by Dr. George Barna. While their study used 51 worldview questions, I'd like to present you with what they list as their "Top Ten." How would you answer these?

1: Do you believe that "having faith matters more than what faith you have?"
2. Do you believe that all faiths are of equal value?
3. Do you believe in karma, i.e., that you get what you give?
4. Do you believe there is no absolute truth?
5. Are you committed to a personal, subjective morality?
6. Do you believe that all people are "basically good?"
7. Do you believe that success is determined by happiness, comfort, goodness, or fulfilled potential?
8. Do you believe that sexual relations apart from marriage are morally acceptable?
9. Do you reject the notion that people are inherently sinful?
10. Do you agree with the conclusion that the purpose of accumulated personal wealth is unrelated to God's purposes?

Yes, these are their "Top Ten" . . . of the most seductive, unbiblical ideas luring people away from the Bible. If you answered 'yes' to any of these, you might want to study God's Word rather than risk being pulled further and further away.

I don't bring this up to question one's salvation. It's not my place to judge, but the idolatries of today in the Western world are found in these false beliefs, Wokeness, critical (Marxist) theory, and humanistic "theology"—anything that opposes what God teaches through His Word. You don't need a man-made idol of rock, wood, gold, or silver set up inside your home to participate in idolatry.

Perhaps you picked up this book because you're fascinated by the "mystery" of the Book of Revelation, and you don't have a personal relationship with Christ. Maybe you wonder how it's even possible to have a relationship with God. I strongly suggest you seek out a faith-based, Bible-believing church in your area and start asking questions. Your eternal destiny depends upon it. For a growing list of such churches, start here: https://drmsh.com/church-directory/

I hope you found this book helpful. Whether you agree, disagree, or only partially agree with me, I'd love to hear your thoughts. Feel free to contact me through my website.

Maranatha!

ABOUT THE AUTHOR

Braxton can't lay claim to wanting to be a writer all his life, although his mother and seventh-grade English teacher were convinced he had what it would take. He went to Duke University, earning a Bachelor's Degree of Science in Engineering with a major in Bio-Medical Engineering, followed by medical school at the University of Cincinnati. After a residency in Emergency Medicine at Madigan Army Medical Center, he served tours as the Chief, Emergency Medical Services at Fort Campbell, KY, and as a research Flight Surgeon at Fort Rucker, AL. Who had time to write?

By the late 1990s, his professional and family life had settled down somewhat, and his mother once again took up her mantra, "Write a book. You're a good writer." Yet, with no experience writing anything other than technical articles, he hesitated to try his hand at fiction. That changed in 1997 when the local newspaper held a writing contest for Valentine's Day. Out of 1100 entries, he made it to the top five finalists and realized that maybe he could write fiction after all.

The next fifteen years saw him learning the craft of writing through local writers' groups, seminars, critique groups, and more. Now, twenty-plus years after that first hesitant start, he can't find enough time to write as much as he'd like. He currently lives in Wisconsin with his wife, Paula. Their two children are grown, and with grandchildren nearby, "Papa" wears many hats.

Books by Braxton DeGarmo:

Still Here Series:
The End Begins - 1
The Shaking - 2
The Beasts – 3
The Trumpets – 4

Non-fiction Study Guides:
Still Here! Surviving the End Times
Still Here! The Apocalypse is Now

MedAir Series:
Looks that Deceive – 1
Rescued and Remembered – 2
The Silenced Shooter – 3
Wrongfully Removed – 4
A Zealot's Destiny – 5
Kidnapped Nation - 6
The Khmer Connection - 7
Resurrected Trouble - 8

Seamus O'Connor Thrillers:
The Militant Genome
Ten Seconds 'Til

Other Books:
Indebted

www.ingramcontent.com/pod-product-compliance
Lightning Source LLC
Chambersburg PA
CBHW060518080526
44586CB00012B/533